Using America Online with Windows 95

Using
America Online with Windows 95

Gene Steinberg

Using America Online with Windows 95

Copyright© 1996 by Que® Corporation.

All rights reserved. Printed in the United States of America. No part of this book may be used or reproduced in any form or by any means, or stored in a database or retrieval system, without prior written permission of the publisher except in the case of brief quotations embodied in critical articles and reviews. Making copies of any part of this book for any purpose other than your own personal use is a violation of United States copyright laws. For information, address Que Corporation, 201 W. 103rd Street, Indianapolis, IN, 46290. You may reach Que's direct sales line by calling 1-800-428-5331.

Library of Congress Catalog No.: 95-71737

ISBN: 0-7897-0594-x

This book is sold *as is*, without warranty of any kind, either express or implied, respecting the contents of this book, including but not limited to implied warranties for the book's quality, performance, merchantability, or fitness for any particular purpose. Neither Que Corporation nor its dealers or distributors shall be liable to the purchaser or any other person or entity with respect to any liability, loss, or damage caused or alleged to have been caused directly or indirectly by this book.

98 97 96   6 5 4 3 2 1

Interpretation of the printing code: the rightmost double-digit number is the year of the book's printing; the rightmost single-digit number, the number of the book's printing. For example, a printing code of 96-1 shows that the first printing of the book occurred in 1996.

All terms mentioned in this book that are known to be trademarks or service marks have been appropriately capitalized. Que cannot attest to the accuracy of this information. Use of a term in this book should not be regarded as affecting the validity of any trademark or service mark.

Screen reproductions in this book were created using Collage Plus from Inner Media, Inc., Hollis, NH.

Credits

President
Roland Elgey

Publisher
Stacy Hiquet

Editorial Services Director
Elizabeth Keaffaber

Managing Editor
Sandy Doell

Director of Marketing
Lynn E. Zingraf

Senior Series Editor
Chris Nelson

Acquisitions Manager
Cheryl Willoughby

Product Director
Mark Cierzniak
Oran Sands

Production Editor
Elizabeth A. Bruns

Assistant Product Marketing Manager
Kim Margolius

Technical Editor
Jim Johnston

Technical Specialist
Nadeem Muhammed

Acquisitions Coordinator
Ruth Slates

Operations Coordinator
Patty Brooks

Editorial Assistant
Andrea Duvall

Book Designer
Ruth Harvey

Cover Designer
Dan Armstrong

Production Team
Steve Adams
Brian Buschkill
Jason Carr
Kim Cofer
Chad Dressler
Terri Edwards
Joan Evan
DiMonique Ford
Trey Frank
Jason Hand
George Hanlin
John Hulse
Damon Jordan
Michelle Lee
Julie Quinn
Bobbi Satterfield
Scott Tullis
Kelly Warner

Indexer
Gina Brown

Composed in *ITC Highlander* and *MCPdigital* by Que Corporation.

*To Barbara and Grayson with love and appreciation.
And to my brother Wally, whom I'll miss always.*

About the Author

Gene Steinberg is an inveterate desktop computer user who first joined America Online in 1989. He quickly became addicted to the new online service and finally earned positions on its computing forum staff. At present, he is Forum Leader of the service's Macintosh Multimedia Forum and curator of AOL Portrait Gallery, a library containing photos of America Online members and their families.

In his regular life, Gene has worked at several occupations. He first studied broadcasting in school and then worked for a number of years as a disc jockey and newscaster. Gene is now a full-time writer and computer software and systems consultant. His published work (in addition to the first editions of this book) includes *Special Edition Using America Online*, *Using America Online with Your Mac* and *Special Edition Using The Macintosh* for Que Corporation, and feature articles and product reviews for *Macworld*.

Acknowledgments

Although the book you hold in your hands includes one name as the author, it is not a project a sane or almost sane person can do alone. I am grateful for the assistance of many, working behind the scenes, who made this book possible.

Among America Online's in-house staff, I have special praise for Dave Baker, Lyn Cameron, Jeff Crowe, Betsy Davison, Keith Deaven, Ken Huntsman, Matt Korn, Ann Kort, Pam McGraw, Kathy Ryan and Deborah Shaw for their ongoing help in making this project a success.

I am also grateful to America Online's Tim Barwick and my friend and sometimes co-writer John Stroud (one of AOL's favorite computing forum leaders) for getting me involved in America Online's forums to begin with.

A number of experts in the computing industry have provided special assistance in researching several chapters of this book. They include Clayton Cowgill of Supra Corporation (the modem manufacturer), Joanne Sperans Hartzell of Insignia Solutions (publishers of SoftWindows) and Pieter Paulson, the computer wizard at Nike, Inc.

Somehow, despite the long hours in front of my computer to write this manuscript, my forums on AOL managed to keep rolling anyway. For that I must give heartfelt praise to my staff at the Macintosh Multimedia Forum (Rob Sonner, Mark Elpers, Marshall Goldberg, Robin Kester, and Trish Meyer) and my staff at the AOL Portrait Gallery (Debbie DeRosa, Adam Lasnik, Michael T. Lester, Lisa Anna Lind, and Tom Wiseman).

I must give special praise to the team at Que Corporation for putting up with my many eccentricities and for allowing me a great deal of latitude in outlining and writing this book. They include Cheryl Willoughby, Mark Cierzniak, Oran Sands, and Elizabeth Bruns. Que's dedicated, fearless technical editor, Jim Johnston, deserves to be singled out for pouring through every written word and every illustration to verify that it was absolutely correct to the last, minute detail.

And last, I wish to offer a heartfelt, loving thank you to my wonderful, beautiful wife Barbara and my extraordinary son Grayson for putting up with the long hours I spent chained to the front of my computer so that my work could be done on schedule.

We'd Like to Hear from You!

As part of our continuing effort to produce books of the highest possible quality, Que would like to hear your comments. To stay competitive, we *really* want you, as a computer book reader and user, to let us know what you like or dislike most about this book or other Que products.

You can mail comments, ideas, or suggestions for improving future editions to the address below, or send us a fax at (317) 581-4663. For the online inclined, Macmillan Computer Publishing has a forum on CompuServe (type **GO QUEBOOKS** at any prompt) through which our staff and authors are available for questions and comments. The address of our Internet site is **http://www.mcp.com** (World Wide Web).

In addition to exploring our forum, please feel free to contact me personally to discuss your opinions of this book: I'm #76245,476 on CompuServe, and **mcierzniak@que.mcp.com** on the Internet.

Thanks in advance—your comments will help us to continue publishing the best books available on computer topics in today's market.

Mark Cierzniak
Product Development Specialist
Que Corporation
201 W. 103rd Street
Indianapolis, Indiana 46290
USA

Contents at a Glance

Introduction

I Let's Get Going

1 How to Get Started on America Online
2. Setting Up Your AOL Windows Software

II Getting Your Feet Wet

3 Finding Your Way Around
4 The Easy Way to Meet People Online
5 How to Stay in Touch with Other Members

III Having Fun on AOL

6 From Music to Sports: Locating Entertainment Information on AOL
7 The Secrets of Safe Online Fun for Kids of All Ages
8 Travel the Stars or Explore Heath Issues: Online Lifestyles & Interest Forums
9 Get Advice, Help and Software from America Online's Computing Forums

IV Information at Your Fingertips

10 How to Find the Software You Want
11 Learning & Reference Sources Online
12 Exploring Your Online Newsstand
13 Say it with Flowers: Secrets of Online Shopping
14 Business or Pleasure: Travel with America Online

V Getting on the Information Superhighway

15 The Internet Connection
16 Internet E-Mail Made Easy
17 The Lowdown on Internet Newsgroups
18 Unmasking the World Wide Web
19 Getting Started on the Web

Table of Contents

Introduction

Who is this book for? 1

The bill of fare 2

Special book elements 3

Shooting at a moving target 5

Part I: Let's Get Going

1 How to Get Started on America Online 9

The history of America Online 10

Here's the fast and easy way to install America Online software 11

Ordering your software 12

    How to install your AOL software 12

    Getting a local connection 15

    Establishing your online account 16

    Create your online mailing address 18

Before you enjoy your first online session 20

    Leaving the starting gate 21

    Let's begin a guided online tour 23

    Examining America Online highlights 23

Just a start 24

Establishing your online account

see page 16

2 Setting Up Your AOL Software 25

A quick and easy modem setup guide 26

How to fine-tune your AOL software 31

    How to set password preferences 32

    Just what are WWW preferences? 33

How to edit pictures with AOL's software 33

Use AOL's FlashBar for easy access   34

Is that all?   37

Part II: Getting Your Feet Wet

3 Finding Your Way Around   41

A brief look at AOL's Departments   42
- The Main Menu is your gateway to all the major features of America Online's virtual city   43
- Today's News   44
- Personal Finance   44
- Computing   45
- Travel   46
- Marketplace   47
- The Newsstand   47
- Entertainment   48
- Education   49
- Sports   50
- Kids Only   50
- ...All this and more   51

4 The Easy Way to Meet People Online   53

Give yourself an online profile   54

Find and meet other AOL members   57
- Locating other America Online members   58
- Viewing other members' profiles   59
- Finding a member online   60

Find and meet other AOL members
see page 57

Getting involved in the People Connection   61
- Entering the Lobby   61
- Visiting private chat rooms   61
- Entering the Center Stage Auditoriums   63

Using abbreviations and shorthand symbols   68
- Online abbreviations   69
- Online shorthand   69

Having a good time?   71

Contents **xv**

5 How to Stay in Touch with Other Members 73

Test the waters: how to write e-mail 74

How to send e-mail 75

How to receive e-mail 76

Sending files with e-mail 78

Saving and printing for posterity 79

Printing your e-mail 80

Setting up AOL's rolodex 80

Using FlashSessions to automate your online visits 82

Scheduling FlashSessions Using Walk-Through 82

Using instant messages for one-on-one meetings 84

The elements of online forums 84

Where the action is: using forum message boards 86

How to find the forum messages that interest you 87

How to post a message in a forum 88

Message threading 89

The elements of online conferences 90

Here's your progress report 91

*Sending files with e-mail
see page 78*

Part III: Having Fun on America Online

Finding movie and television information

see page 99

6 From Music to Sports: Locating Entertainment Information on AOL 95

Your first visit to the Entertainment forum 96

A look beneath the What's Hot icon 97

Visiting top Internet sites 98

Let's fly through MusicSpace 98

Finding movie and television information 99

Reading ShowBiz News & Info 99

A look beneath the Television & Radio icon 99

And that's not all 100

Accessing Hollywood Online 100

Finding music information 101

News from the world of sports see page 106

Accessing the RockNet forum   101
Accessing the Grateful Dead forum   102
Exploring Warner/Reprise Records Online   102
Be your own online critic   103
Checking out online games resources   104
A visit to the PC Games forum   104
Accessing the Online Gaming forums   104
Entering the Conference Center   105
Joining the Federation   105
News from the world of sports   106
Sitting in the Sports Grandstand   107
Online book information   107
The fun is just beginning   107

7 The Secrets of Safe Online Fun for Kids of All Ages   109

Online visits are usually enjoyable, but first...   110
Set Parental Controls to protect your child   111
How to protect your kids when they explore the Internet   113
How to set Parental Controls   114
Finding fun for kids of all ages   117
Internet sites for kids, too   118
Exploring *Disney Adventures* magazine   118
Accessing the Cartoon Network   119
Reading Tomorrow's Morning   119
Online games   120
Special Kids-Only conferences online   120
Chat Room rules   121
Ready to chat?   122
Now for some special forums for parents   122
Visiting the Parents' Information Network   122
Take advantage of the National Parenting Center   123
More than meets the eye   124

How to set Parental Controls see page 114

Contents **xvii**

8 Travel the Stars or Explore Health Issues: Online Lifestyles & Interest Forums   125

Top Internet Sites   127

Forums devoted to special interests   127
    Baby Boomers   127
    National Multiple Sclerosis Society Forum   128
    Religion & Ethics Forum   128
    SeniorNet Online   128

Hobbies and Clubs Online   128
    The Astronomy Club (a.k.a. the Astronomy Forum)   129
    The Cooking Club   129
    The Exchange   130
    The Capital Connection (a.k.a. Politics)   130
    AOL's Genealogy Club   131
    Kodak Photography Forum   131
    Science Fiction & Fantasy area   131
    Star Trek Club   132

Areas devoted to health, home, and the environment   132
    Better Health & Medical Forum   133
    Environmental Forum   133
    Issues in mental health   133
    Network Earth online   133
    Pet Care Forum   134

Areas Devoted to Professions and Organizations   134
    Aviation Forum   134
    Military & Vets Club   135
    National Space Society   135

Visiting leisure & entertainment information areas   137
    Car and Driver online   137
    Dolby Audio/Video Forum   137
    Consumer Electronics Forum   138

Towns and Cities Online   138
    Visiting Chicago Online   139
    Reading the *Chicago Tribune*   139

Pet Care Forum
see page 134

Using the Mercury Center   140
    Reading the *San Jose Mercury News*   141
Reading The *New York Times* Online   141
Just part of the picture   142

9 Get Advice, Help and Software from America Online's Computing Forums   143

Exploring the Computing Forums   144
    Accessing Computing Internet Sites   145
    Get Answers from the PC Help Desk   146
    PC Applications Forum covers your favorite DOS and Windows programs   146
    Explore modems and networking at the PC Communications Forum   147
    Learn about programming at the PC Developers Forum   147
    Visiting the DOS Forum   148
    Play the Games Forum   149
    Illustrating the Graphic Arts Forum   149
    Getting an advanced look at the newest PC hardware   150
    Using the PC Multimedia Forum   150
    Hear new sounds from the PC Music and Sound Forum   151
    Getting the goods on OS/2   152
    Exploring the Personal Digital Assistants Forum   152
    Visiting the User Groups Forum   153
    Explore the possibilities of Windows 95   154
Preview your favorite computer books & magazines   154
    For those who work at home   155
    Your computer is almost a member of the family   155
    On the road with *Mobile Office* Online   156
    Visiting *PC World* Online   156
    Visiting *WordPerfect Magazine* Online   157
Straight from the horse's mouth: seeking company support   158
    Finding a Company   158
    Using Industry Connection Help   160
The results are in   161

For those who work at home see page 155

Contents   xix

Part IV: Information at Your Fingertips

10 How to Find the Software You Want   165

Downloading files from A to Z
see page 169

How to get the hang of AOL's software libraries   166
    The easy way to search for files   167
Downloading files from A to Z   169
    The Download Manager   170
    How do I use the files I've downloaded?   172
What kind of software is available?   173
    Commercial software   173
    Demoware   174
    Shareware   174
    Freeware   174
    Public Domain Software   175
Uploading files from A to Z   175
    Where to upload   175
    How to upload   175
A world of discovery   176

11 Learning & Reference Sources Online   177

Court TV shows how courts really work
see page 182

A visit to the Reference Desk   178
    There are Internet sites for reference, too   179
    And the word you want is…   179
    Ask ERIC   180
    Barron's Booknotes helps you with your studies   180
    A visit to Compton's NewMedia learning center   180
    The Career Center helps you reach a job decision   181
    Court TV shows how courts really work   182
    Access C-SPAN to see Congress in action   182
    Smithsonian Online is your interactive museum   182
Let's explore the Education Center   183
    You can visit top education Web sites   184
    A visit to the Academic Assistance Center   184
    A look at the CNN Newsroom   185
    Using College Board Online   185

Explore the Electronic University Network   186
Attend the Komputer Klinic   186
A trip to the Library of Congress Online   187
Join the National Geographic Society   188
Access National Public Radio Outreach   188
A Visit to the Scholastic Forum   188
The Afterwards Cafe helps you relax   189
AOL Makes Learning Fun   190

12 Exploring Your Online Newsstand   191

A look at Today's News   192
U.S. & World news   193
Business news   194
Weather news   195
U.S. Cities Forecasts   197
Top Internet sites   197
Browsing the online Newsstand   197
The Atlantic Monthly   198
Columnists & Features Online   199
Consumer Reports   199
Cowles/SIMBA Media Information Network   199
The New Republic   199
OMNI Magazine Online   200
Saturday Review Online   200
Stereo Review Online   201
TIME Magazine Online   201
WIRED   201
Woman's Day Online   202
Worth Online   203

Browsing the online Newsstand see page 197

13 Say it with Flowers: Secrets of Online Shopping   205

Your virtual marketplace   206
Top Internet Sites   207
Placing an order with the AOL product center   207
How to get an AOL software upgrade   210

Common sense tips for online shopping
see page 219

Buying a car   210
Sending flowers   212
Buying books online   213
You can buy computer products online, too   214
    Computer Express   214
The online gift shop   215
Using Shoppers Advantage Online   216
Using the Classifieds Online   217
Still more online shopping resources   218
    Home delivery from AOL   218
Common sense tips for online shopping   219
Before you order...   219
After the package arrives   220
Ready for that shopping tour?   220

14 Business or Pleasure: Travel with America Online   221

A visit to the Travel department   222
    Cruise the world on the Internet   222
Using the EAASY SABRE System   223
    First you can view weather reports   224
    Finding the best fares or flights   224
How to use ExpressNet from American Express   225
A trip to Travelers Corner   226
How to Preview Vacations Online   227
A trip to the Travel Forum   227
    Taking a Hike Online   228
Experiencing Bed & Breakfast U.S.A.   229
    Using DineBase Restaurant Listings   229
    In search of an Outdoor Adventure Online   230
Consulting the State Travel Advisories   231
Ready to Leave?   231

How to Preview Vacations Online
see page 227

xxii Using America Online with Windows 95

Part V: Getting on the Information Superhighway

15 The Internet Connection   235

Yes, what *is* this Internet stuff all about?   236
What you get from the Internet   236

Let's explore AOL's Internet features   238
AOL's Mail Gateway is your Internet e-mail center   239
The wild world of UseNet Newsgroups   240
The Internet provides huge resources of information   240
You can join an Internet Mailing list   241
Transferring files on the Internet   241
Experience graphics and sound on the World Wide Web   242

If you want to know more   244

Now that you've entered the on-ramp   244

Let's explore AOL's Internet features

see page 238

16 Internet E-Mail Made Easy   245

How to send and receive Internet e-mail   246
How to send Internet e-mail   247
How to receive Internet e-mail   251
A look at Internet file attachments   251

A look at Internet mailing lists   252

How to join an Internet mailing list   254
How to respond to mailing list messages   255
How to leave a mailing list   255

What to do if your mailbox is filled   256

Bigger than the Post Office   257

How to join an Internet mailing list

see page 254

17 The Lowdown on Internet Newsgroups   259

How to set up AOL's newsgroup reader   260
First, let's set your newsgroup preferences   261
How the messages are displayed   262

Contents xxiii

Then, the order of display   262
What's in a name   263

Internet Newsgroups—the Ground Rules   263

How to participate in Internet newsgroups   266
How to find a newsgroup   267
Use Expert Add if you know the name   268

How to read your newsgroup messages   269
How to follow a message thread   270
Setting message preferences   271
See it all with the List All feature   272

How to reply to a newsgroup message   272
About cross-posting   273

How to post a newsgroup message   273
If the newsgroup has no unread messages   275

Let AOL record your keystrokes   275

Secrets of AOL's File Grabber   276

A favorite newsgroup list   277

18 Unmasking the World Wide Web   279

Hello, Web site!   281
Hold on a second—something's missing!   281
How to get from here to there   282
Let's get past that Home Page   284
A fast way to get there again   285
What do all those fancy buttons mean?   285

Secrets of speeding up Web access

see page 286

Secrets of speeding up Web access   286

And that's not all   287

19 Getting Started on the Web   289

Just a few favorite computing sites (and some other good stuff)   290
IBM   291
Microsoft   292

Novell, Inc.   292

Software Ventures Corporation   293

Ziff-Davis   294

The Howard Stern Show   294

Star Trek: Voyager   295

The Young and the Restless   296

The X-Files   296

The Central Intelligence Agency   297

Finding Web sites on your own   298

Paying a visit to Yahoo   298

More search tools   300

Do it your way   302

How to make your own WWW page the easy way   302

    First, the ingredients for our stew   303

    Getting to the finish line   305

    How to find AOL member home pages   307

Ziff-Davis
see page 294

Introduction

Not too many years ago, I found an interesting offer with my usual collection of junk mail. It was for something called America Online, a service where fellow computer users could meet, exchange messages, find software, and look up information covering a variety of subjects.

In that first year as a member, I found America Online somewhat of a lonely place to be. There weren't many members, and more often than not, I didn't find too many places to occupy my attention, though I enjoyed browsing through the service for software to run on my new computer.

I never anticipated the sort of population explosion that would occur.

As this book was written, there were four million members on America Online, making it the world's largest online service, and the figure was growing by hundreds of thousands each month.

America Online has also rapidly expanded the available services. It made alliances with the major media centers, such as ABC, Simon & Schuster, the *New York Times*, Time-Warner, and others. The simple software it provided was soon expanded to provide a huge collection of additional features, such as fast download of online artwork and the ability to connect to a new, uncharted territory, the global Internet.

You no doubt have read about America Online in your daily newspaper, or seen reports about the service on TV. It's clear the online world has made a tremendous impact on all our lives. And you'll see the changes to America Online continue unabated in the years to come.

Who is this book for?

I've written this book for the beginner and the seasoned online traveler. So even if you've just begun to perfect your mouse-clicking skills, you'll find this book an easy way to get connected to America Online and learn the ropes.

And please don't consider me your teacher, nor this a textbook. Think of me as just a fellow computer user, sitting across the room from you, who is there to discuss ways to make your online experience easier and more fun.

You can read this book like a novel, from beginning to end. Or you can focus just on the chapters that contain the information you need right away. The book is written for both kinds of readers, so you don't have to pore over many chapters to find what you want. If it's necessary to read another part of the book for expanded information, I'll mention it.

The bill of fare

I've divided this book into five parts, so you can easily focus on the chapters that interest you the most. Here's the menu:

Part I: Let's Get Going

In the first two chapters of the book, I'll show you how to install America Online's Windows software, set up your online account, and enjoy your first session on AOL. Then I'll give you some helpful hints on setting up the software to run best on your computer. If you run into any problems along the way, I've offered some hints to solve common connection and software problems.

Part II: Getting Your Feet Wet

Here's where the action begins. First I'll take you briefly through AOL's fourteen departments, then explain how you can meet other AOL members. And then I'll show you what AOL's e-mail, message boards, and online forums are all about. I'll even introduce you to those famous America Online conferences, where some of the most famous personalities from the political and show business worlds have appeared.

Part III: Having Fun on AOL

In the next four chapters, I'll show you how to locate online information and how to introduce your kids to AOL and the Internet. Then I'll cover the lifestyles and special interest areas, which cover loads of subjects from health care to *Star Trek* fans. You'll also get a brief tour of AOL's computing forums and the industry connection areas, where you can contact the major computer manufacturers.

Part IV: Information at Your Fingertips

America Online has tens of thousands of software files available for you. You just need to know where to find them, and I'll show you how in this section. You'll also discover a number of resources for online education and reference information. We'll take a quick stopover at AOL's online newsstand, where some of your favorite publications are available. You'll discover handy sources for buying merchandise online at low, low prices and pay a visit to AOL's travel agency.

Part V: Getting on the Information Superhighway

The worldwide Internet network has become the hot new frontier, and America Online offers a full slate of Internet services. In the final five chapters of this book, I'll show you how to send e-mail through the Internet, how to subscribe to mailing lists, and how to participate in the wild, wacky newsgroup message boards. You'll also learn about the newest Internet feature, the World Wide Web, which offers you pictures, text, and sometimes sound to enhance your online visits.

Special book elements

This book has a number of special elements and conventions to help you find information quickly or skip stuff you don't want to read right now.

Tips either point out information often overlooked in the documentation or help you use your software more efficiently, like a shortcut. Some tips help you solve or avoid problems.

Cautions alert you to potential dangerous consequences of a procedure or practice, especially if it could cause serious or even disastrous results (such as loss or corruption of data).

 What are Q&A notes?
Cast in the form of questions and answers, these notes provide you with advice on ways to solve common problems.

 Plain English, please!
These notes explain the meanings of technical terms or computer jargon.

Throughout this book, I'll use a comma to separate parts of a pull-down menu command. For example, to open a document, you'll choose File, Open. That means Pull down the File menu and choose Open from the list.

And if you see two keys separated by a plus sign, such as Ctrl+X, that means to press and hold the first key, press the second key, then release both keys.

Sidebars are interesting nuggets of information

Sidebars provide interesting, nonessential reading: side-alley trips you can take when you're not at the computer or when you just want some relief from working. Here, you may find more technical details, funny stories, personal anecdotes, or interesting background information.

Shooting at a moving target

I began writing books on America Online for Que in 1994. Each edition has shown major changes from the previous work. America Online, like a large city, is growing and changing constantly. You will find that the service's look and feel will develop and improve over time. Some of the places pictured in this book might look a little different on your screen, too. But the information in these pages will be useful for a long time as a guide to learning about America Online.

As you begin to explore the online community, keep this book at hand. When you have a question or want to learn more about a particular place, you can move directly to that chapter for the information you want.

The online community has, over the years, become my second home. Here I meet and interact with our friends and even conduct many of my regular business affairs. I have made deals and begun work projects with people whom I know only by e-mail.

Indeed, the dream of the information superhighway has, to me, become an up-close and personal reality, and I want you to share that dream, too. Let the pages that follow be your starting point on the road to a learning experience that might be unlike any other you've ever had.

Gene Steinberg
Scottsdale, Arizona

Part I: Let's Get Going

Chapter 1: **How to Get Started on America Online**

Chapter 2: **Setting Up Your AOL Windows Software**

1

How to Get Started on America Online

● **In this chapter:**

- **Join America Online**
- **Create your own online address**
- **Take a fast tour of the services**
- **But first a little history…**

You can begin your online adventure with just a software disk! . . . .

10   **Part I** *Let's Get Going*

So many of our technological marvels had their humble beginnings as toys for hobbyists, engineers and scientists. When their value was demonstrated to the rest of us, manufacturers found ways to make them faster and cheaper and, in some respects, better. What was once an incredible achievement became a regular part of our everyday lives. In the 1980s, we had compact disc players and videocassette recorders. For the 1990s, it's the personal computer. There are tens of millions of computers in our homes, offices, and schools. Airplane seats are filled with folks preparing documents or playing games on their laptop computers. Hotels provide special phone jacks so their guests can stay connected via their computers.

As computers spread across our land, those of us who bought these new appliances sought out ways to connect to other computer users. We bought those little devices that let your computer talk through telephone lines with modems and we signed up with organizations that let computer users link up together via their modems and share messages and receive information.

The history of America Online

The dream of the information superhighway wasn't really in many people's minds in 1985, when America Online was founded as Quantum Computer Services. In that year, the Apple Macintosh was just a low-powered niche computer, and Microsoft Windows didn't exist.

Today America Online is a publicly owned company that offers an online community for well over four million members. The service offers online shopping, information services, such as daily newspapers and magazines, and even virtual reference books, such as encyclopedias.

America Online is like a huge city, with many people hanging out and communicating with one another on a host of subjects, from the time of day and the weather to the state of the nation and the world. The online experience is unlike any you've ever seen. After you have been introduced to America Online, you'll probably want to stick around.

Here's the fast and easy way to install America Online software

Installing AOL's software on your PC is easy. In just a couple of minutes you'll be ready to connect to the service for the first time.

To use America Online software, you need a 386 or faster with 4M or more of installed RAM and at least 4M of free hard-drive space. If you want to use AOL's multimedia features, including access to the Internet's World Wide Web, you'll want at least 8MB of RAM to get good performance.

 Plain English, please!

Multimedia is a term that describes the ability to mix pictures, sound, and text on a computer or even on your home audio system or TV.

Of course, every new PC sold these days more than meets these basic needs.

In writing this chapter, I'm assuming you are comfortable performing the basic functions of using your computer, such as installing new software from a floppy disk onto your hard drive, performing simple file management chores, opening applications, and using the mouse. If you need a quick refresher course, review the instruction manuals that came with your computer or operating system disks. Or get yourself a copy of *Using Windows 95* from Que at your local bookstore.

Before you install the AOL software, though, make a backup of your original floppy disk. (You should do this sort of thing with all your software and valuable disks.) Then lock the original disks in a safe and preferably physically separate place, in case your copies are damaged.

You do need one more thing, of course, and that is a Hayes-compatible modem with a speed of 2400 bps (bits per second) or faster. If you don't have a modem, you'll want to buy one at your favorite dealer.

 Plain English, please!

The word **modem** is short for modulator/demodulator. It's a device that allows you to send and receive computer data over telephone lines. A modem actually converts the binary 1s and 0s of computer data into sounds (although it usually sounds more like an unlistenable mixture of whistles and hisses to most of us) so the phone lines can handle the information.

Part I Let's Get Going

America Online has been rolling out its 14,400 and 28,800 bits per second services, and prices for high-speed modems have dropped, so you'll want to buy the fastest modem you can afford. You also can expect even higher speeds to be supported by America Online in the future.

CAUTION **The descriptions in this book are based on version 2.5 of AOL's** Windows software. As the software is revised, you should expect some of the features and information screens to change too, but the basic setup instructions will still apply.

Ordering your software

America Online (AOL) disks often come free with your new software or computer purchase. Some of your favorite computing magazines also include the software disks from time to time. Lots of disks also are sent by direct mail, so if you're in the habit of tossing out ads you may just want to take a second look at any trim little package with an America Online logo on it.

If you don't have an America Online disk on hand, you can order one by calling 1-800-827-6364. Please tell the operator the kind of computer you have, so you will receive the right software. You will get your disk in a couple of weeks. In the meantime, you can review this chapter and the next one about installing your software, establishing your personal online account, and mastering the America Online program.

Even if you already have telecommunications software installed on your computer, America Online uses its own proprietary software to provide the unique graphic environment and efficient performance. You need America Online's special software to use the service. It does not work with a general-purpose terminal program.

How to install your AOL software

America Online's software is compressed, which is a technique used to make files smaller so they take up less room. That way, the software can be supplied on a single 1.4M floppy disk.

TIP **Before proceeding with your software installation, have your** software's registration certificate and your credit card or checkbook handy. Also, be sure that your modem has been turned on and is hooked up to your computer and to your phone line.

Chapter 1 *How to Get Started on America Online* 13

 Q&A **Help! I haven't upgraded to Windows 95 yet. Does that mean I can't join America Online.**

Yes, you can join America Online. AOL's software looks and runs pretty much the same in Windows 3.1. Just be sure the disk you have isn't specifically designed just to work with Windows 95 (you'll want to check the label). When you're ready to upgrade to Windows 95, the Microsoft installer is smart enough to include all your existing software in the installation process, so you'll be able to log onto America Online without any trouble.

After you've made a backup of your original software disk, you're ready to get the software up and running. Follow these steps:

1. Insert the floppy disk into your PC's floppy drive.
2. Click the Windows 95 Start button.
3. Choose Run.
4. Type **A:\SETUP.EXE**.
5. Then press the Enter key on your PC's keyboard (see fig. 1.1).

Fig. 1.1
America Online's clever installer will gently guide you through the process of installing your new software.

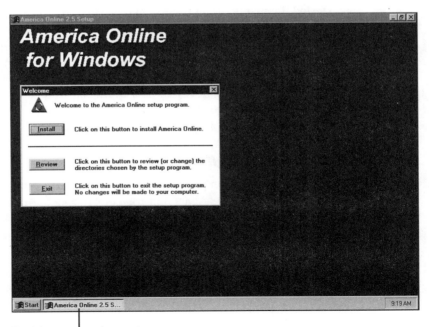

Check here to see what version of the software you're using.

In a minute or two, you receive a message that the software has been successfully installed, and the AOL program will appear on your PC's desktop in an open folder. If you have any problems at this point, you should probably just try to install the software again.

Now let's open your new program and get on with the rest of the setup and enrollment process. To get the process under way, simply double-click on the AOL program icon.

As soon as the program opens, you will be taken step-by-step through the process of setting up your America Online software to work with your modem and telephone (see fig. 1.2), and then you'll enroll as an AOL member. Before making a selection, read the instructions carefully on the information screens. As America Online software is updated, the information you will read is likely to change.

For the next few moments, you see more information windows. It is a good idea to read the instructions carefully before proceeding. If you have any questions or problems, you can choose Cancel to stop the installation and try again later.

During the installation process, AOL's software probed your modem to get a basic picture of its capabilities. For most setups, this will do just fine. But if you have a high speed modem (28,800 bps) or just wish to get the best possible performance, you'll want to do a custom setup before going further.

If you want to check or revise your modem profile, click the No button in the window and continue. If you decide to go this route (and not go with the default setting), you have a few more things to do:

 Plain English, please!

> AOL's modem profile is a file containing instructions that tell your modem how to talk to AOL's host computer network.

1. Although the software has made choices for you about modem speed and the kind of modem profile it's using, you can change these setups to something you feel might provide better performance. AOL software comes with profiles for most popular makes and models of modems, including Hayes, Megahertz, Motorola, Supra, U.S. Robotics, and others. For most users, the default selection should work best. I'll show you how to choose a different modem setup in chapter 2, "Setting Up Your AOL Software."

Fig. 1.2

You can change your modem setup on this screen.

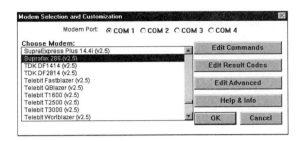

2. If you decide to change your setup options, you are asked whether you want to install the option to disable Call Waiting service when you are online. If you have Call Waiting and someone tries to call you while you're online, the tones you hear in your telephone will quickly dump you from your online connection. You might have to check with your local telephone company, however, before choosing the disable option. Not all services allow you to turn off Call Waiting for a single call.

3. If your online connections are being made from an office, you might have to dial a special number, usually 9, to get an outside line. Be sure to select this option if you need it; otherwise, you can't make your first online connection.

Getting a local connection

Now you want to have America Online's host computer find a local connection number for you. As soon as your modem setup has been completed, AOL's host computer will be dialed up. Once you're connected, you are asked to enter your area code so America Online can hook you up to the closest (and thus the cheapest) connection to your area.

The host computer searches its directory of access numbers for ones that match the area code you entered (see fig. 1.3). If you cannot locate a number in your area code, you have the option to choose another number from a nearby area code. Because America Online is continuously adding new connection numbers, you always have the opportunity to change your connection number later. (See chapter 3, "Finding Your Way Around", for more information about locating and changing your America Online access numbers.)

Fig. 1.3
This is the screen where you pick your first local access number.

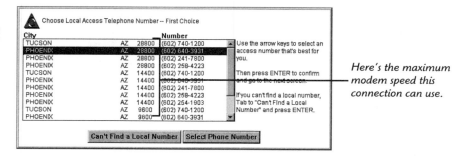

You should select two connection numbers if they are available. That way, if your modem can't make a connection with the first number—perhaps because the number's busy or because of line noise—you have a second chance to connect to America Online.

Once you've joined America Online, you can always get a new set of local numbers in a way similar to what I've just described. Just choose Get Local # from the pop-up menu of your AOL software that lists your screen names (you'll find out about those in the next section), and AOL's friendly host computer will guide you through the process of creating a new set of connection numbers. If you have a high-speed modem, of course, you'll want to choose the AOLNet numbers, which support connection speeds of up to 28,800 bps.

Establishing your online account

From here on, until you log on to the service for the first time, you are guided through several steps that enable you to establish your own exclusive America Online account and set your billing options. (Now you find out why I suggested that you have handy the certificate that came with your software disks and your credit card or checkbook.)

The choices you make now are not etched in stone. If you decide to change your password or billing information later, you can easily do so in the free Online Support area.

To establish your online account, follow these steps:

1 First, examine the registration numbers that are on the folder in which your America Online software was packaged. Enter the certificate number and certificate passwords in the blank Certificate Number and

Chapter 1 *How to Get Started on America Online* **17**

Certificate Password entry boxes (see fig. 1.4). You can use the Tab key on your computer's keyboard to move from one entry field to the next.

Fig. 1.4
Use this screen to start setting up your online account. First, you enter the Certificate Number and Password information.

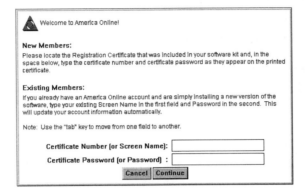

   2 Click the Continue button.

Each step from here on will bring up one or more information screens. Before clicking the Continue button each step of the way, you will want to read the information, because it contains important things you need to know about setting up your AOL account.

   3 Enter your name, mailing address, and telephone number.

   4 Click the Continue button.

   5 Indicate how you want to pay for your America Online service. You can choose Modify Billing Information (see fig. 1.5) and then choose from American Express, Discover, MasterCard, or Visa. Or, if you prefer, you can have your online charges deducted regularly from your checking account (see fig. 1.6), using the Other Billing Method option.

Fig. 1.5
Enter your credit card information here. You can easily change your credit card billing information whenever you want in AOL's Billing area (I explain more about that in a tip a bit later).

Fig. 1.6
You can opt to have your online charges deducted automatically from your checking account for a slight monthly surcharge.

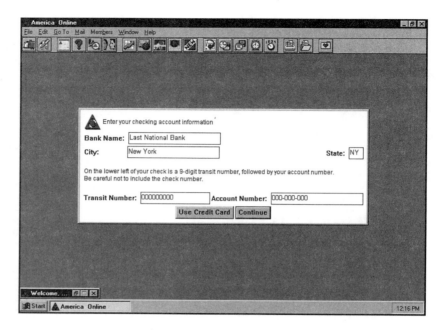

To protect you, America Online verifies all your billing information. If the program encounters a problem in establishing your account, the account is suspended until you are able to update your billing information. This precaution is taken solely for your protection. After all, you wouldn't want to pay for someone else's online charges.

 **If you are billing your service to your checking account, America Online** may take up to a day or two to verify the account before you can connect to the service. If this is the case, you'll see an onscreen message to that effect.

 To check your usage bill on America Online, type the keyword Billing. You are then taken to a free support area where you can check your current bill and make changes to your billing information.

Create your online mailing address

Next, you need to enter your online mailing address—your screen name. This is a golden opportunity to be creative. Your online address can contain from three to ten characters (letters and numbers). You can identify yourself on America Online by your first name, an abbreviation of your name, or even a descriptive word or two that expresses your own unique personality traits, such as The Bear.

The online name you choose for yourself is used by your master account, and the host computer checks that name (along with the password you select) every time you log on to America Online. You can add up to four additional names to your online account, for use by other members of your family, or for yourself if you decide to try on a change of clothing from time to time (or you want to use one screen name for business purposes, and one just for fun). Bear in mind that you can use only one screen name attached to your account at any one time. If you want to log on simultaneously with more than one screen name (to allow, for example, your child to hook up to the service), you need to establish separate accounts.

If someone is already using the name you select, you are given the option of using that name plus a number (the number is randomly selected by the computer). You might, for example, be offered the choice of using GeneS12345 if a number of people online are already using the screen name GeneS.

 **You cannot delete your master account name without deleting** your account, so take as much time as you need to select an appropriate screen name.

As you try to locate an available screen name, America Online searches its database to determine whether someone else already has selected that name. Because America Online is a family-oriented service, names using vulgar language or with a vulgar connotation are not accepted.

After America Online has accepted your screen name, your next step is to select a password. A password is your ounce of protection against someone using your account without your permission, so don't use anything obvious, like a contraction of your name. Select a unique word or phrase that someone would be unlikely to stumble on at random.

> **Plain English, please!**
>
> In the computer world, a **password** is a key that unlocks something, such as your access to an online service or access to a computer network at a typical workplace. This key may consist of letters, numbers, or both (such as UFO, 1234, or UFO23). It is very important to choose a password that would not be easy for others to figure out (a simple name isn't a good idea) but that you can remember without difficulty.

After you've chosen your screen name, you're ready to go out and meet the online community.

Before you are formally welcomed to the America Online family, you are asked whether you accept the Terms of Service. Carefully read the information displayed. You also can check the text of the terms in the Online Support area. Basically the terms request that you be a good citizen during your online visits and avoid using vulgar language and other such things.

Before you enjoy your first online session

Before you connect to AOL for your first session, I want to give you a couple of quick shortcuts for getting around the online community quickly and getting direct online help.

The first shortcut is how to use a keyword. This is a keyboard command you can specify only while you're connected to America Online. You can use keywords to go just about anywhere on America Online, without having to worry about the exact routes for getting there.

To use America Online keywords, press Control-K and then enter the keyword in the entry field of the Keyword dialog box that will appear on your screen (see fig. 1.7). Then press Return or Enter, and in just a few seconds you'll be transported to the place you want to visit. (If the keyword happens to be wrong or is mistyped, you'll get a message to that effect.) I'll give you a thorough rundown on AOL's software in chapter 2, "Setting Up Your AOL Windows Software," in case you still have questions.

TIP **To review AOL's Terms of Service at any time, use the keyword** TOS (Terms of Service). This takes you to an area free of online charges where you can read the terms.

Whenever you're logged onto America Online, you can visit the free online support area to get direct assistance with any problem. To get to the support area, choose the Members, Member Services, or just type the keyword Help. A window will appear asking whether you want to enter this free area.

Fig. 1.7
A keyword is your magic carpet for quick trips along AOL's information superhighway.

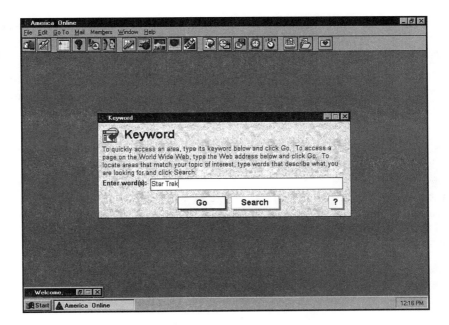

 Q&A *What's a free area?*

It's a special area set aside by America Online to provide support information and assistance to members. Because it's free, you aren't charged for the time you spend online while you're in this area getting the information you need.

Okay, now let's get ready to join the online community.

Leaving the starting gate

The first time you connect to America Online (assuming your computer's sounds are working), you hear a friendly voice intone, "Welcome," and a few seconds later you hear that same fellow say, "You've Got Mail." Yes, when you sign onto America Online for the first time, you indeed find a letter in your mailbox. Just click on the You Have Mail icon, and you see your first letter listed in the directory. Double-click on that directory listing to see the text of the letter on your computer screen. The letter is from Steve Case, the president of America Online. He welcomes you to the service and briefly outlines the special features you might want to examine during your travels.

The first screen you see on your computer, the Welcome screen, is your gateway to all the features offered by America Online (see fig. 1.8). In the middle of the Welcome screen is a list of special announcements, places to visit, and the Top News headline. Just click on the icon to the right of the message that describes something you want to investigate (or on the icon to the left of the Top News Story headline), and you are taken to that area on America Online. The list you see in this Welcome screen changes several times per day as different services are featured and the top news stories change.

Fig. 1.8
This screen is your America Online gateway.

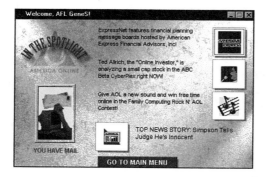

At the bottom of the Welcome screen (also known as In the Spotlight) is a rectangular box labeled GO TO MAIN MENU. When you click on this box you are taken to the window that lies beneath the Welcome screen (see fig. 1.9), which is your gateway to all the major services on America Online. At the left of the Main Menu screen are three icons. Clicking on In the Spotlight returns you to the original Welcome screen. Beneath it is the icon for America Online's electronic mail center, the Post Office. At the bottom is the Discover AOL icon, which I'll explore further a bit later in this chapter.

Fig. 1.9
America Online's Main Menu is the table of contents to all the major features of the service.

At the left of the screen are the AOL logo, the Discover AOL icon, and your personal mail icon. To the right of those icons are two columns of colorful rectangular buttons, each of which takes you to a different department. These buttons are clearly labeled, and you can click on any one of them now to explore. These departments are discussed in detail in chapter 3, "Finding Your Way Around."

For now, I'll just take you on a brief tour of the service.

Let's begin a guided online tour

To explore America Online, click on the Discover AOL icon. The Discover America Online screen appears, as shown in figure 1.10.

Fig. 1.10
You can find all sorts of things on America Online on your very first visit.

You can visit eight different locations, each identified by a unique icon. Clicking once on an icon takes you to the corresponding area on the network.

TIP **Before going further, you probably want to click on the "A Letter From Steve" icon.** Every month or two, America Online's president, Steve Case, writes a status report on the services, telling about America Online's growth and the new features that are available. He also gives a brief preview of the features you can expect in the near future.

Now you're ready to embark on your tour.

Examining America Online highlights

Using the America Online Highlights icon is a quick way to familiarize yourself with the major features of America Online. The services highlighted change from time to time, so you might want to take this little tour again every so often.

The stops along the tour change from time to time, but each window provides information about a specific area on America Online.

These areas, called forums, are discussed in more detail beginning in chapter 3, "Finding Your Way Around." For now, you can either select the Continue Tour button, to go on with the tour, or the Show button, which transports you directly to the area you are reading about. If you decide to visit one of these forums, you can take the tour again later.

When you've gone through all the forum windows, the screen appears, letting you know you have completed the tour. You then are returned to the Discover AOL area.

After you've completed your tour, spend some time poking around the service on your own. At each new location, you can check things out or move on. Literally thousands of services are available to you, covering many interests. This book lists only some of the highlights because new services are added almost daily. You will find every online visit an adventure of discovery and enjoyment.

 TIP If you're watching your budget, type the keyword Clock. You then see an onscreen clock that shows the amount of time you've been online.

Just a start

Now you've officially joined the online community as a member of America Online. You probably want to take some time to explore your new home and get an idea of the vast array of information services now available to you.

After you've become a little more accustomed to navigating through America Online, you'll want to begin to master your America Online software. For a description of all the software features and how to fine-tune the software, you'll want to read chapter 2, "Setting Up Your AOL Software."

Setting Up Your AOL Software

● **In this chapter:**

- Quickly set up your modem to connect to AOL at top speed

- Got connection problems? We'll tell you how to fix them

- Make AOL's software work the way you want it to

- Use your AOL software to edit online graphics

Here are hints and tricks for getting the most out of your AOL time . . . .

26 Part I *Let's Get Going*

When you first drive a new car, you get comfortable before you take it out for a spin. You adjust the seats, the rearview mirror, the side-view mirrors, and maybe the steering wheel. When you install new software, you'll also want to learn ways to fine-tune it to perform to your taste. With America Online's Windows software, you'll want to make several adjustments so the software works exactly the way you want it to.

In the next few pages, I'll cover ways to set up your AOL software for best performance. And you'll get some helpful hints to make your online visits more enjoyable. But first, I want to tell you about a quick method to open your AOL software.

TIP **If you have a problem using your America Online software and you** need some immediate assistance, click the Help menu and choose the item you want to know about from the Help Contents list.

A quick and easy modem setup guide

When you connect to America Online, you usually hear that little box next to a desktop PC (or the one inside your PC) squawking and squeaking during the connection process. I admit it sounds intimidating, because that device (your modem) doesn't always adhere to the Windows 95 concept of plug-and-play. But AOL's Windows software makes using your modem easy.

Before you connect to America Online on a regular basis, you'll want to take a moment or two to be sure your modem is set up properly. When you first install your America Online software, the software examines your modem and sets a default modem profile for it. If you buy a new modem, you'll want to change these settings. Or you might want to change your connection numbers to the America Online network.

TIP **A selection of updated modem drivers is available for download** from America Online's Member Services area (*Keyword:* **Help**). To access these drivers, first click the Members' Online Support icon in the main Member Services window, and then click on Technical Help. Sometimes modem makers will supply an AOL connection file with their own software (so you want to check out the files they give you).

Chapter 2 Setting Up Your AOL Software

To change your connection settings, follow these steps:

1 Click the Setup button in the main America Online window to display the screen shown in figure 2.1. (You can change these settings only when you're not logged onto the America Online network.)

Fig. 2.1
You can easily make changes to your Network & Modem setup for the best connections to America Online.

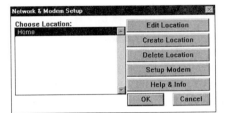

The fastest way to launch

Okay, here's the usual routine. You want to launch an application, so you click the Start menu, choose Programs, and then search through the folder that contains the application you want to run. Here's an easier way. It's called a Shortcut, and it'll put America Online's software icon right on your PC's desktop. Here's how to make one:

1 Open the folder in which AOL's software is installed, or use Windows Explorer and highlight the program.

2 Click the right mouse button, and drag the AOL program icon to the desktop.

3 Choose Create Shortcut(s) Here from the pop-up menu.

If you don't know the location of the program, you can use Windows 95's wizard to find the program from a list of available folders on your PC's hard drive. Here's how:

1 If AOL's icon doesn't line up with your other desktop items, right click the place on your PC's desktop where you want AOL's program icon to appear.

2 Choose New, Shortcut from the menu that appears.

3 Browse through the folders at the left side of the wizard screen to locate the AOL program folder.

4 Then name your shortcut in the text field labeled Command Line.

Once you've made your AOL program shortcut, you'll see the AOL icon on your PC's desktop. When you double-click that icon, the AOL program will launch. Just like that!

28 Part I *Let's Get Going*

 Plain English, please!

On your PC, a **shortcut** is a small file that is actually a reference to the original file (the original can be a document, an application program, or even a networked disk, to cite a few examples). This handy feature allows you to activate a file without having to comb through the Start menu to find it.

2 Click on the Edit Location option.

You can set up two connection profiles (see fig. 2.2). Your America Online software uses the one on the left when trying to make your initial connection to the network. If the connection doesn't succeed for any reason—usually due to a busy connection port or noise on the line—the program dials the number on the right.

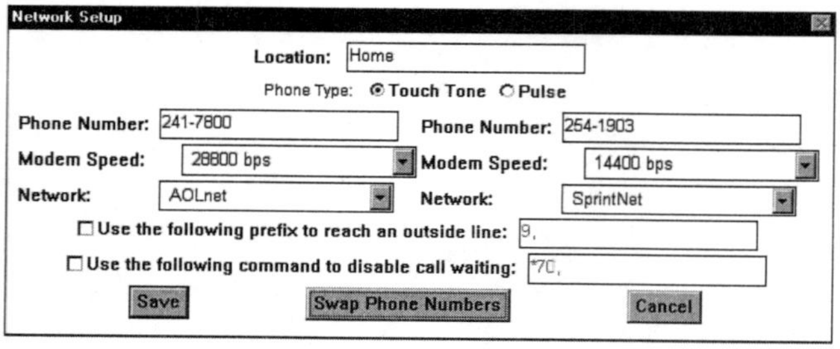

Fig. 2.2
You can quickly change the connection numbers used to access AOL on this screen.

 TIP **If you've moved, or you're traveling, or you just want to see if you** can get a better connection to AOL, you may want to change the number you use to connect to AOL. It's an easy process.

First thing to do is log onto America Online. Then type the keyword Access. You are asked whether you want to enter this free area. Press Return or click Yes. You then see a window with a list of options for finding an access number. For now, just double-click on Search. You see a window with a space for you to enter the area code you want to check. When you enter that number, America Online checks its online phone directory and produces a list of phone numbers for the selected area.

 TIP **A quick way to navigate from one data entry point (field) to** another is to press Tab. To return to the previous field, press Shift+Tab.

Chapter 2 *Setting Up Your AOL Software* **29**

3 The first option, Phone Type, enables you to choose between a standard Touch Tone telephone and a Pulse telephone.

4 Type the new number in the Phone Number box. When you change the number, you also might need to change the Network setting as well. The Network setting is the service that America Online uses to connect to its host computers. When you get a list of phone numbers from America Online for your area, you see such names as AOLNet, SprintNet, or Tymnet attached to the phone numbers. Simply pull down the menu at the right of the Network label, and select the correct name of the service provider.

5 America Online's phone directory also lists the baud rate supported by that phone number. You need to select the correct speed in the Baud Rate box of the Network Setup dialog box, or you can't properly connect to the network. So, if the network supports 14,400 bps, choose that figure (or a higher one) for best performance.

The next two check boxes control how the software uses your modem to dial the service.

6 Some businesses have special phone lines that require a dial out code. Usually it's 9, but you can change that setting if necessary (I've been at some hotels where 8 is used instead). If you need to dial a special number to reach an outside line, check this box.

7 This option allows you to turn off Call Waiting during your online session.

8 The final option you have is to Swap Phone Numbers. Clicking on that button transfers the information from the left to the right side of the dialog box, and vice versa. This feature is useful if you find that you are getting better online performance with your second connection number.

Q&A *I just bought a new V.34 (28,800 bps) modem, and it still connects at 2400 bps. Why?*

Getting a high-speed modem is half the battle. To log onto AOL at high speed, you need an access number that supports that capability. You can search the full listing of numbers while online via the keyword Access.

Q&A How do I know I'm connecting at high speed?

Just look at your AOL software window when logging on. Step 3 shows the speed at which you're connecting.

Q&A Help. My modem won't dial AOL.

If you've been able to connect to AOL before, something might have changed in your setup. Here are some steps to follow:

1 Switch off your modem and turn it back on again. Sometimes the modem's firmware (the chips inside the modem) will freeze due to a software defect or a previous connection problem. When you turn the modem on again, it's the equivalent of restarting your computer, and often has the same result.

2 Try another telecommunications program, such as Microphone with Windows 95 (now called Hyperterminal) or a similar program. If another telecommunications program can successfully make your modem dial out, the problem is definitely related to the way your AOL software is set up (in which case you want to review steps 1–8 earlier in this chapter).

3 Make sure the dial prefix or string is correct.

Click Setup box while logged off. Be sure that the correct Modem Type is selected from the pop-up menu.

Q&A Help! I can't find a nearby phone number in my home town or in the place I'm visiting. What's the best way to get onto AOL?

America Online's telephone access networks are always being updated, but there are some parts of the U.S. without a nearby local access number. If you run into such a situation, you have another choice—an 800 number—that America Online has established to help you get high speed, 28,800 bps access, to its network. The number is 800-716-0023. I want to add that this phone number carries an hourly surcharge (check AOL's Access area for the latest price), but that charge is apt to be less than you'd pay for most long distance phone calls.

How to fine-tune your AOL software

The next thing you want to do is set up your America Online software's preferences. This is how you adjust the program so it looks and feels the way you want it to. Even if everything looks okay to you at first glance, it's worth the effort to try out a few settings just to see whether you can adjust things a bit better.

To set up preferences, choose Set Preferences from the Members menu, or press Control- = . The Preferences window appears, with eight icons that represent preference choices (see fig. 2.3).

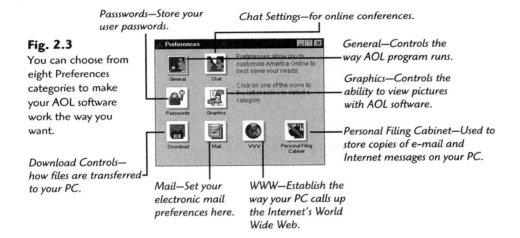

Fig. 2.3
You can choose from eight Preferences categories to make your AOL software work the way you want.

Passswords—Store your user passwords.

Chat Settings—for online conferences.

General—Controls the way AOL program runs.

Graphics—Controls the ability to view pictures with AOL software.

Personal Filing Cabinet—Used to store copies of e-mail and Internet messages on your PC.

Download Controls—how files are transferred to your PC.

Mail—Set your electronic mail preferences here.

WWW—Establish the way your PC calls up the Internet's World Wide Web.

Setting most of your preferences involves the same steps. You click the check box next to an item to select it, and you see an x appear in that box. You click on the box again to turn the feature off, at which time the x disappears. Figure 2.4 shows an example of several options checked in the General Preferences dialog box.

Fig. 2.4
Checking a box is all that's necessary to change your America Online preferences.

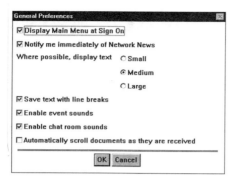

Most of the AOL program settings can pretty much be left intact for now. As you spend more time on AOL, you'll want to play with those preferences and see what effect they have. They are clearly labeled as to what they do, and it's easy to set them back to their original settings, so don't worry if you don't like the changes you've wrought. There is one preference, though, that you'll want to think about carefully. I'll discuss that one in the next section.

How to set password preferences

Here's a feature you'll want to use with caution. When you click the password icon (see fig. 2.5), it brings up a dialog box in which you can store the passwords you select for each of your screen names. That means you can call up America Online and have the program automatically log on for you. But if others are using your computer, and you would prefer not to risk the possibility of someone else using your account without your permission, you should not store your passwords in this manner. If no passwords are stored, you are asked to enter your password at the beginning of your online visit.

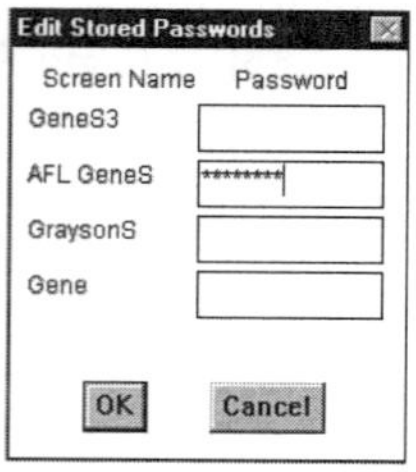

Fig. 2.5
Enter your stored passwords with caution and with no prying eyes around.

If, after reading my warnings, you want to store your online passwords, simply select this option, which brings up a list of your screen names. Enter the correct password in the text entry field next to the appropriate screen name.

Just what are WWW preferences?

The World Wide Web gives the Internet color and style. I'll tell you more about these preferences and how to access the Web in chapters 18 and 19. For now you can get a brief idea of America Online's Internet services via the keyword Internet.

How to edit pictures with AOL's software

When you open a picture file in your AOL software, you can actually edit the image. It's not quite as elaborate as a regular image editing program (such as Corel Draw or Adobe Photoshop), but you can do some simple stuff with it.

To open the toolbar, you have to have a picture file open; otherwise, the command is grayed out. With a picture opened in your AOL program, click Edit, Show Tools (see fig. 2.6). Then a set of graphic editing tools will appear in a movable window. These tools are similar to what you might find in an image editing program (but, as I said, not quite as elaborate).

Fig. 2.6
AOL's image editing toolbar lets you do basic touchups to a picture you've downloaded.

Here's what those tools mean, row by row, from left to right.

- *Rotation Tool.* This tool rotates a graphic image 90 degrees counter-clockwise.

- *Revert Tool.* This tool reverts the image to the last saved version. It's a quick way to undo multiple changes you've made to an image file.

- *Horizontal Rotation Tool.* This tool flips the graphic image horizontally.

- *Vertical Rotation Tool.* This tool flips the graphic image vertically.

- *Brighten Image Tool.* This tool brightens the graphic image by a preset amount.

- *Darken Image Tool.* This tool darkens the graphic image by a preset amount.

- *Increase Contrast Tool.* This tool establishes a higher image contrast level.

- *Decrease Contrast Tool.* This tool establishes a lower image contrast level.

- *Grayscale Tool.* This tool removes the color bits from a color image, and changes it to grayscale.

- *Invert Image Tool.* This tool makes a positive image negative, and vice versa.

- *Fit Image to View.* This tool lets you resize a picture to fill your monitor's screen. But remember, if you are making a picture larger, you expand the little bitmaps that make up the image too, so making a picture bigger can make it look worse also.

Use AOL's FlashBar for easy access

America Online's Windows software gives you a quick way to go directly to an online department or take advantage of the most popular features of your software. This feature is called the FlashBar, and it contains 20 icons (see fig. 2.7). Each FlashBar icon represents a different AOL function or takes you to a particular online area.

Fig. 2.7
The FlashBar and your mouse are a great combination for activating the most-used features of your America Online software.

TIP **If you forget what the FlashBar icons mean, simply place the mouse** cursor above the icon, and you'll see a label that describes its function.

When you first open your America Online application, most of these icons are grayed out. But when you log on, the icons become bright and colorful. Clicking on the appropriate icon with your mouse takes you directly to the listed online area or activates the listed function.

Chapter 2 *Setting Up Your AOL Software* **35**

In table 2.1, you'll see the special functions and destinations attached to each icon. The areas shown match, from left to right, to the icons displayed on the FlashBar. All these areas and features are discussed in more detail throughout the remainder of this book.

Table 2.1 Using the FlashBar

Icon	Destination or function
	Check Mail
	Compose Mail
	Go to Main Menu
	Online Help
	Directory of Services
	Lobby in People Connection
	Stock Link
	Top News

continues

Table 2.1 Continued

Icon	Destination or function
	Go to Center Stage
	Internet Connection
	New Features and Services
	Discover America Online
	Go to Keyword
	Download Manager
	File Search
	Online Clock
	Personal Choices
	Print

Chapter 2 *Setting Up Your AOL Software* **37**

Icon	Destination or function
	Favorite Places Menu

> **TIP** **If you see a little heart-shaped icon at the upper right side of the** title bar of the window that represents an AOL area, there's a quick way to get back to it again. Just click on that icon. You'll get an acknowledgment message that the area has been added to your list of Favorite Places. And you can access that listing just by clicking the right-most icon on your AOL program's FlashBar.

Is that all?

The steps described in this chapter help you fine-tune your AOL Windows software to suit your tastes, just as you adjust the seats and mirrors in a car when you sit in it for the first time. To learn more about AOL's exciting features, you'll want to turn the page to the next chapter.

Part II: Getting Your Feet Wet

Chapter 3: **Finding Your Way Around**

Chapter 4: **The Easy Way to Meet People Online**

Chapter 5: **How to Stay in Touch with Other Members**

Finding Your Way Around

● **In this chapter:**

- All the major departments on America Online
- A quick way to navigate around the network
- A fast look at online spots devoted to entertainment
- A quick visit to the online computing areas
- A look at areas devoted to education and reference information

A vast world of entertainment and information is waiting for you on America Online, so let's dive in. . . . . ➤

Over the first two chapters of this book, you've installed your new AOL software and learned a little something about the features that are offered. I've also helped you fine-tune the software so you can get the most out of your AOL time. Now let's have a look at some of the services AOL offers. I'll flesh these out in the later chapters of this book.

A brief look at AOL's Departments

Now that you've signed onto America Online and learned how to use the software, it's time to do more than just stick your toes in the water.

Every time you log onto America Online, you'll see the Welcome screen (see fig. 3.1), also known as In The Spotlight. This screen shows the major highlights for the moment and perhaps even informs you that you have e-mail waiting.

Fig. 3.1
See the current highlights and check your mail when you first log on to America Online.

You'll know right away if you have mail waiting for you!

In this chapter, I'll dig a bit deeper, beneath the In The Spotlight window, to the Main Menu and beyond, where you'll explore the various virtual neighborhoods, known as *departments*, of America Online (see fig. 3.2). The Main Menu is located just beneath the In The Spotlight window when you first log onto America Online. The fastest way to bring the menu up front is to click on the shaded GO TO MAIN MENU rectangle at the bottom of the Welcome screen.

Chapter 3 *Finding Your Way Around* **43**

The Main Menu is your gateway to all the major features of America Online's virtual city.

Use this icon to send and receive your mail. Keyword: Post Office

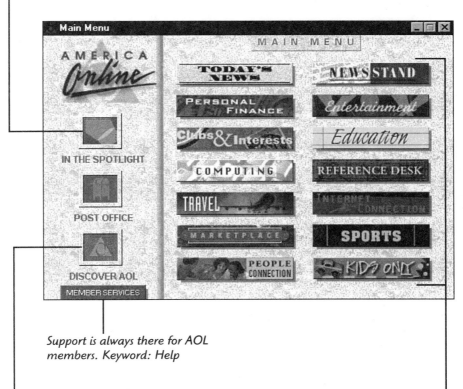

Support is always there for AOL members. Keyword: Help

Discover what's new and what's hot on AOL. Keyword: Discover

AOL features numerous areas for info, data, news, friendship, and just plain fun!

Each of the 14 online departments shown is identified by a major topic of interest. A department contains a number of forums, folders, services, and other areas related (sometimes loosely) to that topic. I'll tell you more about those areas later in this book. For now, I'll just scratch the surface.

TIP If you've closed the Main Menu during your online session, you can bring it up again by simply selecting the Go To Menu and then choosing Main Menu.

Today's News

Keyword: **News**

Here's your online daily newspaper. In addition to providing the top news of the day, the Today's News department (shown in fig. 3.2) has special sections: US and World, Business, Entertainment, Sports, and Weather. You can also use the search window, in the middle right of the department window, to locate stories about a particular item of interest. I'll describe this area in more detail in chapter 12, "Exploring Your Online Newsstand."

Fig. 3.2
Stay on top of the fast-moving events with America Online's Today's News department.

Personal Finance

Keyword: **Finance**

Let's consider this department an extension of Today's News. The Personal Finance department (see fig. 3.3) lets you delve more deeply into all aspects of handling your personal finances, from reviewing the day's business news (and how it may affect your income and investment strategies) to seeking out the profile of a company you may want to add to your stock portfolio. A surface glance at the main Personal Finance department window shows you lots of information resources.

Fig. 3.3
A vast storehouse of business news and advice awaits you in the Personal Finance department.

Computing

Keyword: **Computing**

Because we all use our personal computers to connect to America Online, the Computing department, shown in figure 3.4, is one of the most popular places to visit on AOL. You'll find lots of information and huge software libraries for your PC, and if you have to cross platforms on occasion, you'll also find Macintosh files, too. In addition, many of the major computer manufacturers have fully staffed support areas on America Online. Go to

Keyword shortcuts

Almost every part of America Online can be reached by pressing Control-K and typing a simple keyword. Most keywords are intuitive, such as typing Computing to reach AOL's Computing department or Entertainment to reach AOL's Entertainment department. If the keyword you choose isn't valid, just click on the Search button in the keyword window, and you'll see a list of likely prospects.

Now if you see a little heart-shaped icon at the right side of the area's title bar, you can quickly add that area to your list of Favorite Places (also see chapter 2). To add an area, simply click that tiny icon, and you'll receive an acknowledgment message that it's now a part of your Favorite Places listings. Not all areas, by the way, have these little icons, so don't be shocked if you don't see one.

these support areas to get quick solutions to problems with a specific product, or even advice on how to use that product more effectively. I'll tell you more about this department in chapter 9, "Get Advice, Help and Software from America Online's Computing Forums."

Fig. 3.4
The Computing area is one of AOL's most frequently visited online departments.

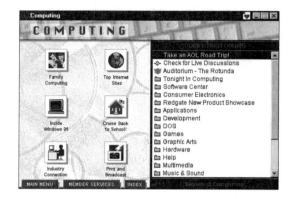

Travel

Keyword: **Travel**

As the name implies, travelers gain gratification in the areas that comprise this department (see fig. 3.5). One of the principal services of Travel & Shopping is EAASY SABRE, American Airlines' computerized travel center. You can book flights on any major airline, reserve rental cars and hotel rooms, or just check schedules and prices during your EAASY SABRE visit. You can plan an entire itinerary simply and quickly with EAASY SABRE.

Fig. 3.5
Book a flight or learn about your favorite tourist spot in America Online's Travel department.

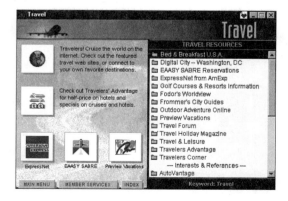

Traveler's Corner brings you information from other wayfaring souls who have already braved the far corners of our country and the farthest reaches of the globe. The Weissmann Travel Reports bring you accurate and enticing reviews of all sorts of places, including such categories as Exotic Destinations, United States Destinations, and International Destinations. The Weissmann Travel Reports you can order through America Online are the same reports used by thousands of leading travel professionals when they counsel clients. I'll cover all this and more in chapter 14, "Business or Pleasure: Travel with America Online."

Marketplace

Keyword: **Marketplace**

The Marketplace is your AOL center for shopping galore! Whether you're looking for America Online goodies such as T-shirts and coffee mugs, wanting to buy or sell a car, or looking for computer training aids, AOL's Marketplace department (shown in fig. 3.6) offers you these things and more. Here's a list of just some of the services offered, many of which are explained in more detail in chapter 13, "Say It with Flowers: Secrets of Online Shopping."

Fig. 3.6
Go shopping and save some cash right on America Online! When you first reach this department, you'll often see a special Spotlight screen showing new features, but the Marketplace will be just a click away.

The Newsstand

Keyword: **Newsstand**

America Online's Newsstand department (see fig. 3.7) offers a vast amount of information about the world today, and the news is as current as it gets. In some cases—such as with *Time* magazine, the *New York Times*, the *San Jose Mercury News*, and many other daily, weekly, and monthly publications—the information is on America Online before the publications themselves hit the streets.

Fig. 3.7
The corner newsstand was never quite like this.

There's so much more in AOL's Newsstand than I can possibly touch on in just this section, so I'll cover it in more detail in chapter 12, "Exploring Your Online Newsstand." I encourage you to explore this immense area of America Online, not only to absorb the day's news but also to expand your own knowledge about the world and current events.

Entertainment

Keyword: **Entertainment**

Movies, television, books, political and funny-pages cartoons, *Disney Adventures* magazine, RockLink, the Trivia Forum, and LaPub—these are just a few of the Entertainment department features that draw huge numbers of AOL members. Almost no other online department has the continuous drawing power of the Entertainment department. Both children and adults frequent Entertainment for its culturally diverse content. Be sure to stop by during your travels across America Online (see fig. 3.8).

As you explore the Entertainment area, be sure to stop by LaPub for a virtual thirst-quencher served by one of LaPub's congenial barkeeps. You may even find time to bounce on their trampoline or soak in the hot tub! (I'll explain what *that* means in chapter 4, "The Easy Way to Meet People Online.")

Fig. 3.8
Here, you can see just a small portion of AOL's Entertainment department.

Education

Keyword: **Education**

Do you need help with that homework assignment, or do you want to take some special courses on a particular topic? You can do these things and more in America Online's active Education department, shown in figure 3.9. Pay a virtual visit to the Library of Congress or the Smithsonian Institution, sign up for a correspondence course, or get information about the next round of college board examinations. For now, I'll refer you to chapter 11, "Learning & Reference Sources Online," for more information.

Fig. 3.9
Sign up for a special course or visit a museum during your visit to the Education department.

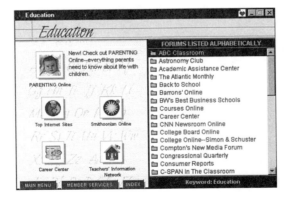

Sports

Keyword: **Sports**

When America's national pastime, baseball, disappeared in the summer of 1994 due to a players' strike, the importance of sports in our lives didn't diminish one iota. We simply talked about the football season instead. America Online's Sports department, shown in figure 3.10, is a repository of the latest sports news, plus discussion groups and regular conferences on your favorite sports. Sometimes you'll be able to converse through cyberspace with some of your favorite sports figures.

Fig. 3.10
If you open your newspaper to the Sports section first, you'll want to make regular stops to this online area.

Kids Only

Keyword: **Kids**

I really haven't discussed special places for kids yet on America Online, so I'll remedy that right now. As shown in figure 3.11, young people have lots of special and very friendly places to visit on America Online. *Disney Adventures* magazine is on hand with a special forum. There's a kids' version of *Time* magazine to explore and also special kids-only versions of America Online's most popular clubs, such as the Astronomy Club and the *Star Trek Club*. I'll cover this all in more detail in chapter 7, "The Secrets of Safe Online Fun for Kids of All Ages."

Fig. 3.11
Kids have a special area to call their own on America Online.

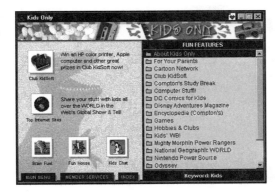

...All this and more

By now, you realize that America Online's departments contain vast areas to explore, and this chapter has highlighted only a few of them.

One of the remaining departments, People Connection, is among the most popular areas on America Online. I'll cover it in depth in chapter 5, "How to Stay in Touch with Other Members." All 14 America Online departments are described in depth in the remaining chapters.

As you read through this book, you'll also find chapters devoted to other important online features, such as e-mail, the Internet (including the World Wide Web), AOL's forums and how to get the most value from them and much more.

For now, just look around and get comfortable with the general layout. When the time comes to explore your chosen areas of interest, the later chapters will guide you through your journeys of discovery.

4

The Easy Way to Meet People Online

● In this chapter:

- Make yourself "known" to the rest of the online community

- Be discovered when your friends are online

- View other members' online profiles

- Find online areas where you can meet people

- Find other members with similar interests

- Follow proper online etiquette while meeting other members

At all hours of the day or night, thousands and thousands of folks like you are connected to America Online. Let's make contact . . . . ➢

One of the most enjoyable parts of becoming an America Online member is the ability to meet others with similar interests, whether computer-related or not. A number of resources are available to aid you in your quest for meeting other online members. You find out about these features in the following paragraphs. But first, you want to learn how to introduce yourself to others.

Give yourself an online profile

Every single member of America Online has at least one screen name. You can create up to five screen names to use when the mood strikes you, or for use by other members of your family. Every member also can create an online profile for each of those online names, for other members to view (see fig. 4.1). Your first step toward meeting people is complete when you fill out your own online profile.

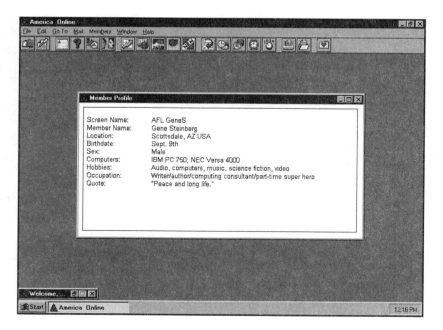

Fig. 4.1
This sample online profile shows the kind of information you can provide in your profile.

Besides the expected information, such as your real name, screen name, and location, you can enter personal information about yourself to indicate your interests to others. Hobbies, favorite quotes, your occupation, and computers you use are some of the entries you might want to provide for your profile.

Chapter 4 *The Easy Way to Meet People Online* **55**

To create or change your profile, choose Edit Your Online Profile from the Members menu of your America Online software. A complete list of the data you can enter is shown in figure 4.2.

Fig. 4.2
Use this data-entry screen to write your personal online profile.

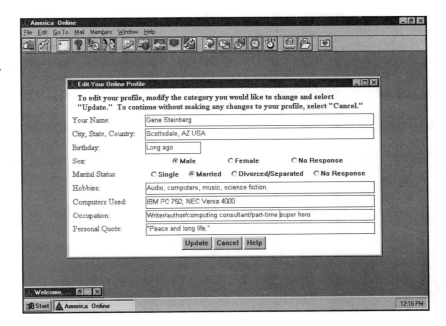

CAUTION **The first time you create a profile, it defaults to include your full** name. You are free to change it to anything you want to have appear there. AOL will respect your privacy.

As you look at the Edit Your Online Profile screen, make a note to yourself about which of the entries you want other people to be able to see when they look up your profile. You might or might not want to reveal certain information, such as your gender, real name, marital status, and so on. Fill in only the information you would not mind telling a stranger. In figure 4.2, for example, I listed my city, state, country information as a region rather than display specific information about my residence.

If you do not want to reveal your gender, be sure to click on the No Response button on that line. (If your name happens to be Pat, you could sure keep 'em guessing!) Also click on No Response for your marital status if you want that information to remain undisclosed.

TIP After you learn how to look up other people's profiles, take some time to look through a few other members' entries for ideas.

The remaining four fields are your basic "essay" answers. Here is where you tell other people about yourself as a person in a few pithy sentences instead of simply stating factual information.

After completing your online profile, review it for spelling accuracy. This step might seem as if it would be fairly obvious, but after you look at a few random profiles, you'll know why I mention it.

After you've reviewed your completed profile and are satisfied with it, click on the Update button to finish the job and move on to more exciting online activities.

Q&A *Whenever I try to check a profile, or open an AOL forum or message window, I get a message saying the system is busy. What's wrong? Is it me or them?*

This is a common problem. Your online session involves communication between your PC and AOL's host computer. If the lines of communication are clogged, you'll see a message that the system is busy (or that the host failed to respond if you're using an older version of AOL's software). The problem may be at AOL's end; its host computer network is indeed busy. It may be due to a problem with your local AOL access number, or it may be due to a system glitch.

When this problem happens, try the following:

1. Log off America Online immediately and then try to reconnect.

2. Try another access number.

   If you cannot get back online, choose Get Local # from the Locality pop-up menu on your AOL log-on screen and Click the Sign-on button to have AOL help you select new connection numbers from your home town.

3. If the connection problem continues, try logging on again at a different time. The evening hours on AOL are prime time for the service, just as they are on the major TV networks, which means higher numbers of users are online.

Chapter 4 *The Easy Way to Meet People Online* **57**

4 If you still keep getting those busy messages, use the AOL keyword System Response to access an area where you can get further assistance, and report your problem to AOL's customer service.

If you have several local access numbers to choose from, you can create separate Locality profiles (see chapter 2) for each pair of phone numbers. That way, if you cannot get connected or get poor performance from one number, you can select a different set of numbers from the pop-up menu at the right of the Locality label.

When you create an online profile for yourself, feel free to be humorous, but also try to be accurate and truthful.

If you are not sure about your entries or have second thoughts about revealing yourself, you might prefer not to complete your online profile. In this case, click on the Cancel button. Your profile is not saved, and your entries vanish. If you want more information about the Edit Your Online Profile screen, click the Help button to get additional information.

How come when I try to get a member's profile, I get a message that there isn't a profile online for that member? I know their membership is still active; I get e-mail from the person.

An AOL member doesn't have to make an online profile. Some choose not to do so, perhaps because they just want to preserve their privacy as much as possible. Their wishes should be respected, and the lack of a profile shouldn't reflect upon how you judge a fellow AOL member. You can also decide not to have a profile displayed, if you wish.

Find and meet other AOL members

Meeting people on America Online has had some interesting outcomes over the years since the online community was launched. The syndicated television program, *The Jerry Springer Show*, once spotlighted a number of AOLers who had met and married. America Online users often inhabit the various People Connection rooms, such as the Flirt's Nook and Romance Connection, in search of friendship, camaraderie, and, yes, even love.

58 **Part II** *Getting Your Feet Wet*

After you've looked around at the dozens of areas where other people congregate, you'll have a hard time tearing yourself away from America Online and the friends you will soon meet!

Are you ready to dive in? Saying hello to people you meet on America Online is certainly a lot easier than opening a conversation with a stranger, because on America Online, remaining alone is difficult.

Locating other America Online members

On busy evenings in recent weeks, America Online has had literally thousands of members in "interactive areas" at one time! But as you stare at the Welcome to AOL screen, you aren't able to see any of these people. It's akin to entering an office building; you need to know where the people are and go there before you can meet anyone. At first, everyone is behind "virtual" closed doors, and those doors are soundproof. Your first step to finding other people is to open these doors and look around. By far, the easiest place to find other members is in the People Connection area of America Online. The People Connection department houses most of the non-computing-related chat rooms where members like to congregate and socialize. Are you ready to take a peek into one of these rooms?

First, select Go To, Lobby (or simply type Ctrl+L). You are immediately transported to the "foyer" of America Online's People Connection, as shown in figure 4.3. This window represents a place in which up to 23 people can gather and get to know one another by exchanging chat. (If the Lobby is full when you enter, the room expands to additional rooms, and the room name has a number after it, such as Lobby 3.) The mechanics of chatting involve typing what you want others to see in the small box in the lower portion of the chat window, and sending it by clicking on the Send button or pressing Return on your keyboard.

If you're like a lot of folks who are new to the online world, don't worry about starting a conversation right away; just hang around the Lobby and watch what other members type to each other. While you're waiting, chances are that someone will say hello to you (it'll show up in the chat window). Don't worry about sending a reply if you aren't comfortable; no one will mind. (Experienced online visitors call it lurking, but don't get the wrong idea about the word. It just means you're hanging out.)

Chapter 4 *The Easy Way to Meet People Online* **59**

Fig. 4.3
America Online's Lobby in the People Connection area is one place you can chat with other members.

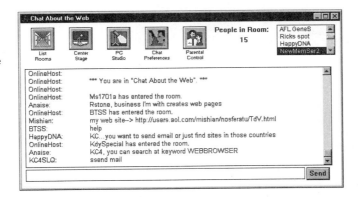

 TIP **When visiting People Connection rooms for the first few times,** you might get a better feel for the rooms' atmospheres by just watching for a few minutes or more.

Look at the Lobby screen shown in figure 4.3. This window contains some items of interest apart from the text you type and the text other people have typed. For one thing, now that you've located some people online, you can find out a little more about them.

Viewing other members' profiles

If you want to view another member's profile, you need to know the member's screen name or be in the same chat room with that member. The Lobby is as good a place as any to start.

Members' screen names are shown at the beginning of each line as it is displayed in the chat window of the Lobby. And if you choose the appropriate option in your AOL software's preferences files, that amorphous Online Host (a euphemism for AOL's host computer system) will announce on the screen the arrival and departure of members to the chat room.

You also have a way to view a list of everyone in the chat room you occupy. The list of those in the chat room is located at the upper right portion of the chat window. Simply scroll through the list and double click on a fellow member's name to find out more about that person. The resulting window contains a list of all the America Online members currently in that room, as shown in figure 4.4. The list is updated as people enter and leave.

Fig. 4.4
The People list tells you which members are currently in the chat room with you.

TIP Use the keyword Help or select Go To, Members' Online Support to view and search the member directory from anywhere online at any time.

Now, you can find out about someone! Select any of the names shown in the list, and click on the Get Info button on the right side of the window. If the person you selected filled out an online profile, you see it in just a few seconds. If that member has not filled out a profile, you receive a message indicating There is no profile available for that name. In that case, try using some of the other names in the list until you find someone who has provided profile information. Depending upon how much information the selected person provided, you see one or more lines of information in the Profile window.

Finding a member online

As you become more comfortable using the conference rooms and People Connection rooms of America Online, you will most likely begin to recognize some of the regulars. Perhaps you also know someone who uses America Online and want to find out if that person is signed on at the same time as you.

America Online provides a fast, easy method of locating people using the service. Select Members, Locate a Member Online, or press Ctrl+F and type the screen name of the person you want to locate (see fig. 4.5).

Fig. 4.5
Select the Locate a Member Online option to find a member.

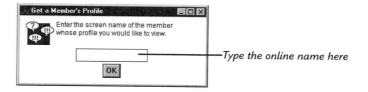

If a person you seek is online when you attempt to find him or her, the America Online host computer tells you that the person you want to find is online but not in a chat area, or you receive the name of the chat or conference room where the person is. If the person is not online, the software tells you exactly that (smart software, very smart).

Getting involved in the People Connection

Of all the areas where people congregate, the People Connection's Lobby is far and away the place you find most of the people who want to talk. On a busy evening, you can easily find thousands of people in the various lobbies in People Connection.

Entering the Lobby

You might be saying to yourself, "Hey, wait a minute—didn't you say earlier that only 23 people can gather in a room at one time?" Well, yes, that's correct as far as it goes. What happens after the 23rd person enters the Lobby is that a new room is automatically created to hold the 24th and all the other people soon to follow. That room is called Lobby 1; after it reaches 23 people, other rooms follow it with names like Lobby 2, Lobby 3, and so on.

The People Connection Lobbies are usually bustling, crowded areas. Think Grand Central Station here; people are constantly coming and going. Often they are leaving for other People Connection rooms with specific themes or to go to Computing & Software conference rooms to discuss the latest industry news. And private rooms are also available; you learn more about that later.

 TIP **As with most public areas in real life, the People Connection rooms** have their own etiquette and rules of conduct. You should take some time during your first sessions to acquaint yourself with AOL's Terms of Service (or TOS). Use the keyword **TOS** to go to AOL's free help area and look over the Terms of Service, which are displayed in separate text files, according to category. Spend at least a few minutes reviewing the contents of this area.

Visiting private chat rooms

If you are like many of the People Connection's regular visitors, you'll eventually meet someone online with whom you want to communicate further. You want more privacy than the public People Connection rooms are able to offer, but in a fashion more convenient than instant messages and e-mail. (Instant messages and e-mail are discussed in more detail in chapter 5.) Here's what to do:

62 Part II *Getting Your Feet Wet*

1. First you will want to go to the Lobby in the People Connection.
2. Click the List Rooms icon on the left side of the Lobby chat window.
3. Alongside the list of rooms that appears is a button titled Private Room. Click on that button.
4. You'll see a request for you to enter a room name. Here you can make up your own room name (so long as it doesn't contain objectionable language). You'll want to remember this room name so that you can send it in an instant message or e-mail to those members you care to have join you.
5. Once you've entered the name, a click on the Go button magically transports you to that room.

TIP **If you don't want someone to accidentally stumble into your** private room, you should choose a name that cannot be guessed easily (or by accident). Maybe something known only to you and your friends.

Private rooms look and feel exactly like any chat room, such as the Lobby or forum conference rooms (see fig. 4.6).

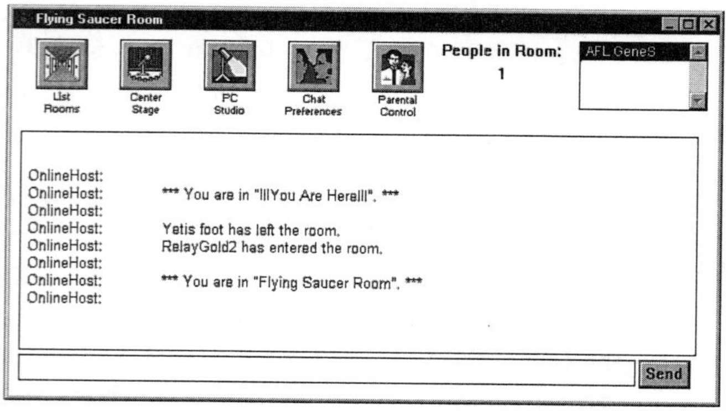

Fig. 4.6
This screen shows an example of a member's private room, named "Flying Saucer Room".

The only difference between a public chat room and a private one is that the name of the room does not appear in any of the People Connection room lists. To join another member already in a private room, you must first know the exact name of that room (or take a very lucky guess, which is why you want to be careful about selecting the name).

Entering the Center Stage Auditoriums

The People Connection staff have also invited some extremely popular celebrities to pay a visit. AOL has featured such personalities as Bob Hope, Mick Jagger, and Teri Hatcher (star of ABC's *Lois and Clark: the New Adventures of Superman*).

Because the regular People Connection rooms hold only 23 folks before another room is automatically opened, a solution was needed for events that would be more popular. Another problem was that with so many people in one room, so many comments and questions would be typed by members wanting to talk to the guests that tracking the conversation with the guests could be next to impossible.

Many of AOL's forums have chat rooms structured just like those in People Connection, except they hold 48 members (so my instructions about the Lobby apply to these rooms as well).

To solve the dilemma of seating capacity, and to make the sessions more structured to handle a larger audience, America Online and People Connection came up with a unique interactive concept: the AOL Auditoriums. Figure 4.7 shows the screen for one of a number of auditoriums that have been established. At any one time, several online conferences may be in progress.

Enter AOL's Rotunda Auditorium

America Online's Computing department has a similar type of auditorium for large gatherings, known as The Rotunda (keyword: **Rotunda**). You'll want to visit the Rotunda often to check on conference schedules and download logs of the meetings you've missed.

The Rotunda is devoted to computing-related subjects. I've been a guest myself there from time to time (to tell AOL members about my books and about the service), and I've also sponsored meetings featuring computing industry leaders, such as those from Compaq Computer (who once actually gave away a multimedia computer to an AOL member during an online session).

The instructions that follow about how to use AOL's Center Stage apply equally to your visits to the Rotunda as well.

Fig. 4.7
One of the People Connection Auditoriums, where thousands can gather. Here's a busy online conference, already in progress.

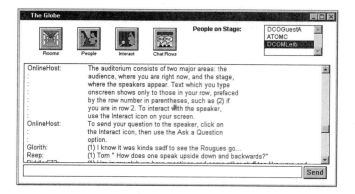

The Center Stage auditoriums are America Online's largest gathering places; each room is capable of accommodating thousands of guests for fun-filled game shows and special events.

When you first log onto AOL, you'll often see an icon announcing a featured conference that's in progress, and clicking on that icon will take you to the center stage area for fast entry to the conference room. Upon entering a Center Stage auditorium, the service reminds you that only those in the same "row" as yours can see the text you type to the screen. If you find that the typing of members in the same rows is distracting or inconvenient to your concentration on the event, you can turn off that feature. Just click the Chat Rows icon; then click on the Turn Off Chat button in the window that appears (see fig. 4.8). When the Chat feature is turned off, you can enjoy the event while seeing only text that appears from the "stage"—text from your hosts, guests, and contestants.

Recording your favorite conferences for posterity

During your visits to America Online, you may want to have a record of that special online conference (or even one of AOL's message boards) so that you can read it on your computer or print it later on. This feature is like having a pair of tape recorders at your beck and call to record your visits to AOL. Let's take a look at the logging options of your America Online software, as shown in figure 4.9.

Chapter 4 *The Easy Way to Meet People Online* **65**

Fig. 4.8
More chat controls for the Center Stage Auditoriums are found in the Chat Rows window.

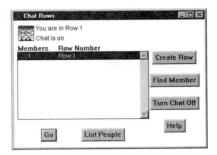

From this window, you also can look for other members who might be online (so you can tell them what a great time you're having on Center Stage), list people in your chat row or any other row, and create a new chat row.

Fig. 4.9
Recording your America Online visit is easy with the program's Logging feature.

- The first option is the Chat Log. During your online travels, you might attend a chat in America Online's People Connection or an online conference. The Chat Log enables you to record the entire conversation.

- The second option is a Session Log. With this log, you can record all the text you read during your visit to America Online. The log doesn't record the mail you send or the messages you post, but you can save those anyway, using File, Save. (You also can log instant messages if you check that option at the bottom of the Logging dialog box.)

To use your online tape recorder, follow these steps:

1 Choose File, Logging, which opens the Logging dialog box.

2 Select the kind of log you want to record.

3 Click the Open button. You then see a dialog box much like the Save As... dialog box, where you are asked to name your file and indicate where it is to be saved (see fig. 4.10). The log is given a default name, such as session.log, but you can give the file any name you want, as

Part II *Getting Your Feet Wet*

long as it contains no more than eight characters (and includes the same file extension).

Fig. 4.10
Name your open log here. You'll want to use a descriptive title, to help you know what to look for when you want to open the file later on.

4 If you want to end the online recording process, return to File, Logging, and choose the Close button in the Logging dialog box.

5 When you decide to resume the logging process or add to a previously created log, click the Append button in the Logging dialog box.

6 When you are finished logging, choose the Close button in the Logging dialog box.

The logging process is flexible. You can open both logs at once if you prefer. What's more, you can append (add to) or close each log separately, depending on which one you've highlighted when you make your choice.

Remember, America Online software can read only 64,000 characters in a single text window. When you want to read additional segments of a long file, you need to select the More option in your Open dialog box.

Many areas besides People Connection hold regular chats and conferences. Look in the Computing forums for other chat schedules (see chapter 9).

The Gallery is a collection of photos that are put in computer-readable form and uploaded for all to see. Thousands of America Online members have already uploaded their portraits or sent their photos to the Gallery's staff to digitize for free. As you get to know some of the regulars online, chances are good that you'll be tempted to find out what they look like, and the Gallery is the place.

A separate library is also included in the Gallery for family-album types of pictures. Perhaps you should gather your own clan's photos and send them to the gallery. If you have a scanner (or access to one at the office), you can scan your own photo and upload it in GIF or JPEG format directly to The Gallery's software libraries, or submit your photo to be scanned and uploaded for you by the Gallery's staff. The address to which you should send your photos for scanning is listed in the library.

To make viewing these photos easy for all America Online users, regardless of the type of computer, the Gallery photos are provided in GIF and JPEG formats.

 Plain English, please!

GIF (pronounced JIF, like the peanut butter brand and short for **Graphic Interchange Format**) is a cross-platform image format that offers a high-quality image with a small file size. The small size keeps your download time short and makes it more convenient if you want to see photos of a number of your fellow members.

JPEG (pronounced JAY-peg) is a standardized image compression mechanism. JPEG stands for **Joint Photographic Experts Group**, the original name of the committee that wrote the standard. The JPEG is tailor-made for either full-color or gray-scale images of natural, real-world scenes. It works beautifully for photos (but not so well for text). A JPEG image is smaller than GIF, but yields a higher quality image.

The very latest versions of your Windows AOL software allow you to actually see a photo gradually appear on your screen while it's being downloaded to your computer, just as I've shown in figure 4.11. To view the photo files after you've downloaded them, simply choose Open from the File menu and then select the file you wish to see. Once the file is opened (or has appeared on your computer's screen right after the download process is over), you'll be able to print it just the same as any other document.

 TIP **If a photo has been uploaded with the newest version of AOL's** software, you'll be able to see a thumbnail of the photo when you view the file description in the Gallery's libraries. **Thumbnails** are not available for photos sent using older versions of AOL's Mac and Windows software. A thumbnail lets you preview the image before you download it, so you can decide whether or not to retrieve the file. But if you don't see a preview, don't assume there's anything wrong with the image or your software. It'll take a while before older image files are updated and replaced with newer ones.

 Plain English, please!
A **thumbnail** is a miniature copy of a photo or graphic image, similar to the contact prints you get from a photo studio when you have portraits made. The use of the word thumb here is appropriate, since the images you see online are sized about the same as the average person's thumb (or at least my thumb).

Fig. 4.11
As you download a file from The Gallery, the photo begins to display on your computer's screen. The complete photo is shown when the download is finished.

For more information about including your own photos in the Gallery, read the Get Framed document in the Gallery's main forum window.

Using abbreviations and shorthand symbols

This section provides a partial listing of some of the more popular abbreviations and shorthand symbols you might see while online in the People Connection, in chat rooms, or on message boards. They have grown out of the need to show what cannot be shown when online—facial expressions and body language.

Online abbreviations

Often when chatting, America Online members will shorten long phrases into a few letters so that they can be typed quickly. Here are some of the more common online abbreviations:

Abbreviation	What it means...
LOL	Laughing out loud
ROFL or ROTFL	Rolling on the floor laughing
AFK	Away from keyboard
BAK	Back at keyboard
BRB	Be right back
OIC	Oh, I see
IMO	In my opinion
IMHO	In my humble opinion or In my honest opinion
TTFN	Ta-ta for now
TTYL	Talk to you later
NIFOC	Nude in front of computer
GMTA	Great minds think alike
IHTBHWYG	It's hard to be humble when you're great
<g>	Grin
GA	Go ahead

Online shorthand

When you're communicating with others online via instant messages, chat rooms, or e-mail, it's often difficult to convey body language and tone of voice. As a result, some brilliant individual invented online shorthand—keyboard symbols that convey human expression. Tilting your head toward the left will help you to see most of the symbols; for example, the characters :) form a sideways smiley face. Here are some common (and, well, not so common) examples:

Part II *Getting Your Feet Wet*

Shorthand	What it means...
[ ]	A hug, repeated as needed for degrees of enthusiasm, such as [[[[[[[[ ]]]]]]]]
:)	Basic smile
:(	Frown
:/	Ho-hum smile
;)	Winking smile
:D	Smile with a big grin
:*	Kiss
8)	Wide-eyed smile
B-)	Wearing glasses
:>)	Big nose
:-)8	Well-dressed
%-)	Cross-eyed
#-)	Partied all night
:-*	Just ate a sour pickle
:-'|	Has a cold
:-R	Has the flu
:-)'	Tends to drool
P-)	Getting fresh
|-)	Falling asleep
:-D	Talks too much
O:-)	Very innocent
M:-)	Saluting (symbol of respect)
-=#:-)	Has wizard status
M-):X):-M	See no evil, hear no evil, speak no evil
>:-(	Sick and tired of reading this nonsense

Shorthand	What it means...
|-O	Bored
:-@	Extremely angry
:-o	Shocked
:-(O)	Yelling
. .	Lying down

Having a good time?

You learn more about forum conferences, such as how to log and print conference proceedings, in the next chapter. You also find out about the formal chat protocol that many forums use and how to look up the conference schedule to find ones that might interest you.

If you have young children in your household who use America Online, be sure also to read chapter 7, "The Secrets of Safe Online Fun for Kids of All Ages," where you'll find some common sense advice to make your children's AOL visits more enjoyable.

How to Stay in Touch with Other Members

● In this chapter:

- Secrets of e-mail and instant messages
- Join conferences and chats on America Online
- The lasting power of message boards
- Run automatic online sessions to save money
- Save information to read offline

Your favorite online activity may very well be getting to know your America Online neighbors . . . . ➤

Although you don't see it when you log onto America online, there are thousands of members in the various chat rooms of People Connection, Computing conference rooms, and other online gathering places at any given time. You can't see e-mail, but millions of such messages fly across cyberspace at all hours of the day and night.

Test the waters: how to write e-mail

You can start writing your e-mail message on America Online with a single, simple step: selecting Compose Mail from the Mail menu bar item. Keyboard enthusiasts may simply press Control-M to begin a new mail message. The resulting message form, shown in figure 5.1, is the jumping-off point for all your original e-mail. Later, I'll show you how to reply to e-mail without using a new mail form.

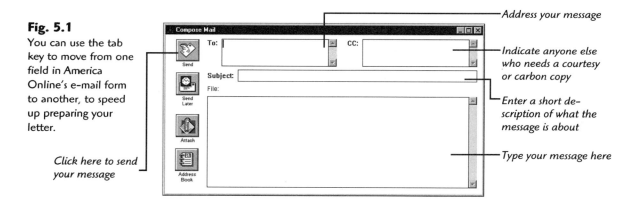

Fig. 5.1
You can use the tab key to move from one field in America Online's e-mail form to another, to speed up preparing your letter.

Click here to send your message

Address your message

Indicate anyone else who needs a courtesy or carbon copy

Enter a short description of what the message is about

Type your message here

When you first conjure up a new e-mail window, the cursor is automatically positioned within the To: field of the form. Although it seems presumptuous, most folks actually do begin composing electronic mail by first addressing it. If this does not suit your tastes, simply press your Tab key to move the cursor to any of the other fields contained in the e-mail window, or click in the desired field with your mouse.

The address fields of the e-mail window can contain literally hundreds of electronic mailing addresses. If you send a message to more than one person, each person's screen name must be separated by a comma or a Return. When you use the Return key to separate multiple names, the window list is easier to read than when separated by commas. In the example shown in figure 5.2, the To: field shows names separated by commas, whereas the CC: field uses the Return.

Fig. 5.2
When you address e-mail to more than one person, each name can be separated by a comma (or a return).

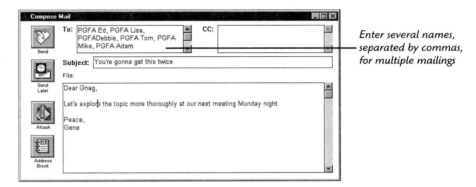

Enter several names, separated by commas, for multiple mailings

If you've entered any addresses in your AOL Address Book, you may also click on the Address Book icon to select names for this e-mail. The use of your AOL Address Book is described later in this chapter, in the section entitled "Setting up AOL's rolodex."

> **Plain English, please!**
>
> AOL's **Address Book** is simply a list of the screen names of your favorite online friends and business associates.

Now, move to the Subject field and let the recipient know what your message is about (without making him read it to find out!). This step is both convenient and considered normal e-mail etiquette.

Next, move the cursor to the message body, and compose your message.

How to send e-mail

 Once your e-mail is composed, you can send it along its merry way by using one of a number of methods. The easiest, if you are connected to America Online, is to click on the Send Now icon on the left side of the e-mail window. The mail is sent immediately, along with any attachments you may have enclosed. We talk more about file attachments later in this chapter, in the section titled "Sending files with e-mail."

76   Part III   Having Fun on America Online

 Plain English, please!

> **Attachments** are files that you can connect to your e-mail, so that they can be sent at the same time you send your e-mail message. This is an important feature that separates AOL from some other online services, where files must be sent as a separate piece of e-mail.

If you composed your outgoing e-mail offline, or signed off while composing it, you may choose to use the Send Later feature that saves the outgoing mail on your hard drive. You can send your saved mail manually on your next online visit, or automatically during your next automated mail session, using AOL's marvelous FlashSession feature (I'll talk about that more later on in this chapter) Please note, however, that if you enclosed an attached file, you cannot move or delete that file you're sending until after your mail transfer is done.

 Plain English, please!

> By **offline**, I'm referring to the ability to write e-mail while not logged onto America Online.

How to receive e-mail

This is the easy part! All you have to do is log on to AOL and, if you have mail, the happy guy that lives inside the AOL program tells you, `You have mail` (that is, assuming that you have your Mail Sounds turned on in the Member Preference settings). A special mail icon is also displayed on the Welcome screen (see fig. 5.3).

Fig. 5.3
When you have e-mail in your mailbox, AOL's handy welcome voice announces it to you and puts up a notice on the opening screen.

AOL lets you know you have mail waiting to be read

Chapter 5 *How to Stay in Touch with Other Members* **77**

You can click on the icon directly above the You have mail message on the Welcome screen, or you can press Control-R to view a list of new mail (see fig. 5.4). You can then double-click to open each piece of mail as you wish.

Fig. 5.4
Here's a listing of e-mail waiting for you to read.

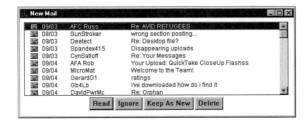

You may also click on the Next arrow icon on the mail form to advance to the next message awaiting you (see fig. 5.5). The Previous arrow lets you move backwards through the mail. The left and right arrow keys on the keyboard are equivalent to clicking on the Next and Previous arrows.

Fig. 5.6
The Read e-mail form. When you move from one message to another, the the document window containing the previous message closes.

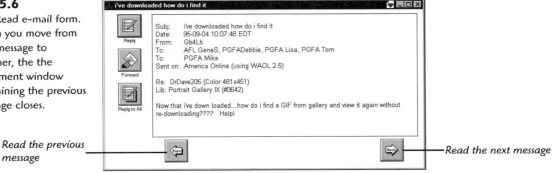

Read the previous message

Read the next message

TIP **If you want to send a letter you just received to another online** address with your added comments, use the Forward icon.

Here are some other AOL e-mail features:

- As you read each piece of mail, a check mark is placed in front of the item as it appears in the New Mail window. If you do not read all your mail in one session, the pieces that have the check mark do not show up the next time you open the New Mail window. Only those items you have not previously read appear there.

- The Ignore button does just what it says. Of course, the person who sent you the e-mail, if they check the status of the message, will know that you ignored the message.

- The Delete button removes the message from your list of incoming mail, unread. Of course, the person who sends you e-mail will know, in checking the message status, that you have deleted the message.

- The Keep As New button allows you to keep the message among your list of waiting mail even after you've read the message. It's useful if you want to use that message as a reminder of an upcoming event or as a specific bit of information you want to review the next time you visit America Online.

Sending files with e-mail

America Online's e-mail system allows you to attach files from your computer to a piece of e-mail (the online equivalent of stapling separate items together). When you send your e-mail, you also send the files you attached to it.

To attach a file when composing e-mail, simply click on the Attach File icon, and use the accompanying dialog box to select the file you wish to attach (see fig. 5.6). If you have file compression software you may also send more than a single file by combining the files into a single archive.

Plain English, please!

Compression is a process that uses a software technique to shrink a file so it's smaller in size. The compression scheme used by AOL, based on PKZip software, will automatically **expand** the file back to its original form when you disconnect from AOL (it's an option in the program settings or preferences that's turned on by default).

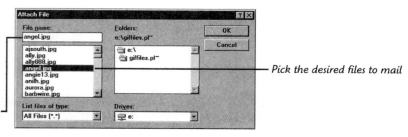

Fig. 5.6
Selecting files to attach is easy in this split window

This window shows the files you've selected to attach to your message

Pick the desired files to mail

The file you attach must be on a disk drive connected to your computer or a mounted network drive, and you must attach the file before you send the e-mail. The recipient sees two extra buttons at the bottom of the received e-mail window, Download File and Download Later. Selecting the Download File button transfers the file from America Online's host to the recipient's computer. Selecting Download Later marks the file for your Download Manager to transfer at a later time. For additional information on the Download Manager, see chapters 3 and 10.

When you send attached files through e-mail, you are charged only for the time needed to send your message and the attachments to the AOL mail-processing area. Similarly, the recipient of the attached file is charged for the time needed to transfer the file from AOL's host to his or her computer. Because this costs money on both ends, it is a good idea not to send unnecessarily large files through e-mail.

Use file-compression whenever possible, and if you believe other AOL members could make use of the file, consider posting the file to a forum library instead of sending it in e-mail. By posting the file to a forum, you are not charged for the connect time spent sending (uploading) the file to AOL's host. Read chapter 10 for more information about uploading files to an AOL software library.

TIP **If you are transferring a GIF or JPEG image file to another AOL** member, compression is probably not going to provide much benefit. These files are already internally compressed and won't get much smaller.

TIP **The Attach File icon changes to Detach File after you attach a file** to your e-mail. If you decide not to send the attached file, but you still want to send the original e-mail message, you can click on Detach File to break the link between the unsent e-mail and the file. At this point, you can still attach a different file to your letter before it's sent.

Saving and printing for posterity

After reading each piece of your e-mail, you have a few options. The first is to simply click the close box of the window, which sends the mail into oblivion. (Well, not quite—you can always find and read mail you've previously viewed from the Check Mail I've Read menu item, found on the Mail menu.)

Another option is to save mail to your Flashbox, a file stored on your hard drive that can hold tons of saved e-mail. To save to your Flashbox, click on the icon just above the appropriately worded Save to Flashmail legend. You can retrieve this e-mail item at any time, whether you are offline or online, by selecting Read Incoming Mail from the Mail menu.

Plain English, please!

AOL's **Flashbox** is a mailbox that's created on your computer's hard drive when you install AOL's software. As I'll explain later in this chapter, this mailbox (or file folder, which is what it looks like) is filled with e-mail you receive during a FlashSession.

You can also save your e-mail as an individual file. America Online has two special file types for e-mail—one for outgoing mail and one for incoming mail. By selecting Save As from the File menu you may choose to save your e-mail as one of these types of files, or as plain text. Saving your mail as plain text allows you to view or change the contents of the e-mail in any text processor, such as your favorite word processing program.

One useful feature found in AOL is the ability to save text to a file. If you ever want to save some text from any of AOL's text windows, not just e-mail, simply select the text with your mouse, and then select File, Save As. This feature is especially handy for saving addresses or lists contained in e-mail that you want to open or import into other applications.

Printing your e-mail

To print a hard copy of your e-mail, choose File, Print. This works the same way as in almost every other Windows 95 application that supports printing. Remember, however, that if you changed printers since the last time you printed anything from AOL, you first need to select Page Setup to verify your printing options.

Setting up AOL's rolodex

Your America Online Address Book is the best way to store mail addresses that you use regularly so that they are available at the click of a mouse. Use this feature to build a file card system to keep track of your online friends.

Chapter 5 *How to Stay in Touch with Other Members*

Suppose that you have an online friend named Jesse Dunn. Her screen name on America Online might be Ogyr, and you exchange e-mail with her often. You'll probably find it more convenient to store her name in your Address Book rather than manually typing it each time you compose mail to her. To do this:

 1 Select Edit Address Book from the Mail menu.

 2 Click on the Create button. A new address entry form appears on-screen (see fig. 5.7).

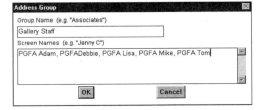

Fig. 5.7
Here's the AOL Address Book screen name entry form. Notice that your friends and business contacts are identified strictly by their screen names.

 3 Type the name of your friend in the Name field; for example, type **Jesse Dunn**.

 4 Type the screen name of your friend in the Account field; for example, type **Ogyr**.

Now, the next time you want to send a piece of mail to Jesse, open a new mail window, click on the Address Book icon on the left side of the window, and click on her name.

You can also include group addresses in your AOL Address Book. This is useful if you want to easily send the same message to friends or business associates that you contact regularly. Just Select Edit Address Book from the Mail menu. Then click on the Create button, which will bring up a new address form. You then name the group (such as **Bowling Team**), and then enter the screen names of those whom you'd like to include in this list. Piece of cake!

Now whenever you select **Bowling Team** (or whatever name you've selected) from your Address Book, all the names you entered for that group appear on the e-mail address field you designate on your Mail form.

Using FlashSessions to automate your online visits

FlashSessions are a terrific way to let AOL's software do the log-ons for you at the times you set (so you don't have to be at your computer) as well as send and retrieve all your e-mail and attached files. By automating your sessions, you can save money by making your visits more efficient (of course you cannot visit forums this way yet, but that may come in the future).

To set your FlashSession preferences, select FlashSessions from the Mail menu. The first time you choose this option, America Online will guide you through the process of scheduling your automated session, using a special feature called Walk-Through, as shown in figure 5.8.

Fig. 5.8
America Online's FlashSessions Walk-Through will quickly guide you step-by-step through the process of activating automatic e-mail sessions.

Scheduling FlashSessions Using Walk-Through

Here are the choices you can make when you set up your AOL FlashSession.

- Whether you want to receive your unread mail during automatic log-ons.

- Whether to automatically download files attached to your e-mail during a FlashSession.

- Whether to send your outgoing e-mail automatically during your FlashSession.

Chapter 5 *How to Stay in Touch with Other Members*   **83**

- Whether or not to retrieve the files selected via AOL's Download Manager during your FlashSession.

- Whether to download Internet newsgroup messages during your FlashSession. You'll want to read chapter 17 to learn more about this entertaining and informative aspect of Internet access.

- Whether to send your responses to newsgroup messages during your FlashSession.

- Whether to store your user passwords. This option is a must to run an automated session on AOL.

- Whether to run your FlashSessions at automatic intervals.

When you set up the automatic FlashSessions feature, you'll bring up several screens that will allow you to select which accounts to use for those sessions, how often they will be run, and on what days of the week.

When you save a stored password with your America Online software, anyone who has access to your computer can log onto the service with your account, and use online time that will be charged to your monthly bill. Before using this option, be certain your computer is not easily accessible to others without your permission. You may want to consider, for example, using a security program to prevent unauthorized access to your computer.

America Online's internal log-in calendar is now working and will connect to the service at the times you scheduled. To turn off automatic connections, select FlashSessions from the Mail menu, click on the Schedule FlashSessions icon, deselect the Starting At check box, and click OK.

I want to reduce my online billing. Is there any way to forward e-mail sent under one screen name to another screen name?

By the time this book gets into print, it's quite possible such a feature may be developed or under development. But as of right now, you can't. So you may want to schedule your e-mail sessions to include only those screen names where the messages you receive must be answered as soon as possible, and schedule sessions with the other accounts less often.

Using instant messages for one-on-one meetings

Instant messages are used for two-way, immediate, private, person-to-person communication. It's the method that's closest to actually talking to someone online. To send an instant message while online, select Send Instant Message from the Members Menu or press Ctrl+I. You see a new window in which to address and compose your message (see fig. 5.9).

Fig. 5.9
The originator's Instant Message window.

If you receive an instant message, respond to it by clicking on the Send button, entering your reply in the lower portion of the Instant Message window, and clicking on the Send button.

You can have a two-way conversation with any AOL member by leaving the Instant Message window open after you send a response. When a new message arrives from your friend, it appears in that window. (If your online sounds are turned on, the arrival of the message follows a pleasant musical tone.) The actual conversation appears in the upper text field, while the responses you type appear in the lower portion of the window. You can hold numerous instant message conversations simultaneously.

As with other types of text windows in AOL, you can print or save the Instant Message window's contents by selecting Print or Save from the File menu in your menu bar.

The elements of online forums

America Online's meeting places are called forums. They are places where staff and members focus on a specific interest. There are more than a dozen forums, for example, in the PC and Windows side of the Computing department (see chapter 9 "Get Advice, Help and Software from America Online's

Chapter 5 *How to Stay in Touch with Other Members* **85**

Computing Forums"). There's a special forum, Help Desk, that will help guide you through the computing forums (see fig. 5.10). It's definitely worth a visit.

Fig. 5.10
America Online's friendly PC Help Desk is a place where beginning AOL members can receive help for common questions about the service.

A few thoughts about instant messaging

Using instant messages is a simple and unobtrusive process. If you are typing in a different window at the moment an instant message arrives, for example, you can automatically send the incoming instant message behind the top window with your next keystroke, provided you turn off the option to bring instant messages to the front (in your AOL application preferences, as I described in chapter 2, "Setting Up Your AOL Windows Software").

If you choose to let instant messages come to the front in your AOL settings, just be careful. If that message comes through while you're closing another text window on AOL, you may close the instant message by mistake, and lose the message in the process, since it can't be retrieved (unless you know who sent it and can ask them to send it again).

In case you'd rather not get an instant message (perhaps you're busy researching material from AOL's Reference or Education departments, for example, and don't want to be disturbed), AOL has a a fast way to turn off this feature. Just open up a blank instant message window, and enter **$im_off** in the To field of the message box. Enter anything you want in the blank message field (one letter or number is sufficient), and send the message.

You'll soon get a message from AOL's host computer that you've turned off instant messages.

This feature will be turned off for the rest of your online session; instant messaging will be active again next time you call up AOL.

If you do want to restore instant messages for your current AOL visit, just open up a blank IM form again, and type **$im_on** in the To field, and again at least one character in the blank message field and send it on its way.

You'll then be able to receive instant messages again.

One more thing: AOL's own staff can still reach you in an instant message even if you've turned off the feature.

All the forums have their own chat rooms, software libraries, and message areas configured to focus on the special interests of that forum.

Where the action is: using forum message boards

The message areas are where members and AOL staff leave messages about the forum's field of interest. One advantage of message boards is that you are not constrained to communicating only with members who are online at the same time as you. When you leave a message, you can wait several minutes, hours, or even days before checking back to look for responses. In that sense, a message board isn't terribly different from an announcement you may put up at a neighborhood community center.

Plain English, please!

A **message board** is an online area that contains short statements in text form from members or AOL staff about a particular topic. A message may be a request for information or for help, or an opinion about a hot issue that's under discussion.

Over the next few pages, I'll describe how message boards are set up and the simple methods involved in posting messages in them. You'll find many of the steps are very much the same as writing up your e-mail message, except that you have to think of a wider audience when you put something in a message board.

Before posting anything in the computing forums' message boards, you should learn about the forums and what their topic or subject covers. To do this, you need to explore. Most forums have a Forum Update file you can read online to find out what is new and what is happening in them. For an example, check out the Weekly Forum Update file in the PC Telecommunications Forum; the keyword is PC Telecom.

 **Before you respond to a message, read the other responses first.** It's possible that the message has already been answered, or your question has already been dealt with by another member. Also, don't type your message in ALL CAPS (like that!). It makes it difficult to read, and it's also the online equivalent of shouting (which isn't terribly polite).

How to find the forum messages that interest you

Once you've located a forum that covers topics you want to know about, you'll want to focus on getting to the messages you want to read. First, click on the Message Boards icon. You see the general subject matter of the forum described briefly.

You have four icons at the bottom of the window, one of which takes you further along the road to finding messages you want to read. The Help & Info icon is your route to the PC Help Desk (again see fig. 5.10). For now, let's click on the List Categories icon, which opens a list of discussion topics (see fig. 5.11). I'll explain what Find New and Find Since is all about in a moment.

Fig. 5.11
The forum messages shown here are divided into folders, each of which represents a category.

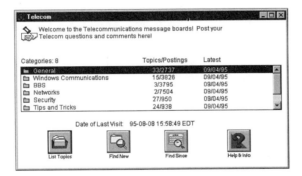

Each forum divides its message boards into a group of overall topics that relate to the forum's field of interest. If you're looking for a particular type of message, check here for the general category. To get to the next step in your message-reading process, click on the List Topics icon (see fig. 5.12).

Fig. 5.12
Here's a list of discussion topics in a typical message category.

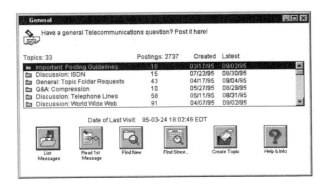

In most message boards, you have a Create Topic option that allows you to make your own folder, name it, and describe the subject matter. In the directory shown in figure 5.12, you have a list of topics created by the forum staff and fellow AOL members. This list is your direct-entry point to a message on the topic in which you are interested.

Now let's get to those other icons I described earlier:

- **Find New.** This icon brings up a display of posted messages and the topics created since the last time you entered that forum (AOL's host computer keeps a record of your previous visit).

    If you are visiting a forum for the first time, choosing this icon can produce literally dozens of topic folders and hundreds of messages. You may be better off using the next option.

- **Find Since.** This icon lets you set a limit for the amount of time spent searching for new messages. Its default is one day, but when you enter a forum for the first time, you might want to read all messages added in the previous 30 to 60 days, so you can get a taste of the flavor of the forum and the kind of messages the board contains.

- **Read 1st Message.** When you open a directory of recent messages (see fig. 5.12), you can highlight a folder's name and click on this icon to see the first new message in the folder.

> **TIP** After you open your first message, use the arrow keys on your keyboard to move to the next or previous message.

- **Create Topic.** This choice allows you to make your own folder, name it, and describe subject matter.

- **List Messages.** This choice brings up a directory that shows the subject of each message. Double click the message itself to open that message window.

How to post a message in a forum

Posting a message is not unlike writing e-mail. You click on the Add Message icon (or Post Response in some forums), enter the subject in the first field, and insert your comment in the second field. By default, the subject of the message you were reading before you choose the Add Message button

Chapter 5 How to Stay in Touch with Other Members   **89**

appears, preceded by the reference (Re:). You can, however, delete this subject and choose one of your own, if you are not responding to a previous message (see figure 5.13).

Fig. 5.13
Here's your completed message, ready to be posted in a forum. Don't forget to spell check before you send it.

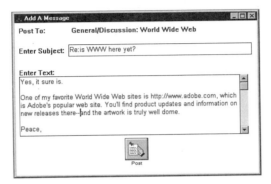

After you write your message, click on the Post icon, and the message is added to the topic folder you were viewing. When your message is actually posted, your screen name and the time it was sent appear at the top of the message.

TIP As with regular e-mail, it's considered good online etiquette to sign the messages you post in a message board.

CAUTION Posting a message more than once in a single forum is considered bad online etiquette. Some AOL members may even get upset having to read the same message over and over again on billable time. When you have something to say, take a moment to choose the topic folder or directory that closely matches what you want to write about. In many forums, you can create your own topic to begin a discussion.

Message threading

If you are a frequent visitor to user group bulletin board systems or some of the other online services, you may be familiar with a feature called **message threading**. This technique lets you read all messages devoted to one subject in a single group, rather than having them mixed in with other messages on other subjects.

When you post a message, you get the option to respond or reply to an individual message rather than just post a new one. There's an important difference between responding and posting. In the first case, your message is added to the "thread," so other members will be able to read the original message and all the responses it brings in one group. If you post a message, it is simply added to the message folder or directory in chronological order without regard to which message you're responding. Even where message threading is available, you'll want to post a message if you prefer to begin a new topic.

You'll find message threading available in America Online's Newsgroups area (*keyword:* **Newsgroups**). Since I will discuss Newsgroups in much more detail in chapter 17, for now I'll just tell you that message threading is spreading to different message boards throughout America Online. In most ways, it's not terribly different from a regular message board. But the ability to keep all the messages on a single subject together makes browsing through messages much easier.

The elements of online conferences

In this section, I'm going to describe the last of the four ways you can communicate on America Online—online conferences, or chats, as they are more commonly called. In many ways, an online conference is the most fun-filled activity you can experience online because it take place in real time.

Within the chat window, you type text in the bottom part of the window and click on the Send button to send it into the upper, main portion of the chat window. (Don't choose Send until you are sure you want to send your text.) Figure 5.14 is a typical chat window.

Fig. 5.14
This forum chat window shows an online session already in progress.

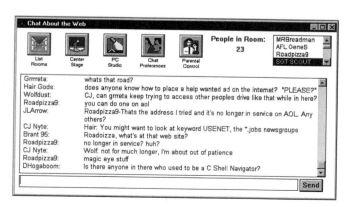

Some forums' chats are formalized, following chat protocol. This decreases the confusion that arises when you get 30 people trying to talk at once. When using **chat protocol**, if you have a question, you raise your hand by sending a question mark (**?**) to the screen. The conference emcee recognizes you in order, and calls on you when it is your turn to speak. You can then send your question. Let the conference host know that you want to make a comment by sending an exclamation mark (**!**) for recognition rather than a question mark.

To keep a text record of the chat, select Logs from the File menu. Here, you can open a chat log to record to a text file everything you see in the chat window. I described the logging process in more detail in chapter 2.

The System log records all messages received by your computer while online, except instant messages and chat text. The other two logs handle those two categories.

Here's your progress report

If the '80s was the decade of the Information Age, the '90s is the Communication Age. Instant access to people all over the world is a reality, regardless of their location or time zone. America Online's fast, flexible methods to communicate with other members and even to send e-mail around the world, gives you the power to express your thoughts to millions just by typing messages on your PC. These indeed are exciting times.

Part III: Having Fun on America Online

Chapter 6:   **From Music to Sports: Locating Entertainment Information on AOL**

Chapter 7:   **The Secrets of Safe Online Fun for Kids of All Ages**

Chapter 8:   **Travel the Stars or Explore Health Issues: Online Lifestyles & Interest Forums**

Chapter 9:   **Get Advice, Help, and Software from America Online's Computing Forums**

6

From Music to Sports: Locating Entertainment Information on AOL

● In this chapter:

- Find the latest news from the world of entertainment
- Become a critic right here on America Online
- Find information about online games
- Visit forums devoted to sporting events

This chapter takes you to areas where you can discover online entertainment resources . . . . ➢

In America Online's terms, the world of entertainment covers everything from a television show to your daily horoscope. In this chapter, you explore such diverse topics as movies, television, music, games, sports, books, and more. You find out what America Online has to offer in those areas and how you can find it. Wherever your interests lie, America Online surely has a place where you can find the entertainment you seek.

Your first visit to the Entertainment forum

Regardless of what facet of the world of entertainment interests you—catching a movie, watching a soap opera, sitting down in front of a warm fireplace with a good book in your hands, or playing a video game—America Online can be your first and best resource for information.

Start your search for entertainment-related information in America Online's Entertainment forum. To access this area, type the keyword **Entertainment**. The directory window shows just a few of the areas you'll visit in this chapter (see fig. 6.1). During your online visits, you discover many more locations that provide you not only with information, but also with an opportunity to participate in discussions on a host of related subjects, and even to post your own book and movie reviews.

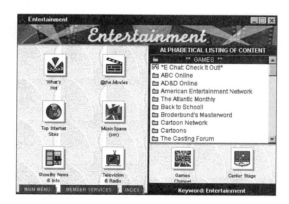

Fig. 6.1
The Entertainment department is America Online's gateway to the world of entertainment.

Throughout this chapter, you'll learn about most of the places listed under Entertainment Features. New features are added regularly to America Online's resource roster, so you can expect this directory listing to change often.

Chapter 6 *From Music to Sports: Locating Entertainment Information on AOL* **97**

You can survey the features of the Entertainment department in two ways. There's an alphabetical listing of the areas available on the directory at the right of the screen. On the left, there are six icons that will quickly transport you to one of your favorite areas. We'll cover some of these first.

A look beneath the What's Hot icon

This icon changes periodically to reflect the latest additions to the Entertainment department and to areas that are running special promotions or introducing new features. As this book was written, featured areas (shown in fig. 6.2) included Center Stage, the area where famous entertainment figures attend online conferences; *Court TV*; *Nick at Nite*; *Hackers*; and *Image Exchange*.

Fig. 6.2
Just some of the forums featured in AOL's Entertainment department. This list is updated regularly.

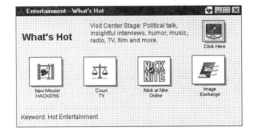

Q&A *How come I have to endure the download of new artwork every time I visit a new online area? What's it doing to my online bill?*

America Online is a graphic-oriented online service; artwork is needed to set off the special features and flavor of a particular department or forum. When you enter an online area for the first time, new artwork is automatically downloaded to your computer. When you revisit that area again in the future, the artwork update won't be repeated—unless further artwork changes are needed.

If the new artwork is on the opening screen you see when you log onto AOL, you'll experience the artwork download when you first log on. But those updates seldom take more than a few seconds to finish.

Yes, it's true that you pay a few pennies here and there for those artwork updates. But this is the most economical way to provide this new artwork to you (although some of it will be included in AOL's CD-ROMs, which will be distributed from time to time). If the artwork resources are extensive, sometimes you can opt out by not entering the area and choosing the Cancel button instead.

Visiting top Internet sites

Not all of the areas you access from America Online are actually part of the service's own features. America Online has an extensive selection of Internet-related services, too. The places shown in the Top Internet Sites listing are part of the Internet's World Wide Web. For the complete story on accessing the World Wide Web from AOL, see chapter 18, "Unmasking the World Wide Web" and chapter 19, "Getting Started on the Web."

Let's fly through MusicSpace

The MusicSpace forum combines AOL's own music-related forums and major sites on the World Wide Web into a colorful, fun-filled, exciting area. From the beautiful artwork (see fig. 6.3) to the extensive list of resources, you can spend hour upon hour in this area and not cover but a small portion of the features available.

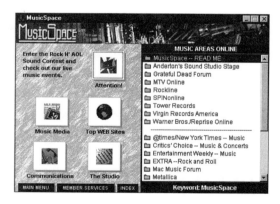

Fig. 6.3
AOL's MusicSpace area is a huge repository of music-related information.

In addition to learning about new recordings from your favorite stars, you'll be able to order your favorite recordings courtesy of Tower Records, the nationwide recorded music chain. Just click the Tower Records listing in the Music Areas Online directory, and you can review a selection of the latest releases or search out older favorites.

Finding movie and television information

Whether it's your favorite flick or a popular TV network, you can access information about it in AOL's Entertainment department. Let's explore it further.

Reading ShowBiz News & Info

The popularity of entertainment news programs on broadcast and cable TV networks and newsstand magazines means we all have an insatiable hunger for news about show business. When you click the ShowBiz News & Info icon in AOL's Entertainment department (see fig. 6.4), you're presented with a large resource of such information.

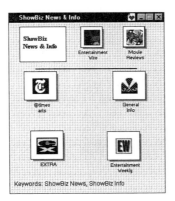

Fig. 6.4
From newsstand magazines to entertainment-related TV programs, you'll find the information you want on AOL.

A look beneath the Television & Radio icon

The Television icon on the bottom of the Entertainment department screen provides the same sort of information about some of your favorite television shows. Before you decide what you want to watch or tape, America Online gives you a chance to preview what's coming up on the tube.

When you click this icon, you see a directory that offers you several forums devoted specifically to radio and television. Let's look into the one labeled Networks first. From the Networks icon, you can choose online forums for such diverse services as the ABC Online (see fig. 6.5), the CBS Network's site on the World Wide Web, AOL's Radio forums, and additional forums related to other broadcast and cable TV networks. From the Shows icon, you can access information about popular programs. MTV Online gets a special, highly stylized, online forum (see fig. 6.6).

Fig. 6.5
There are several television and radio features to choose from at this site.

Fig. 6.6
MTV Online tells you all about the network's programming schedule, and also features chats featuring some of your favorite musical stars.

And that's not all

Still more online resources with an entertainment slant are available from the Entertainment department's directory window at the right. Some of the areas shown, such as the one devoted to the movie *Batman Forever*, appear only to support a specific movie or program and will be withdrawn when that production is out of circulation. Others, while ever-changing in appearance and organization, are more-or-less permanent fixtures on AOL. Following is an overview of some of these resources.

Accessing Hollywood Online

Keyword: **Hollywood**

At any one time, literally dozens of current motion pictures might be playing at your local theaters. New flicks are released weekly. During the summer

Chapter 6 *From Music to Sports: Locating Entertainment Information on AOL*

and Christmas seasons, scores of pictures vie for your attention and your ticket dollars. What to do?

You can use America Online's Hollywood Online forum (see fig. 6.7) to learn about these films before they are released.

Fig. 6.7
Hollywood Online is Tinseltown's own forum on America Online.

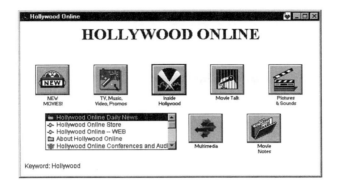

Finding music information

Keyword: **Music**

If you dig rock n' roll music or if you prefer country, classical, or jazz, you will appreciate America Online's music-related forums. They are your resources for information and online discussion about your favorite performers. The keyword Music (or the Music icon in the Entertainment department window) is just a gateway. It's a stopping-off point where you can visit the special online areas that cater to music lovers of all persuasions.

Accessing the RockNet forum

Keyword: **RockNet**

When I was a kid, it was just plain old rock n' roll. But this musical form represents many tastes and styles. So now you see references to Classic Rock, which emphasizes the music that was popular in the late 1960s and early 1970s (such as the Beatles and the Rolling Stones), and Alternative Rock, which represents performers at the cutting edge of musical development (such as Aphex Twin and Nine Inch Nails).

No matter what sort of rock n' roll music you prefer, you can read about it in the RockNet forum on America Online. You can share your feelings about your favorite bands here or just read reviews and gossip about them.

Accessing the Grateful Dead forum

Keyword: **Grateful Dead**

Until bandleader Jerry Garcia's death at the age of 53, the Grateful Dead had the distinction of being one of the longest surviving rock and roll bands. Their concerts were sellouts, and so they've set up their own special area on America Online for the Deadheads among you to visit, read about the band's musical legacy, its influence on our pop culture, and even share messages with other fans (see fig. 6.8). The Winterland: Dead Chat room is just what it says: a place where you can have online chats with other members of the online community.

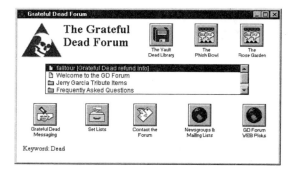

Fig. 6.8
Even the Grateful Dead have their own special place on America Online.

Exploring Warner/Reprise Records Online

Keyword: **Warner**

Warner/Reprise Records spans generations of music lovers. This forum covers the entire Warner/Reprise artist roster (see fig. 6.9).

Chapter 6 *From Music to Sports: Locating Entertainment Information on AOL* **103**

Fig. 6.9
This screen appears when you visit the Warner/Reprise Records forum on America Online.

Be your own online critic

Keyword: **Critics**

Before many people buy a book, see a movie, or even rent a videotape, they want to know what the reviewers have to say about it. America Online's Critics' Choice (see fig. 6.10) is a compendium of thousands of reviews and discussions about the entire spectrum of the world of entertainment.

Fig. 6.10
The Critics' Choice area is where you can read what the critics say and where you can become one yourself (if it suits you).

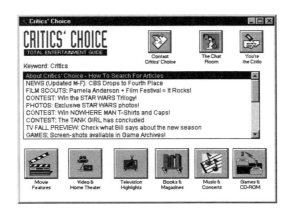

Checking out online games resources

Still another icon on the Entertainment department window is Games, and it represents, among other things, one of the most popular categories of software sales. They appeal to the young and the young at heart. A computer game enables you to turn your PC into an outer space battleground, a deep, dark dungeon, or even a maze. You can pit yourself against evil creatures and machines or even other human players in a quest to right wrongs, locate a secret castle, or save the world from destruction.

A visit to the PC Games forum

Keywords: **PC Games**

The PC computing forums are discussed in chapter 9, "Get Advice, Help and Software from America Online's Computing Forums," but the games forums deserve a special place here, because they are a special resource that any fan of computer games will want to visit often. Figure 6.11 shows the games forum screen.

Fig. 6.11
The PC Games forum is for computer game enthusiasts. It's a place where you can learn about the new games, and download game software you can run on your PC.

Accessing the Online Gaming forums

Keyword: **Gaming**

Whether you are interested in a casual game of checkers or are involved in a heavy-duty game of strategy, America Online's Online Gaming Forums area is a place you surely want to learn about and visit often.

As you can see from the forum's main directory window in figure 6.12, this forum serves as an entranceway to a number of areas that deal with gaming.

Chapter 6 *From Music to Sports: Locating Entertainment Information on AOL*

Fig. 6.12
The Online Gaming Forums screen is your first stop for information on all sorts of games.

Entering the Conference Center

The Online Gaming Forum holds regular conferences. Along with online members and forum staff, you can attend these conferences to participate in chats and attend debates and panel discussions featuring experts on the subject. To enter the conference center, click the Conference Center icon in the Online Gaming Forums main window.

Joining the Federation

Keyword: **Federation**

In addition to learning more about your games, you can actually get in on the action, with online role-playing games. AOL's role-playing games let you become a character in a far-flung fantasy, one you share with other members. The Federation (see fig. 6.13) is an adult space fantasy where you gain points through economics and politics rather than by slaying monsters and destroying your opponent's space craft.

Fig. 6.13
Federation interactive online game that lets you explore far-flung worlds in search of power and wealth. You play by entering text into a window that looks much like a chat room window.

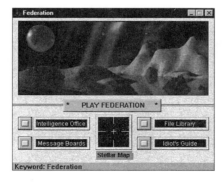

News from the world of sports

Keyword: **Sports**

If you played Little League sports when you were a child, have children interested in sporting activities, watch sports events regularly on television, or have been known to attend a game or two, you might want to visit America Online's virtual sports page frequently. To do so, choose Sports from AOL's Main Menu window to display the Sports department screen shown in figure 6.14.

Fig. 6.14
Whatever your favorite sport's activity, you'll find information about it on America Online.

The major sports are listed in the directory window at the right of the screen. To the left to you can check the latest news from the world of sports, by clicking the Sports icon. DataTimes Sports Reports, at the bottom left, is another major sports news resource. To the right of this icon is an icon that represents the most popular sport of the current season; it was football at the time this chapter was written. And then there's The Grandstand, which is shown in figure 6.15.

Fig. 6.15
Take your seat in The Grandstand to enjoy your favorite sport.

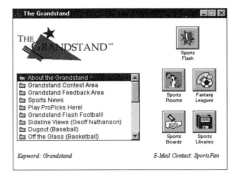

Sitting in the Sports Grandstand

Keyword: **Grandstand**

The Grandstand is where all you sports lovers can find the latest news about your favorite games, learn how your favorite teams fared the night before, and participate in online conferences with other fans. It is the entrance to America Online's sports stadium.

Highlights of The Grandstand include message boards and chat rooms where you can discuss your favorite sports. And the best feature of all is the Fantasy Leagues, where you can play your favorite games in cyberspace. And since it's all make believe, you can have a wrestling match without ever breaking into a sweat, and participate in an auto race without ever having to drive a car around a track.

Online book information

Keyword: **Books**

Whether you prefer fiction or nonfiction, you should check the Book Bestsellers first to see how your favorite author's works are faring in the marketplace. Choose Book Bestsellers from the main Entertainment Forum window to display the Book Bestsellers. From there you can find out more about this area of America Online, check out the bestseller lists, and see what's soon to be released. Your Book Reviews is the place to post your own book reviews and read about the choices of other members of the online community.

The fun is just beginning

As with other areas on America Online, you don't have to restrict yourself to searching one area for the information you want. Chapter 11, "Learning and Reference Sources Online," and chapter 12, "Exploring Your Online Newsstand," will take you to related information resources. And in the next chapter, you'll learn about the special online resources devoted to kids and how you can exert parental controls to govern your child's conduct on AOL.

The Secrets of Safe Online Fun for Kids of All Ages

● **In this chapter:**

- **How to access the special kids-only areas of America Online**
- **How kids can play online games**
- **All about special conferences for young people**
- **Online areas devoted to parents and child care**
- **Introduce your children to the Internet**
- **Set Parental Controls on your child's online visits**

America Online isn't just a playground for adults. Kids can join in, too. Before your kids dive into the forums head first, though, you will want to review some useful information. . ▶

America Online, as you've seen so far, is basically a warm, friendly place that you might think of as your hometown in cyberspace. But, like in your hometown, there are some folks who don't always think about common sense and courtesy toward others. And when you, as a parent, allow your kids to enter the online universe, you want to be sure their visits are always friendly, fun, and educational.

TIP You can save and print any text item in an AOL information window for later reference. Just click the text item first.

Online visits are usually enjoyable, but first...

The online experience should be friendly and fun, and it's just that for most AOL members. As with other parts of our society, however, there are a few people who don't have the best interests of you and your child in mind. The first part of this chapter outlines the methods to help protect your child. You'll want to read them and discuss them with your children before they begin to explore AOL's online community.

Although problems seldom occur, here are a few things you and your child should watch out for during your travels on AOL:

- **Inappropriate material**—As explained later in this chapter, nude or explicit photos and related text material are not allowed on AOL. That does not stop some people from exchanging such files, however. You should instruct your child to bring information about such files directly to your attention, so that the proper authorities at America Online can be informed about it.

- **Face-to-face meetings**—You should instruct your child never to give out personal information, such as your home address or telephone number, to another AOL member (however friendly that member may seem) without your approval. Personal meetings between your child and another AOL member should be done under your supervision at a public location.

Chapter 7 *The Secrets of Safe Online Fun for Kids of All Ages* **111**

- **Online harassment**—If your child receives instant messages or e-mail that is threatening or intimidating or that contains objectionable content, have your child bring the material directly to your attention so that you can file a complaint against the member who sends such material.

- **Internet access**—The Internet is largely unregulated and is not subject to Parental Controls or America Online's Terms of Service. As a result, you'll want to instruct your child carefully about both the benefits and the potential downsides of Internet access before your child begins to explore that area.

In the next few pages, you'll learn how to set restrictions upon areas your child may visit and how to deal with problems if they occur.

Set Parental Controls to protect your child

Keyword: **Parental Controls**

As a concerned parent, you may want to restrict the access of your child to certain areas of America Online. That's the purpose of Parental Chat Controls. This feature permits the original account holder (the screen name created when you first established your AOL account) to block or restrict access by users of other screen names on your AOL account from certain areas and features on America Online (see fig. 7.1). Setting these limits can help protect your child against possible exposure to objectionable material and possible online harassment in some areas of the service.

Fig. 7.1
The Parental Controls center lets you set limits on your child's access to AOL forums and the Internet.

In order to activate Parental Controls, you must be logged on with your master account name (the name that's listed first among your list of available accounts in the main window of your AOL software).

CAUTION **Your account password and billing information should be** considered confidential. You'll never be asked by an AOL employee online to give out this information. If you ever receive such a request, report it to AOL's Terms of Service area immediately. The keyword is TOS.

You can establish controls for just one or all screen names on your account. After Parental Control is set for a particular screen name, it's enforced every time that screen name logs on. The master account holder can make changes to Parental Control settings at any time.

While you're logged on with your master screen name, you can activate one or more Parental Control features. Just click the Chat Controls button from the main window of the Parental Controls center. Here are the options you'll want to consider:

- **Block Instant Messages**—Turns off Instant Messages, which are the immediate, one-to-one communications that can only be viewed by the sender and receiver of the message.

- **Block All Rooms**—Blocks access to the People Connection. The People Connection is the live, interactive chat area of America Online; it doesn't include the chat rooms in the Computing area.

- **Block Member Rooms**—Only blocks access to the member-created rooms within the People Connection. Other People Connection rooms, such as the Lobby, Romance Connection, and so on, are still accessible when this Parental Control feature is activated.

- **Block Conference Rooms**—Blocks access to the more focused rooms found around various departments on America Online, such as the classrooms in Learning & Reference, the technical forums in Computing & Software, and the NeverWinter Nights role-playing game in Games & Entertainment. It does not affect access to rooms in the People Connection.

CAUTION If your child commits repeated violations against AOL's Terms of Service, your account may be closed without notice. You will have to make telephone contact with the customer service department to restore the account. You should monitor your child's activities carefully.

How to protect your kids when they explore the Internet

The Internet is a huge, multifaceted, exciting, but largely unregulated place. A whole section of this book—Part V, "Getting on the Information Superhighway"—is devoted to Internet issues. This section briefly discusses common parental concerns about children making online visits.

The important thing to realize is that the Internet is not a single large online service, but a huge number of smaller networks linked by computers, modems, and telephone lines. When you visit America Online's Internet Connection (*Keyword:* **Internet**), you are, in effect, leaving the service and visiting places where America Online's Terms of Service simply does not apply. Of course, this doesn't mean that you and your child can behave any differently than when you visit one of America Online's regular areas. Your conduct reflects on the service, and violating the Terms of Service during an Internet visit on AOL is the same as violating those terms in the regular areas on AOL.

But visiting those Internet areas mean that you and your child will encounter areas where the rules and regulations of this service do not necessarily apply and where others might act in ways you don't approve. One example is the Internet areas devoted to sexually explicit material. In addition, it is not uncommon to find material in Internet mailing lists or newsgroups that contains language you might consider offensive. What to do?

Here are a few common-sense ideas:

- Before your child enters the Internet area, set limits on the kind of material your child is allowed to see.
- Review Internet e-mail newsgroups, mailing lists, and other information before your child is allowed to participate in them.

- Although your child is entitled to some measure of privacy, stay in touch with your child's online activities. Take the time to be with your child during online sessions—not just to monitor his activities, but also to share online experiences with him.

How to set Parental Controls

Despite the precautions I've just outlined, you may decide it's better for your child not to have access to certain Internet-based features. So, AOL has established a set of Parental Controls for this area too, activated in much the same way as the regular Parental Controls described earlier in this chapter.

The are two ways to activate these controls. First is simply to click the News Groups button when you visit AOL's Parental Controls center (shown in fig. 7.1). Or, if you've already opened AOL's Newsgroups window, at, *Keyword* **Newsgroups**, you can click the Parental Controls button (see fig. 7.2).

CAUTION **As with AOL's regular Parental Controls, you can't activate the** ones in the Newsgroups area unless you have logged on using your master AOL account.

Fig. 7.2
AOL's Newsgroups area.

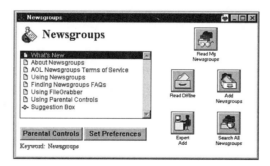

After selecting the person for whom you want to establish Parental Controls (by clicking the button next to his or her screen name), click the Edit button. You'll see the dialog box shown in figure 7.3.

Fig. 7.3
These choices are available via Internet Parental Controls.

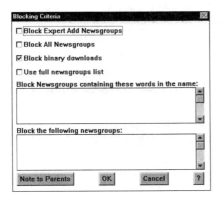

You can click the options shown in the preceding figure to control access of other members on your account to specific Internet Newsgroup features. Each option can apply to any screen name you select. Here's the run-down:

- **Block Expert Add Newsgroups**—Use this feature to prevent someone from adding newsgroups that are not a part of AOL's standard listing.

- **Block All Newsgroups**—For the ultimate level of protection, you may choose this option so your child has no access whatsoever to this feature.

- **Block Binary Downloads**—Use this feature to prevent a member from downloading encoded files in an Internet Newsgroup. Such files are a possible source of objectionable graphic files.

- **Use full newsgroups list**—Select this option for the full list of Newsgroups. This feature affords full access to all newsgroups, but you can selectively change their availability by selecting one or both of the next two items.

- **Block Newsgroups containing these words in the name**—You can use this feature to specify certain words, such as sex or erotica, that may represent newsgroups that offer material that's not suitable for your child.

- **Block the following newsgroups**—You can use this feature to specify the names of the newsgroups you want to block for a specific AOL screen name.

- **Note to Parents**—Click this button to get an overview of Internet Newsgroups and the best ways to participate in this exciting Internet feature.

By using one or more of the above Parental Controls, you can allow your child limited access to the Internet within the guidelines you set, and you can help provide a safe online experience. Remember, though, that these changes can only be made when you're logged on using your master account name (the first screen name shown when you click the pop-up list of names in your Windows AOL software).

Why is my account already signed on?

Even if you have the full slate of five screen names on your account, you can only use one of those names at a time. So if your child is using another screen name and you want to log on, you'll have to ask your child to log off first. If you want to be able to use America Online at the same time as your family members, you may want to consider setting up an extra account.

Just one more thing: If you get accidentally disconnected from America Online (perhaps because of trouble on the phone line), AOL's host computer may take a minute or two to get the hint. You'll get a message that your account is logged on, even though it's not. If that happens to you, just wait a few minutes and try again.

Provide an instruction session

Before you introduce your child to the online world, it might be helpful to provide a brief instruction session on creating an America Online screen name, logging on, and maneuvering around the service. It is a good idea to go over basic computer troubleshooting tips as well, in case your computer crashes in your absence—something that's apt to happen with any personal computer. There's a detailed tutorial on using America Online's Windows software in chapter 2.

Finding fun for kids of all ages

Keyword: **Kids**

America Online offers a variety of online activities for your kids where they can enjoy a number of entertaining and educational activities. You'll find discussions of some of them in the remainder of this chapter. Our first stopping point is AOL's Kids Only department, shown in figure 7.4. Not only can kids have fun, they can also learn a few things and become more adept at working with a computer.

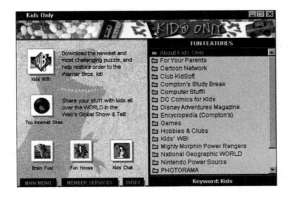

Fig. 7.4
Kids Only is a special place for children to participate in activities right on America Online.

Many of the areas discussed so far in this book have special kids-only departments as well—areas developed strictly for young people. The Kids Only department window in figure 7.5 shows just a few of the areas available, all specially designed for kids ages 5 through 14.

As with all America Online sessions, you should teach your children how to conduct themselves online. Discuss with them the basics of using America Online software, such as navigating through the network, reading and posting messages, and participating in online conferences. Your child should know how to act responsibly online and refrain from the use of vulgar language. In addition, you should establish limits as to the amount of time your children spend online because you are responsible for any charges they run up during their visits.

The next section covers some of the forums on America Online that are just for kids.

Internet sites for kids, too

Just like other areas of America Online, AOL has set aside a selection of Internet sites that cater to a particular interest. Just click the Top Internet Sites icon in the Kids Only area (see figure 7.5), and you'll see a specially selected range of sites on the Internet's World Wide Web that will provide hours of fun and education for your child.

Fig. 7.5
Just some of the World Wide Web pages that are available through direct access via AOL's Kids Only area.

Exploring *Disney Adventures* magazine

Keyword: **Disney Adventures magazine**

Every month, *Disney Adventures* brings exciting stories to your children (see figure 7.6). America Online is the place for your child to read about those many adventures and learn more about the world. The magazine even offers online conferences such as D.A. Live (which takes place in the forum's Odeon Auditorium), where your child can meet other kids with similar interests and enjoy an online chat.

Fig. 7.6
Disney Adventures magazine is a special resource for your child on America Online.

Accessing the Cartoon Network

Keyword: **Cartoon Network**

One of the exciting aspects of cable television is the availability of programs devoted to just one subject or one category of entertainment. Chapter 6, "From Music to Sports: Locating Online Entertainment Information," describes a number of the popular networks of this type that are represented on AOL. This section is devoted to the Cartoon Network forum (see fig. 7.7). Cartoon entertainment appeals to people of all ages, from children to adults. America Online has a special library of cartoon art in GIF (Graphic Interchange Format) format. See chapters 3, "Finding Your Way Around," and 5, "How to Stay in Touch with Other Members," for further information.

Fig. 7.7
America Online didn't forget cartoons.

Reading Tomorrow's Morning

Keyword: **Tomorrows Morning forum**

The folks who run the Tomorrow's Morning forum on AOL call it America's coolest (and only weekly home delivery) newspaper written and designed just for kids (see fig. 7.8). Your child has probably received an offer to subscribe at school. Highlights of each edition are available online, and there are additional areas worth exploring too.

Fig. 7.8
Read Tomorrow's Morning, the popular weekly newspaper for kids.

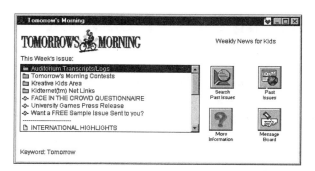

Online games

The last chapter introduced you to the various online gaming forums and told you how to search for the secrets of your favorite computer games. This chapter concentrates on games designed strictly for online visitors in the 5 to 14 age group. To reach this resource, choose Games & Computers from the Kids Only department window, and then click the Online Games icon.

- You'll find a number of fascinating games you'll want to try. There's a choice of trivia games, puzzles, and other fun-filled activities. And sometimes prizes are awarded to those getting the top scores. The list changes frequently, so rather than list them here, let me just suggest that you read the ground rules before you plunge in. Then sit back and enjoy.

CAUTION **Online games can run very fast, and they're exciting for young** people to play, but that doesn't mean the rules of good online conduct are forsaken. If too many online participants disrupt the contest, the host may decide not to award any prizes. So please urge your child to behave properly during the contest.

Special Kids-Only conferences online

Among the most popular online activities are chatting, interacting with other AOL members, and attending an online conference (where you can sometimes meet a famous personality and ask questions). AOL's Kids Chat (see figure 7.9) is the youthful equivalent of the popular People's Connection area and is designed strictly for members ages 5 to 14. It is carefully monitored by an enthusiastic band of online staffers, whom you'll recognize by the KO in front of their screen names.

Fig. 7.9
Participate in special youth-oriented chats on AOL.

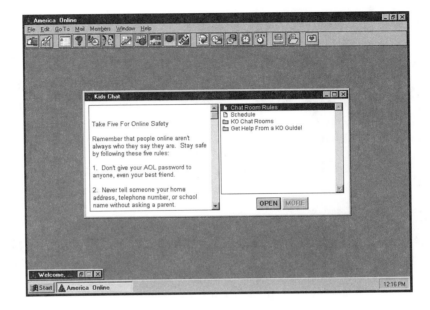

Chat Room rules

Before your youngster attends a Kids Connection event, it's a good idea to discuss the guidelines with your child. And you should attend a chat or two yourself to get a feeling for how they're conducted. As with any chat room or auditorium on AOL, the Terms of Service apply, so you'll want to review those terms (*Keyword:* **TOS**) that cover the common-sense guidelines for online conduct. The Chat Room Rules listing in the directory window of the Kids Connection area also summarizes some of these simple requirements.

The most important thing to consider, of course, is respect for other online members. Everyone should be treated equally and given equal opportunity to participate in an online session, free of interruptions. Someone else's misbehavior is not an invitation for others to disturb the chat as well. Each conference is monitored by a staff of online hosts who try to make sure the rules of proper online conduct are observed.

TIP If your online session is interrupted for any reason, just log on again. Usually, you'll be able to reconnect the second time without further trouble.

Ready to chat?

There are several conference halls in the Kids Chat area: Each posts a schedule of regular chats, so consult the Calendar listings before you enter the chat room of your choice. And if you miss a really important chat, don't despair. There's also a library where you can download logs of previous chats. You'll find those logs useful when two or more interesting chats are being held at the very same time.

TIP You can make your own chat log. Simply choose File, Logs and select the appropriate option to start recording your log.

Now for some special forums for parents

It's a complex world, which makes the problem of bringing up children more and more difficult. America Online has set up several areas in which parents can learn more about coping with the problems of daily living and how to deal with the problems and concerns of their children.

Visiting the Parents' Information Network

Keyword: **Parents**

America Online's Parents' Information Network is a fully integrated collection of online services dedicated to parental interests and concerns (see fig. 7.10). There are a number of special areas you'll want to consult from time to time in this forum.

One icon deserves a special mention. Click the Child Safety Brochure icon, and a colorful photo and a short, informative booklet providing helpful advice for your child's visits along the Information Superhighway appears (see fig. 7.11).

Chapter 7 *The Secrets of Safe Online Fun for Kids of All Ages* **123**

Fig. 7.10
A visit to the Parents' Information Network on AOL.

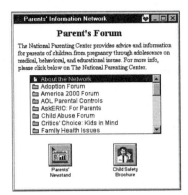

TIP Most of the photos you see online are in full color. To view them that way, you not only need a computer that supports color, but also a color monitor to view the photo on.

Fig. 7.11
A brochure about child safety online.

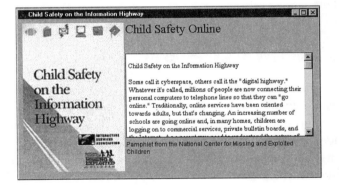

You'll want to review this material carefully; it summarizes many of the concerns parents should have about their child's participation in an online service. The entire text of this booklet can be saved or printed simply by choosing the appropriate commands from the File menu.

Take advantage of the National Parenting Center

Keyword: **TNPC**

AOL's National Parenting Center forum is designed to provide parents with useful information to make their jobs easier (see fig. 7.12). The center was founded in 1989, and the online area provides a large library of helpful information that deals with common problems and concerns of modern parenting.

Fig. 7.12
This forum offers comprehensive advice for parents.

After reading about the activities of the National Parenting Center, you may want to consider becoming a member. Full membership information is provided in this online support area; AOL members are offered a special membership rate.

More than meets the eye

As with other areas on America Online, you don't have to restrict yourself to searching one area for the information you want. For more useful information on children-related resources on AOL, visit the Entertainment, Education, and Learning & Reference departments, too. You'll find that many of the forums designed for adults also have special departments kids will want to check further. You should also read Part IV, "Information at Your Fingertips," for more details.

Travel the Stars or Explore Health Issues: Online Lifestyles & Interest Forums

● In this chapter:

- Share hobbies ranging from home theater to science fiction

- Discover the latest news on health-care issues

- Discuss the important issues of the day

- Learn about things to do in many major cities

Let's roam the stars, explore new developments in health care, seek out information about whatever hobbies or special interests intrigue you, America Online probably has set aside a space place . . . . ▶

You can explore the worldwide Internet, upgrade the sound of your stereo, research your family history, and debate with other America Online members on subjects ranging from the top news of the day to whether your PC or Macintosh is the better computer (and I'm sure what your answer will be). It can all happen in the various Lifestyles forums on America Online.

Figure 8.1 shows the Clubs & Interests main window, which you can find by typing the keyword Clubs. As you can see, the features you can reach from this point are numerous, diverse, and intriguing.

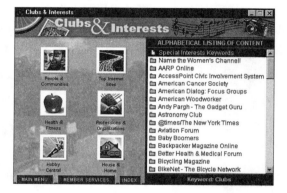

Fig. 8.1
The Clubs & Interests department on America Online leads you to a diverse group of features. (The artwork you see here will change often as new areas are added or changed.)

When I sat down to write this chapter, I spent many, many hours exploring all the areas on America Online that cater to lifestyles, hobbies, and special interests (some of these places were also discussed in chapter 6). You learn more in this chapter and finish the little tour in chapter 12.

My survey seemed to be never-ending. For this reason, this chapter just touches on the highlights of America Online's Lifestyle areas, and the rest is left for you to explore at your leisure.

To make it easier to find an area that caters to a specific interest, all of the forums in this area of America Online are grouped by category, as represented by the icons at the left of the Clubs & Interests screen. Let's explore the highlights.

Top Internet Sites

As with other departments on America Online, the Clubs & Interests department has hot links to the World Wide Web, which you can begin to explore simply by clicking the Top Internet Sites icon (see fig. 8.2).

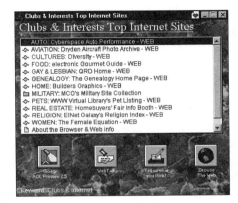

Fig. 8.2
If a special interest area isn't on AOL, you're likely to find it surfing the World Wide Web. The list you see here will change often as the Internet is a fluid place.

As you can see from the list in figure 8.2, the forums you visit on America Online are but a portion of the fascinating places you can explore during your online visit. Using AOL's World Wide Web browser software, you can take off and fly across the world in search of other sources of fascinating information.

Forums devoted to special interests

You'll find many online forums that cater to special interests. Here are just a few of the more popular areas. As I list them, I'll show you some of the more visually arresting artwork adopted by these forums.

Baby Boomers

Keyword: **Baby Boomers**

The focus on this forum is strictly interaction. You can share your experiences on a host of subjects with others who were born in the same frenetic generation.

National Multiple Sclerosis Society Forum

Keyword: **NMSS**

The National Multiple Sclerosis Society has set up this forum on America Online to provide information about the disease, including updates on medical research into finding a cure. A host of information is available for you to read about this topic. You can also find a message center, and health and medical chat rooms where you can interact with other members, including health-care professionals.

Religion & Ethics Forum

Keyword: **Religion**

The Religion & Ethics Forum doesn't favor a particular religion or belief system. It has message boards devoted to many faiths, including New Age philosophies. In the Religion and Ethics Message Center, you can debate with other online members.

SeniorNet Online

Keyword: **SeniorNet**

SeniorNet Online should demonstrate to everyone that reaching one's senior years is often when life truly begins. In a special Computer Learning Center, you can learn how to master your computer. SeniorNet Online also includes active message areas, a Community Center, where you can interact with other online members and forum staff, and a wealth of information you can read and download.

Hobbies and Clubs Online

Whether your interest is recreational or professional, America Online has a hobby or club forum for you. Let's visit a few of them.

The Astronomy Club (a.k.a. the Astronomy Forum)

Keyword: **Astronomy**

America Online's Astronomy Club (see fig. 8.3) is hosted by a real astronomer, Mr. Astro, better known as Stuart Goldman, who is an associate editor at *Star & Telescope* magazine. If you want to learn more about the stars and planets, explore the Ask Mr. Astro message board. There, you can interact with other America Online members who share an interest in astronomy, or even ask experts such as Mr. Astro about what is on your mind.

Fig. 8.3
You can explore the stars with a little help from America Online.

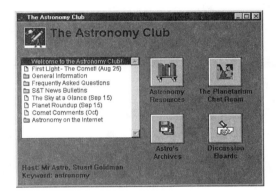

The Cooking Club

Keyword: **Cooking**

Whether your efforts at cooking are limited to boiling water and warming a TV dinner (hmm, sounds like me!), or you are a culinary expert, you can find a wealth of useful information in America Online's Cooking Club. The forum includes message boards where you can share your favorite recipes or pick up a tip or two from other online gourmets. You can even enter a conference room, the Kitchen, where regular meetings are held on food preparation or new recipes.

The Exchange

Keyword: **The Exchange**

The Exchange is a place where you can express yourself on a wide variety of special interests. There are discussion areas related to men's and women's issues, gardening and other outdoor activities, politics, philosophy, crafts, careers, coin collecting, and other topics.

CAUTION As with other areas on America Online, make sure to approach the debates in the Exchange and other message board areas with a bit of care. Don't use vulgar language, don't insult other America Online members (even though the discussions have been known to get hot and heavy), and, most importantly, just have a good time.

The Capital Connection (a.k.a. Politics)

Keywords: **Capital, Politics**

You can find information and debates on all sorts of issues in many places on America Online, from company support forums in the Computing & Software section, to the special places that are devoted solely to news and debate about the issues that affect us the most. The Capital Connection is one of those special places (see fig. 8.4).

Fig. 8.4
America Online's Capital Connection area gives you a chance to speak your mind about the important issues of the day.

AOL's Genealogy Club

Keyword: **Roots**

This special corner of the America Online community, the Genealogy Club, provides advice and useful information to help you search your family tree. In active message areas, you can share information and experiences with other online members as you try to find just who your ancestors were.

The software library includes programs that help you catalog information about your family history. You can review the findings of many genealogy experts who assist you in your quest. Or you can attend the regular chats in the Ancestral Digs Conference Hall to interact with other online members.

Kodak Photography Forum

Keyword: **Kodak**

The Kodak Photography Forum, shown in figure 8.5, is conducted by Ron Baird, a photography specialist from Kodak who writes many of their technical manuals. Ron, along with fellow online members, provides you with hints and tips that can make your picture-taking experience more rewarding. If you're looking to sell that old camera and get something better, you can even check out a buy & sell section.

Fig. 8.5
America Online's Kodak Photography Forum is the place for shutterbugs of all kinds.

Science Fiction & Fantasy area

Keyword: **Science Fiction**

Science fiction is the art of taking present-day science, imagining how it will develop in the future, and building an exciting story around that sort of speculation. America Online's Science Fiction & Fantasy section is an active pit stop for fans of books, comics, movies, and TV programs. You can share your views and learn about upcoming events. Figure 8.6 shows the main Science Fiction & Fantasy directory window.

Fig. 8.6
Explore new, exciting worlds without ever leaving your computer's screen in AOL's Science Fiction and Fantasy forums.

Star Trek Club

Keyword: **Star Trek**

America Online's *Star Trek* Club is a meeting ground for Trekkers, where you learn about upcoming TV shows and conferences and can participate in discussions and chats with other fans. One chat I recently attended featured one of the special effects experts on the *Star Trek: Deep Space Nine* program, who let us in on just how those incredible visual illusions on the show are created. Now that another *Star Trek* program is on the air, *Star Trek: Voyager*, you'll find an even greater variety of information in this active online area.

Areas devoted to health, home, and the environment

Here are the parts of America Online that are devoted to the subjects that are uppermost in the minds of most of us.

Better Health & Medical Forum

Keyword: **Health**

Whether you are a health-care professional or are just seeking the route to better health and a longer, more productive life, the Better Health & Medical Forum is a place you might want to visit often. The Better Health & Medical Forum contains a large store of text files on all sorts of health-related issues. It's not intended to replace a regular visit to your family physician, but is designed to give you a better range of knowledge about the issues that are of the most importance to you.

Environmental Forum

Keyword: **eforum**

The news media refers to the 1990s as the Decade for the Environment. The Environmental Forum is America Online's response to the attention on the environment. This forum has an active message board divided into four main categories. And because the best way to deal with environmental concerns can become hotly contested at times, one board is called The Water Cooler. There, you can approach all these subjects with calm and reason.

Issues in mental health

Keyword: **IMH**

Relationships are probably the most difficult problems you are asked to face. Whether it's your spouse, your children, or just coping with each day's events, the task often can be challenging. Issues in Mental Health is a place where you can learn about how to deal with everyday problems. Active message boards enable you to interact with other online members and professionals concerning the problems of daily living.

Network Earth online

*Keyword: **Network Earth***

Network Earth is a weekly television program broadcast on the Atlanta-based TBS Super Station, which is offered through cable TV systems around the country. This program features reports about the progress made in dealing with the problems of the environment.

Pet Care Forum

Keyword: **Pet**

Most of you probably think of a pet as a dog or a cat, or even a fish, but many other animals qualify for pet status. The Pet Care Forum on America Online is devoted to helping you find better ways to care for all your animal friends (see fig. 8.7).

Fig. 8.7
Learn more about caring for your pet in America Online's Pet Care Forum.

Areas Devoted to Professions and Organizations

A number of professional societies have formed special areas on America Online that cater to members, as well as casual visitors who want to learn more about a specific topic. I'll discuss a few of them in the pages that follow.

Aviation Forum

Keyword: **Fly**

Whether your interest in aviation is limited to reading about it in your living room, building a model plane, or piloting a craft yourself, the place where you can find others who share your interest is America Online's Aviation Forum (see fig. 8.8).

Fig. 8.8
The Aviation Forum is a fascinating place for both armchair and active aviators.

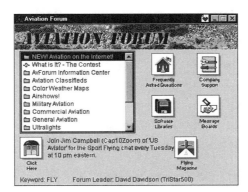

 TIP **If you can't find the specific forum that interests you on America Online,** try locating it with a keyword. Most keywords either contain the name of an area or its subject, so if you don't know which keyword is correct, don't hesitate to try a few out for size. Suppose, for example, that you want to learn more about Dolby Surround sound. Type the keyword Dolby and guess what? It takes you directly to the Dolby Audio/Video Forum on America Online.

Military & Vets Club

Keyword: **Military**

America Online's Military & Vets Club is dedicated to those of you who have served the country in the armed forces, whether in war or peace. You can find message areas for both veterans and for those still serving in the military.

National Space Society

Keyword: **NSS**

The National Space Society is devoted to promoting research and exploration of space (see fig. 8.9). Its Board of Governors features such luminaries as Hugh Downs, Arthur C. Clarke, Jacques Cousteau, John Glenn, Nichelle Nichols (Uhura, the communications officer from the original *Star Trek* TV show and movies), and Alan Shepard.

Fig. 8.9
America Online's center for space-related research is the National Space Society.

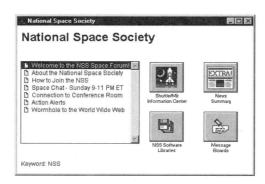

Downloading graphic images

Many of the forums I've described in this chapter (and throughout the book, for that matter) contain lots of beautiful artwork that you can download and view on your computer, or print if you prefer (but a color printer would be nice if you want to see a hard copy representation in all its glory). The forums devoted to photography and space travel are special examples of where artwork will be located. These files are usually offered in GIF and JPEG formats, which are graphic image formats that are used to provide the highest possible quality and keep the file sizes small (and shorten download times). The neat thing is that your Windows AOL software can read these files in the same way you can read simple text files. You'll see the graphic images appear on your computer when you download them, and, if you want to see a file you've already downloaded, just choose File, Open, and select the file you wish to see. It's that simple.

Some images, such as AOL's weather maps, are available in a special format called ART, which is a very compact file conversion technique developed by Johnson-Grace Company that produces a picture file you can download in just a few seconds. You can tell if it's an ART file simply by the fact that just clicking the file icon (or double clicking the file name), rather than choosing a Download option, starts the file download (and the download is very, very fast).

Visiting leisure & entertainment information areas

Of course, not every part of America Online is quite as serious as the places I've just discussed. Here are some examples that provide a more entertaining outlook on life.

Car and Driver online

Keywords: **Car and Driver**

Before you buy a new car, you'll want to keep up to date about the new models and how they perform on the road. *Car and Driver* is one of the oldest magazines that caters to automobile enthusiasts. Their online forum, shown in figure 8.10, includes feature articles from the magazine itself, complete test reports of the hot new models, and an active message area where you can learn about the experiences other AOL members have had with these models. Oh, and by the way, we don't want to ignore them, but *Car and Driver*'s sister magazine, *Road and Track*, has its own AOL forum too. Keyword is Cars.

Fig. 8.10
Car and Driver magazine tells you how the new cars really perform before you take that test drive.

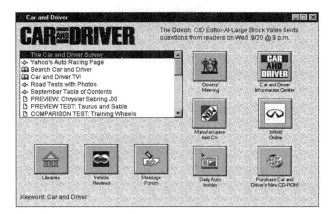

Dolby Audio/Video Forum

Keyword: **Dolby**

The name Dolby was originally synonymous with techniques to provide better-quality sound with reduced background noise (or hiss) on audio compact cassettes and professional studio recordings. It also describes a technology (Dolby Surround) that provides uncanny realism in your favorite motion pictures. If you've ever watched a movie in a theater equipped with Dolby Surround, you heard sounds emanating not only from your screen but also from your left, your right, and behind you. The Dolby Audio/Video Forum on America Online features experts from the audio and video industries and active fans who interact on a whole range of issues, from where to hear the best movie sound to how to set up a Surround sound installation in your home.

Consumer Electronics Forum

Keyword: **CE**

Consumer Electronics (see fig. 8.11) is a comprehensive forum that covers everything from household gadgets to home theater (and many, many possibilities in between). Whether you want to buy a new telephone pager, or a satellite receiving dish for your TV, you'll find information and fascinating discussions in this forum.

Fig. 8.11
Home electronics of all sorts are at the forefront in this fascinating AOL forum.

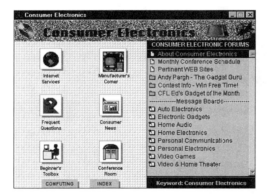

Towns and Cities Online

Some of your favorite cultural centers are now participating in forums on America Online. You can travel to Chicago, New York, the San Francisco Bay area, or even the nation's capital simply by clicking an icon, or entering the appropriate keyword. For the rest of this chapter, I'll cover a few of the forums devoted to these areas.

Visiting Chicago Online

Keyword: **Chicago**

Much like the city for which it's named, this forum is a huge, sprawling place with many areas to visit. This section just covers the highlights and leaves you to explore the rest at your leisure.

When first visiting Chicago Online, click on the Chicagoland Calendar listing in the main forum directory (see fig. 8.12) for the latest news and event information. If you're traveling to Chicago for business or pleasure, you'll probably want to read the *Chicago Tribune* News & Features area (which we'll get to shortly) for latest forecasts and for important information you need to know when you get there.

Fig. 8.12
Chicago Online is the gateway to information about happenings in the Windy City.

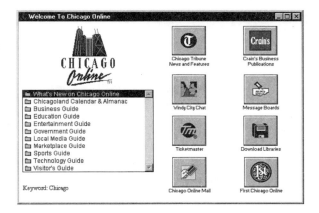

The Ticketmaster icon takes you to the Ticketmaster gateway, a special area where you can learn about concerts and other special events, not only in Chicago, but in the state of Florida too (and it's expanding to other parts of the country as time goes on). Once you've found the event you want to attend, you can order your tickets right from the keyboard and mouse of your personal computer.

Reading the *Chicago Tribune*

Keyword: **Chicago Tribune**

One of the biggest challenges for the large daily newspapers has been to decide just how to deal with the Information Superhighway. The *Chicago Tribune* Forum is the way one publisher is meeting the challenge.

The *Chicago Tribune* Forum (run by the sponsors of Chicago Online) delivers the same news, sports, and features that you find in the printed editions. One section is even devoted to classified ads. You can view, save, or print text files that you select. And you can search the contents of each daily edition for specific news items.

Using the Mercury Center

Keyword: **Mercury**

Like Chicago Online, Mercury Center is a resource run by a large daily newspaper, in this case, the *San Jose Mercury News*. As you can see in figure 8.13, Mercury Center is designed to provide a full range of information about the San Francisco Bay area (which includes the Silicon Valley).

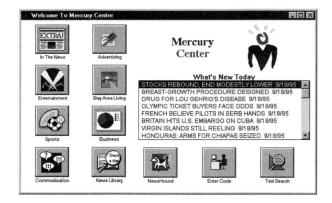

Fig. 8.13
Mercury Center is the center for news, views, and more for visitors to the San Francisco Bay area.

When you first visit Mercury Center, you might just want to look at the top news. It is shown in the What's New Today listing at the right of the Mercury Center screen, which you can view online or save and print, the same as any other text document on America Online.

Each icon on the main Mercury Center screen takes you to another special part of Mercury Center. You can check the latest Bay Area entertainment news and then review the Bay Area Living section for a list of things to do when you visit the area, including a list of popular restaurants.

Other sections are devoted to sports and business information and another of America Online's unique message boards, where both fellow members and Mercury Center staff discuss the important issues of the day, or whatever else is on their minds.

One really fascinating feature is Newshound (shown in the Mercury Center window in fig. 8.13), a search tool that will seek out information from the *San Jose Mercury News* and other sources behind the scenes. When the information is found, it'll be sent directly to you via e-mail. Give it a try and see.

Reading the *San Jose Mercury News*

The instructions here are a bit involved, but bear with me; it's the best way to get to this area: When you click on the In the News icon on the main Mercury Center screen (see fig. 8.13), and then click on the Extra icon that appears in the next window, you bring up a copy of the current edition of the *San Jose Mercury News* (see fig. 8.14). You can read the entire news, sports, and features sections and interact with the paper's editors.

Fig. 8.14
Your virtual daily newspaper comes right to your America Online doorstep.

Reading The *New York Times* Online

Keyword: **times**

Start spreading the news and be a part of it—The *New York Times* is on America Online (see fig. 8.15), with an emphasis on the top features and lifestyle news from each daily edition of the paper. All the top stories from the newspaper itself are available for you to read online, or save and print for later review.

Fig. 8.15
The New York Times offers the best of its daily editions on America Online.

 CAUTION When you want to find *The New York Times* on America Online, don't forget the keyword is times. If you forget the s, and type time instead, you'll be taken to the *Time* magazine forum instead.

If you live in New York, or are planning a visit, click on the Leisure icon. You'll find news and views about the top dining and entertainment spots in New York. And don't forget to check out In The Region, a special area devoted to the rest of the tri-state New York metropolitan area.

Just part of the picture

New Clubs & Interests forums are being added regularly to America Online, so if you don't find an area that caters to your special interest, check back often. A number of the special forums mentioned briefly in this chapter, and other information pertinent to your lifestyles and interests needs, are also discussed in more detail throughout this book.

Get Advice, Help, and Software from America Online's Computing Forums

● **In this chapter:**

- **How to get the latest scoop about Windows 95 and other stuff**
- **Read your favorite computing magazines**
- **Visit AOL's popular computing forums**
- **Get free support from computer manufacturers**

You interact with America Online by computer, so the online service is a natural place to learn how to make your computer work better for you . . . . ➤

Whether you want to download a fancy new shareware program, solve a specific problem, or if you just need some advice on how to upgrade your computer for better performance, America Online can help you find the answers.

Suppose, for example, that you try to run a new program and your computer crashes every time. It's Friday evening, and the manufacturer's technical support people have gone home for the weekend. You need that new software to finish a special project. What do you do?

Or suppose that you're looking for a program that can help remind you of special events. Relief is just a download away in America Online's vast software libraries. AOL has thousands of different software applications to offer, with more being added daily.

Just log on to America Online, where you can find both members and manufacturer's support people ready and willing to help you out of your jam.

Exploring the Computing Forums

Keyword: **Computing**

You've had it happen. Your computer is crashing whenever you try to open a new document. Or you want to learn to use your computer more effectively, or just talk computers with fellow online members. Well, the place to go to deal with all these matters is one of America Online's Computing forums (see fig. 9.1).

The hardworking folks who run these forums are truly the unsung heroes of AOL. They are available day and night, often on weekends. They are indeed the backbone of our favorite online service.

It's true that the computing forums don't necessarily offer the razzle-dazzle graphics of some of the other areas of the service, nor does their content make the front pages of the newspapers as other online areas do. But they provide the help you need when your computer isn't working properly, and they offer huge resources of information to help make your computer run better. And there's always that cool new software posted in their software libraries, with tens of thousands of choice files from which to choose.

There's an AOL computing forum covering every facet of personal computing, from PC games to the latest hints and tips about using Windows 95. You'll find active message boards, huge listings of helpful information, and ready answers to the questions you have. In addition, these forums hold regular conferences, featuring the people who run the forums as well as industry experts who often come by to tell you about a new product or simply to hang out and chat with you about a variety of computing subjects.

Because a picture is truly worth a thousand words, look closely at the figures that follow for a brief idea of many of the services that these forums offer.

Accessing Computing Internet Sites

Many of the major computing manufacturers and publishers have created home pages on the World Wide Web. By clicking on the Top Internet Sites icon, you'll have a direct passage to many of these information resources. The listing of available sites changes so often that I am not giving you a lineup, except to tell you that you'll always find such companies as IBM, Intel and Microsoft on the list.

> ### Plain English, please!
> On the World Wide Web, a **home page** is the first or main screen at a Web site. The home page will often present introductory material about the site, and offer hot links to access additional information (and sometimes software files) from this location. In some cases, you'll even see a list of other sites containing related information. Chapters 16 through 20 cover AOL's various Internet-related services.

Fig. 9.1
A number of World Wide Web sites are directly accessible from this convenient area of AOL's Computing department.

Get Answers from the PC Help Forum

Keyword: **Help Desk**

Every PC computing forum on America Online has a little icon with a shaded question mark. It's labeled Help & Information, and it's your entry to the PC Help Forum (see fig. 9.2).

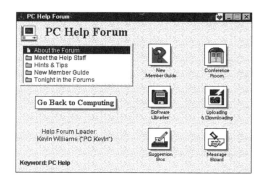

Fig. 9.2
When you need a helping hand, the PC Help Forum on America Online is there for you.

TIP Before you post a question, read older messages in the same message folder or in other message areas dealing with a similar topic. You might find a response and a solution to a question much like yours.

PC Applications Forum covers your favorite DOS and Windows programs

Keyword: **PC Applications**

The market offers a bewildering array of PC applications. Knowing which word processor to choose, which financial planning software works best, and which spreadsheet crunches numbers most efficiently is difficult to determine. The Applications Forum (see fig. 9.3) tries to bring a little order and helpful advice into its active message board.

Chapter 9 *Get Advice, Help, and Software from America Online's Computing Forums* **147**

Fig. 9.3
The Applications forum offers computing advice, free-wheeling discussions, and software for you to download.

Explore modems and networking at the PC Communications Forum

Keyword: **PC Telecom**

If you're thinking of buying one of those newer, high-speed modems, or finding a better way to network your computer with a printer or another computer, pay a visit to the Telecommunications forums on America Online. Figure 9.4 shows the PC Telecommunications Forum screen.

Fig. 9.4
The Communications Forum is your America Online headquarters for PC, modem, and networking issues.

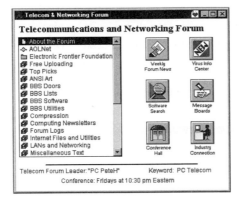

Learn about programming in the PC Development Forum

Keyword: **PC Development**

If you want to write your own software, or you're a professional looking for advice on dealing with a specific problem in writing code, America Online's developers' forums are resources you can use again and again. Figure 9.5 shows the Development Forum screen.

Fig. 9.5
When you want to write your own software for DOS, OS/2, and Windows, the Development Forum is a place you want to visit.

Visiting the DOS Forum

Keyword: **DOS**

When Microsoft introduced MS-DOS 6.0, America Online established a special Resource Center in the DOS Forum to offer advice and suggestions on updating your PC computers to take the best advantage of this new operating system. You can even download the latest DOS update and take advantage of the new features and "bug fixes" that are offered.

The DOS Forum on America Online (see fig. 9.6) is not just an information center to help you make your computer run more efficiently.

Fig. 9.6
Advice and updates are available on America Online's DOS Forum.

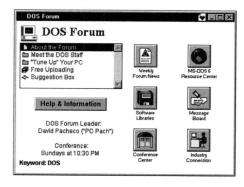

Play the Games Forum

Keyword: **PC Games**

In chapter 6, "From Music to Sports: Locating Online Entertainment Information on AOL," you were introduced to many of the ways you can have pure, simple fun on America Online. The Games forums contain shareware games, add-ons, demos of many popular commercial games, and, just as important, helpful advice on how to make your playtime (for adults and children) more rewarding. Figure 9.7 shows the Games Forum screen. (For more information, refer to chapter 7, "The Secrets of Safe Online Fun for Kids of All Ages.")

Fig. 9.7
You have time for a little fun with a game downloaded from the PC Games Forum.

Illustrating the Graphic Arts Forum

Keyword: **PC Graphics**

If you are a computer artist or want to become one, you need to drop in to visit the PC Graphic Arts Forum on America Online. This forums contain huge resources of information to help you learn your craft and produce better work (see fig. 9.8).

Fig. 9.8
The PC Graphic Arts Forum is America Online's resource for graphics professionals.

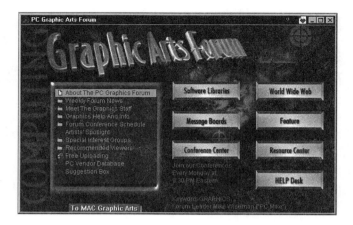

Getting an advanced look at the newest PC hardware

Keyword: **PC Hardware**

New computers are coming out so often that keeping a scorecard is difficult. Before you buy a new model only to learn that it will be outdated the next day, check out America Online's PC Hardware forum, shown in figure 9.9.

Fig. 9.9
Find out which PC can run Windows faster in the PC Hardware Forum.

Using the PC Multimedia Forum

Keyword: **PC Multimedia**

The word *multimedia* has been bandied about the computer world for quite a number of years. Multimedia refers to the marriage of audio and video (still

Chapter 9 *Get Advice, Help, and Software from America Online's Computing Forums*

or moving) on your desktop computer. As computers have become more and more powerful, the tools to manipulate the sometimes huge audio and video files have become cheaper and easier to use.

Major movie production houses have been using desktop computers for their work. The newest PCs offer special tools for multimedia use, ranging from CD-ROMs to video capture expansion cards. The PC Multimedia Forum (see fig. 9.10) is your meeting ground for both amateurs and professionals to share experiences and learn more about this growing art.

Fig. 9.10
Video and sound combine to produce multimedia, and this forum is where you can keep up-to-date with the emerging technologies.

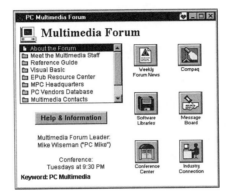

Hear new sounds from the PC Music and Sound Forum

Keyword: **PC Music**

In the 1980s, music came into its own on a desktop computer. More and more recording artists (some whose names are household words) have begun to use personal computers to create and store sounds. With a few inexpensive add-ons, you can even make your computer into a miniature, multitrack recording studio and produce digital-quality audio.

The PC Music and Sound Forum on America Online provide helpful advice and tips on how you can use these tools to create professional-sounding music presentations (see fig. 9.11).

Fig. 9.11
The PC Music and Sound Forum on America Online gives PC music buffs a chance to explore musical tools.

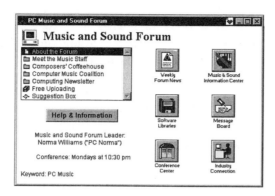

Getting the goods on OS/2

Keyword: **OS 2**

IBM's OS/2 is an efficient multitasking operating system that is gaining more and more popularity in the PC world. Even if you aren't ready to switch just yet, you might want to visit America Online's OS/2 Forum to learn just what all those computer magazines are writing about and find out whether OS/2 is something you want to use. Figure 9.12 shows the main OS/2 Forum window, from which you can access all the forum's resources.

Fig. 9.12
The ins and outs of OS/2 are explained in this America Online forum.

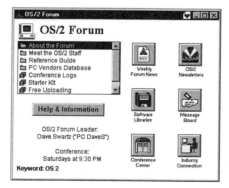

Exploring the Personal Digital Assistants Forum

Keyword: **PDA**

PDA is an abbreviation for Personal Digital Assistants, and it refers to a computer that you can hold in the palm of your hand, such as a Sharp Wizard or an Apple Newton. Whether you have just bought one of these neat examples of electronic wizardry or you are wondering whether it's something other than a high-priced toy, you can visit this forum to learn more (see fig. 9.13).

Fig. 9.13
Learn about hand-held computers in this America Online forum.

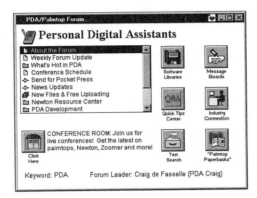

Visiting the User Groups Forum

Keyword: **UGF**

When you first buy a personal computer, you're no doubt anxious to meet other computer owners to receive advice and share tips and tricks to make your computer run more effectively. A *user group* is a club, pure and simple. It's an organization consisting of computer owners, usually devoted to one specific platform, such as PC or Macintosh. If you're a user group member, or just want to learn about joining one, pay a visit to America Online's New User Groups Forum (see fig. 9.14).

Fig. 9.14
Meet with fellow computer owners, right here on America Online.

Explore the possibilities of Windows 95

Keyword: **Windows Forum**

Microsoft Windows 95 has caught the PC world by storm, providing an easy-to-use point-and-click metaphor to the way you interact with your computer. America Online's Windows forum provides an extensive library of public domain and shareware, an active message board, and regular conferences where you can interact with fellow members and experts alike (see fig. 9.15). With Windows 95 being loaded on millions of PCs, this is the place where you'll find out what it means for your computing experience.

Fig. 9.15
You can make Windows work better by consulting the Windows Forum.

Preview your favorite computer books & magazines

When you want to learn more about how your computer works, find out how to use a specific piece of software, or just sneak a preview of upcoming products, you are likely to venture into your local bookstore and purchase a book such as this one.

America Online gives you a chance to preview some of those publications before you buy them. You can even search through back issues of many of your favorite computing magazines for a specific article of interest, all during your online session. Here are a few choice publications you'll want to check out further.

For those who work at home

Keyword: **Home Office**

If you are like many people and work from an office located in your own home, you might want to read *Home Office Computing.* This magazine caters to small-business folk, offers advice on buying new hardware and software, and provides helpful tips on making your office run more productively (see fig. 9.16).

Fig. 9.16
Home Office Computing's forum on America Online is a valuable resource for small businesses.

Your computer is almost a member of the family

Keyword: **HomePC**

The personal computer has taken over almost every area of our lives. Our children work with computers at school, and low-priced computers are now available not only at specialty stores, but also at discount stores and consumer electronics chains. *HomePC* magazine (see fig. 9.17) is for users of both the Apple Macintosh and IBM PCs and compatibles, with an emphasis on the home, rather than business, user.

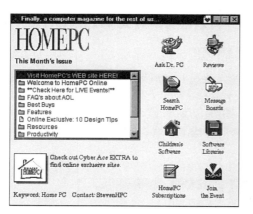

Fig. 9.17
HomePC magazine takes a personal approach to the world of personal computing.

On the road with *Mobile Office* Online

Keyword: **Mobile, Portable**

The proliferation of laptop computers has made it possible for you to do your work almost anywhere in the world (even in the middle of a desert) so long as you have a spare set of batteries or an available source for AC power. *Mobile Office* Online, as shown in figure 9.18, is the AOL counterpart of the popular newsstand magazine that caters to this new generation of traveling workers.

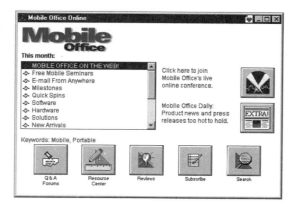

Fig. 9.18
Mobile Office magazine keeps tabs on the growing world of laptop computing.

Visiting *PC World* Online

Keyword: **PC World**

PC World magazine is one of the most popular computer magazines available. It provides its own unique slant to information on new PC hardware and

Chapter 9 Get Advice, Help, and Software from America Online's Computing Forums **157**

software products. A typical visit to the forum might offer you news about a special contest, a new family of chips from Intel, or the latest operating system upgrade from Microsoft. The PC World Online screen is shown in figure 9.19.

Fig. 9.19
PC World Online is an information resource for users of IBM PCs and compatibles.

Visiting *WordPerfect Magazine* Online

Keyword: **WPMag**

If you are a user of WordPerfect, the popular cross-platform word processing program published by Novell, the monthly WordPerfect magazine, shown in figure 9.20, is your source for advice and information about this popular program. It comes in two flavors—the regular version, and a special Windows edition.

Fig. 9.20
OnLine Access features *WordPerfect Magazine.*

Straight from the horse's mouth: seeking company support

Keyword: **Industry Connection**

If you've ever waited long minutes listening to voice mail when you tried to telephone a hardware or software manufacturer for some help, you'll appreciate America Online's solution. More than 200 firms, ranging from small utility software publishers to the major manufacturers of computer hardware, are represented in America Online's Industry Connection areas, as shown in figure 9.21. What's more, additional firms are being added almost daily, so it's likely that most of the publishers you want to contact are online now or will be shortly.

Fig. 9.21
Get help right from the source using America Online's Industry Connection.

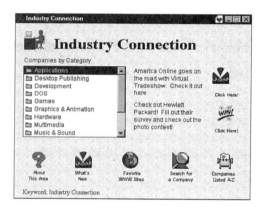

These support forums are places where you can get advice on how to use a company's product more effectively and how to solve problems when they arise. The company's own support personnel usually staff the forums, and they are often ably assisted by knowledgeable America Online members.

Software publishers often give you free maintenance updates to their products in their support areas, so you don't have to wait for that product update to be mailed to you. You'll also want to check the software libraries often in case they contain an update that you need.

Finding a Company

You can also find computing industry support areas in the computing and software forums that cater to the kind of product the companies support.

Suppose, for example, that you want to access a modem manufacturer in the Hardware and Communications forums. Click on the Industry Connection icon to see whether the firm is represented.

But the fastest route might simply be to use a keyword to go directly to the firm you want. If you want to find Diamond Multimedia, which manufactures multimedia and video expansion cards for both PCs and Macs, type the keyword **Diamond**. In just a few seconds, you are transported directly to the front door of the company's America Online support forum (see fig. 9.22).

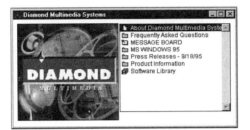

Fig. 9.22
One of the larger manufacturers of expansion cards is Diamond Multimedia, who supports their many customers through their AOL forum.

AOL is for both PC and Mac users!

Crossing platforms? It's very common these days for folks to have to work on both Macs and PCs in an office or home setup. America Online's software is designed to look very similar on both platforms (although the available features are somewhat different), so you can interact with the service in a similar manner. You'll find all the differences spelled out in full detail in my other AOL book, *Using America Online with the Mac*.

You'll also find that the computing forums for the other platform and magazines that cater to the other platform are easily accessed from both sides of the fence. So you don't have to worry about not being able to get to the Mac forums while using your PC, and vice versa. The Computing department, (*Keyword*: **Computing**), offers a cross-platform gateway. Or you can reach a specific area by its keyword, which is usually the same whether you're logged on with a Mac or PC.

Using industry connection help

A technical support person can't help you solve your problem if you don't give enough information about your setup and the difficulties you're having with the product. This typical letter is often found in the message boards:

```
Help! My computer is crashing all the time. I can't get any
work done when I use your software. I need help.
Signed: Harried Harry
```

This sort of letter is only going to postpone the process of helping you, because the letter lacks any information to enable a technical support person to diagnose and, if necessary, try to reproduce your problem. Remember that the only information a manufacturing rep has to go on is what you provide in your letter, because he isn't present at your worksite to see what exactly is going wrong.

The following list gives you some helpful hints on how to ask a company support person for help:

1 Describe the kind of computer you have, including the model number.

2 Briefly describe your setup, including the operating system version and the amount of installed RAM, and list the accessories attached to it, such as a video card or an additional hard drive.

3 Identify the manufacturer's product by model or version number. Quite often a problem might affect only a single version of a program or piece of hardware.

Posting—Once is enough!

Don't cross-post. In other words, don't post your message in more than one message folder in a single forum. America Online members don't always take kindly to reading the same message over and over again. Before you issue your plea for help, take a few moments to find the right place to post it. Look for a computing forum or a company support area that's appropriate (the Hardware forum, for example, for a malfunctioning printer), and leave your message there.

Chapter 9 *Get Advice, Help, and Software from America Online's Computing Forums*

4 Describe the kind of problem you're having. If your computer is crashing, report whether an error message appears on your computer's screen. That kind of message might be crucial to finding out what went wrong.

5 If the problem can be reproduced, describe the steps you've taken to reproduce it. That way, if the problem is unique to your setup, the steps can give a clue for the support person to attempt to reproduce the problem.

6 If the problem started after you made a change in your setup, such as a new hardware addition or a software installation, mention that, too. That new installation might have caused your troubles.

7 Finally, don't expect miracles. These products are manufactured by human beings and they have the same shortcomings as the rest of us. No hardware or software product is ever perfect, but you want to get it to work as efficiently as possible in your home or office.

Sometimes a problem is just too complex to deal with by e-mail or a message board. In that case, the company invites you to contact their technical support people directly for further assistance.

The results are in

If you want to learn more about your computer and how to use it more effectively, America Online is your best resource for interacting not only with hardware and software manufacturers but also with many savvy computer users.

Part IV: Information at Your Fingertips

Chapter 10: **How to Find the Software You Want**

Chapter 11: **Learning & Reference Sources Online**

Chapter 12: **Exploring Your Online Newsstand**

Chapter 13: **Say it with Flowers: Secrets of Online Shopping**

Chapter 14: **Business or Pleasure: Travel with America Online**

10

How to Find the Software You Want

● In this chapter:

- Find software in America Online's libraries quickly and easily

- Transfer that software directly to your computer

- Search the vast array of software you can find on America Online

- Upload your own files to America Online's huge software libraries

America Online is like a software playground, with tens of thousands of files available for you to download. . . . . ▶

166 **Part IV** *Information at Your Fingertips*

As you continue to explore America Online, you'll discover that there are thousands upon thousands of DOS, OS/2 and Windows 95 software files for you to download. If you cross computing platforms on occasion, you'll find large numbers of Macintosh software files as well. Whether it's an arcade game, a program that lets you create a to-do list, or an update to commercial software you own, America Online is the place to find it.

How to get the hang of AOL's software libraries

When I first joined America Online in 1989, I was the owner of a brand new computer, and I wanted to stock up on software. As an inveterate software junkie, I was a frequent visitor to the service's vast software libraries. It took me a while to discover the rich array of information services available elsewhere online.

Before we go on, let's define a couple of computer terms you'll see often in this chapter.

- **Downloading** a file is simply the act of transferring a file from an online service's host computer (or another modem), through the telephone lines, and to your computer by way of your modem.

- **Uploading** a file is the process of sending a file from your computer directly to an online service or another modem.

A fast primer on virus protection

Because there is always the danger that a file can be contaminated by a computer virus, America Online's forum staff checks all uploaded files with an up-to-date virus detection program before posting them online. You should, however, always install and use the latest virus detection software so that all your files are safe and sound.

Chapter 10 *How to Find the Software You Want* **167**

CAUTION Not all software that you can retrieve during your AOL session comes from AOL's own software libraries. Through AOL's Internet feature, you can access world-wide software repositories. Since the quality of managing such libraries may not be as stringent as on America Online, you should use virus detection software to analyze those files before you try to use them. You can check out the latest information on computer viruses in AOL's Virus Information Center (*keyword:* **Virus**). Remember, if you have just upgraded to Windows 95 from an earlier version of Windows, you will need to upgrade your virus detection software, too.

The easy way to search for files

The fastest way to locate software you want is to let America Online's host computer do the searching for you. So let's bring up America Online's File Search window:

1. Press Control+K and type the *keyword:* **File Search**. Or choose Search Software Libraries from the Go To menu of your AOL software.

2. In seconds, you see a large window on your computer that gives you a number of search options (see fig. 10.1).

Fig. 10.1
You can find the software you want from a specific forum or over a specific time frame (so you can see all the newest files listed at once).

3. You can search for software in many ways. You can limit your search to a specific category, such as Games or Graphics. You can even restrict the search to a specific time frame; for instance, perhaps you only want to find a file that was posted in the past month.

4 If you want to locate a file by name or subject, enter the information in the List files field. If you want to find a screen saver, for example, you'll enter screen saver as the subject of your search

In this example, I'm trying to locate a Windows arcade game that my son requested.

I looked for the file by its category, Arcade Games, and came up with lots of possibilities. But with thousands of games to look for, I was presented with an unwieldy list of files to pick it from. Best thing to do is be as specific as you can. If you know the name of the game you want, that's the most specific search string to enter.

5 If files matching your description cannot be found, you'll see a message window that notifies you that a match to your search request is not available.

6 If files meeting your description are located, you'll see a File List window on-screen (see fig. 10.2). A file may be listed more than once if it is in more than one library on America Online. Because only 20 files are loaded to the File List at one time, you might need to click on the List More Files button to see additional entries.

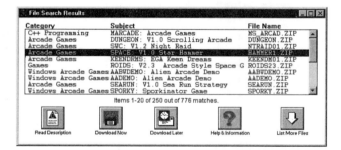

Fig. 10.2
Here's the list of files that match your search description. There are lots of possibilities to check here.

7 To learn more about the file that interests you, either highlight the file name and double-click on it, or select the Get File Description button, either by clicking on it or by pressing Return or Enter. You'll see a window very much like the one shown in figure 10.3.

Fig. 10.3
To learn more about the file (including how fast a PC you need and what operating system it requires), review the file description first.

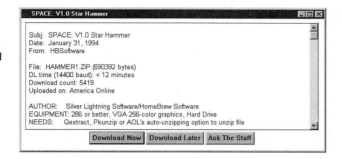

Downloading files from A to Z

Now that you've found a file you'd like to download to your computer, the next step is to start the download process. Your first option is to create a file queue, which is a list of files to download. That list or directory will be stored in America Online's Download Manager (which I'll describe in more detail a bit later in this chapter). Your second option is to download the file immediately.

 TIP Before downloading a file, check the File Description (shown in fig. 10.3). This description not only tells you more about the file, but contains information about what kind of computer it works on.

Now that you've found the file you want, the next step is to transfer that file to your PC. Here are the steps you'll follow:

1 The default selection in the software list (at the bottom of the file description window) is Download Now. This brings up a standard Save dialog box that allows you to indicate where you want to store the file that's being transferred to your computer (see fig. 10.4).

Fig. 10.4
Select the place where you want the file sent.

2 You have the option to rename the file, simply by entering the new name at the bottom of the Save dialog box.

3 Click on the Save button or hit the Return or Enter key to begin the download process.

 TIP **To speed up file transfer times, you may want to log on to** America Online at a non-peak hour, perhaps early in the morning, when network traffic is less busy.

4 When your file download begins, you see a progress bar showing approximately how much of the file has been sent, and an estimate of how long it will take to transfer that file to your computer.

 TIP **Although your PC can multitask, it's best to avoid CPU-intensive** tasks, such as calculating a spreadsheet, while downloading. Doing so could slow down or even interrupt the download process.

5 When the file has been transferred, America Online's friendly narrator will (if the sounds are enabled) announce File Done.

 Q&A *Help! Performance is really slow on AOL right now and the download is taking forever. Can I stop the download and start it again later?*

If you decide you don't want to download the file after all, hit the Finish Later button. In a minute or two, the download will stop. If you intend to resume the download at a later time, don't delete the partial file that has been transferred to your computer; if you do, the Download Manager cannot resume downloading at the point where it left off.

There's another advantage in choosing to finish your download at a later time. If AOL's network traffic is high, you can run a FlashSession at another hour, when performance is better, thus reducing the time it takes to retrieve the files you want.

The Download Manager

You can build a download queue or list by using the Download Manager, and you can start the download any time during your online session or when the session ends. When you add a file to the list, you see an acknowledgment message.

Chapter 10 *How to Find the Software You Want* **171**

TIP **You can download files and do other online tasks at the same time.** While performance is slower (it'll take a while for a text window to show up, for example), you can use this technique to get more value out of your online time. One thing: You cannot upload a file and do anything else at the same time on AOL.

To use the Download Manager, choose the second option available to you when downloading a file—Download Later. As I mentioned earlier, you find that button in a file description window (refer to fig. 10.3).

Check the Download Manager any time after adding files to the queue to see if you want to make changes in the listing before downloading begins. The files will be shown in the order that they will be downloaded (this isn't something you can change, except by removing a file from the list).

CAUTION **If you log on to America Online as a guest using another member's software,** the Download Later function will not work, nor will you be able to use AOL's FlashSession feature.

Q&A *Some of the files I find in a forum don't show up with AOL's file search feature. Why?*

As this book was going to press, some areas of AOL weren't a part of the file search capability. These included specialty forums in departments other than the Computing area, and company-support forums. By the time you read this book, you may find that these libraries are also part of the file search feature.

Also, it can take 12 to 24 hours for the file search database at AOL's host computer to update its directory. So newly posted files may not always show up.

America Online's Download Manager lets you manage the entire download process from a single window. You can open the Download Manager window when notified that a file has been added to the download queue by selecting the Download Manager button, or you can use America Online's File menu. The Download Manager displays all files you've selected for downloading (see fig. 10.5).

Fig. 10.5
The Download Manager window lists the total size of the files you've selected for transfer to your computer and gives an estimated transfer time at your modem connection speed.

Read a more detailed description and decide if you want the file.

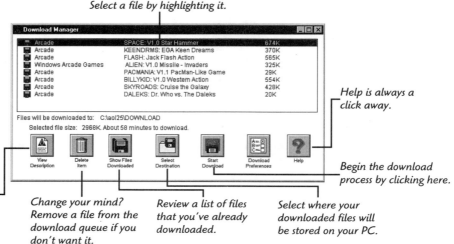

Select a file by highlighting it.

Help is always a click away.

Begin the download process by clicking here.

Change your mind? Remove a file from the download queue if you don't want it.

Review a list of files that you've already downloaded.

Select where your downloaded files will be stored on your PC.

How do I use the files I've downloaded?

Most larger files in America Online's software libraries are compressed to save disk space and to reduce transfer time, thereby reducing online charges.

America Online's software can be set to automatically expand files that you've downloaded as soon as you log off. Because some files may be compressed in a format that isn't supported by the software, those files will have to be expanded before you use them.

Before you pick a file to download, read the file description carefully to make sure that your computer, operating system, and software setup are compatible with those of the file. If you make a mistake and download a file you can't use, type the keyword Credit to request a rebate to your account for the time you wasted online.

 TIP **Use Windows 95 multitasking capabilities to their best advantage** while on AOL. If you are downloading a long file, you can go ahead and switch to another program and continue working in that program till the download finishes.

If you get a message that the file has been damaged after download, you need to remove the file from your computer and download the file again (you can request account credit at any time for a bad file). Although files are not damaged often, sometimes a file may not arrive in perfect condition due to noise on the telephone lines or to a network-related problem.

CAUTION **If your download is interrupted for any reason (perhaps your** connection was terminated because of poor phone-line conditions), a fragmented or partial file is left on your computer's drive. If you want to resume the download when you log on again, don't delete or move the partial file. Otherwise, you won't be able to resume your download where it left off.

Q&A *I downloaded some files. Now I can't find them. Where are they?*

When you install your AOL software, the Download Manager sets a default location for downloaded files. It's the aol25/DOWNLOAD folder. You can change this destination by activating the Download Manager (from the File menu) if you prefer, of course.

Another point: Sometimes the file that you download has a different name than the title it's shown under in a forum's software library. You can click on the Show Completed Downloads icon of AOL's Download Manager to recheck the actual file name (or while online, return to the forum from which you downloaded the file, to check the actual file name as shown in the file description).

If you still cannot locate the file, use the Find, Files or Folders feature that's available from your Windows 95 Start menu to determine where it is.

What kind of software is available?

Before you begin to fill your software library, let's discuss the kinds of software that are available and the types of software you are apt to find on America Online.

Commercial software

Commercial software is a retail product. You can find it at your local computer dealer, software reseller, or at one of the mail order firms that cater to this type of merchandise. You can even order commercial software on America Online through a publisher's company support area or through forums devoted to shopping.

You will not usually find commercial software in America Online's software libraries, but you can, from time to time, locate a free update program. The author or publisher of a software product can make an update program available so that you can revise your copy of the software to a newer version, usually to fix some bugs.

Demoware

Demonstration software is designed to let you try out all or most of the features of a software product before you buy it. Demoware, as it's known, may be either a commercial or a shareware program. In most cases, you can use the software for a limited period of time, ranging from a few days to a week or two; it then expires and you cannot use it again until you buy a copy. Some demoware may simply lock out some program features (such as the capability to save and print a document), which become available in the version you buy. When you purchase the program, you will often receive a special password that allows you to turn the demo program into the full-featured version.

Shareware

Shareware exemplifies the original try-before-you-buy concept. The author or publisher of a software product gives you a fully functional version (though a feature or two may be restricted). You can try it out on your computer for a period of up to a month. When that period expires, you are asked to pay the author or publisher a small fee for a license to continue to run the program.

Shareware is one of the last vestiges in our society of an honor system. The publisher has no way of knowing whether you are continuing to use the software. If you decide to continue to run it, consider the time and energy the author put into writing and testing that software. Also, consider how you would feel if you were not paid for your work.

Freeware

This category covers a wide range of products. Freeware is available to you without cost, but the author retains all rights to the program, including how it is to be distributed. Freeware may include a fully functioning program or an update to an existing product. Don't attribute cost to value. You can often find a wealth of very useful programs in this category.

Public Domain Software

Public domain software can be used and distributed freely. The author has given up all rights to this program.

Uploading files from A to Z

America Online's computing forums have a special department labeled New Files and Free Uploading. This department allows you to upload software to America Online's software libraries without being charged.

 **Demoware and shareware can contain restrictions on whether** they can be uploaded by anyone other than the author, so read the instructions that come with the software before you decide to upload it to America Online. In general, commercial updates, such as system-related software from Apple Computer, may be uploaded to America Online only by the publisher.

Where to upload

You must do a little research to find out the appropriate place to upload the file and to verify that you have the right to send it. Each computing forum has a description file that tells you its purpose and the kind of software wanted. Rather than waste your time and the forum's by uploading to an inappropriate location, read the description files to be sure that you are uploading your software to the most suitable forum. A screen saver, for example, will likely go in a Utilities forum.

Before uploading the file—especially if you are not the author—use America Online's File Search feature (described in the section "Using File Search," earlier in this chapter) to make sure that the file you want to send isn't already posted somewhere on America Online.

How to upload

When you visit a computing software library (see chapter 9, "Get Advice, Help and Software from America Online's Computing Forums"), you'll see a button at the bottom of the software directory labeled Upload File. When you want to send your file, click on the button, which opens the window shown in figure 10.6.

Fig. 10.6
Enter information about the file you're sending here. This material will become part of the file description when your file is released by a forum staff (though they may edit the material sometimes).

TIP Before filling out the Upload File Information window, review the descriptions of other software to become familiar with the way the descriptions are written and the kind of information required.

The Upload File Information window has several fields that you need to fill out. Enter the title of the file in the subject field, then the name of the author of the file, and the kind of equipment needed to use it. Next, give a brief description of the file you're sending. You can enter a list of suggested keywords so that others can locate the file easily. (You don't have to include keywords, though. The forum staff will do that if this field is left blank.)

When you upload the file, you'll see a File Transfer window that's very much like the one displayed when you download a file. After the file is received, it is reviewed by forum staff members who decide whether it's suitable for their forum. The file description you give may be edited.

Because many of the staff members who review these files are volunteers, expect several days to pass before you hear of the forum's decision. If posted, your file will turn up in their New Files and Free Uploading library.

A world of discovery

Okay, now you have the basics on how to get software and other files from America Online, and how to post your own files as well. Virtually all of the forums you visit on AOL have software libraries. You'll find a huge store of files from which to choose.

11
Learning & Reference Sources Online

● **In this chapter:**

- Tap the resources of huge libraries

- Check your spelling with AOL's dictionary

- Consult an online encyclopedia

- Find help for your child's homework

- Take diploma and degree-granting courses without ever attending a classroom

You can learn something about almost anything on America Online . . . .

Part IV *Information at Your Fingertips*

Combine the vast resources of a major encyclopedia, home study schools, libraries, museums, and dozens of other information centers, and you'll find nearly all the information you need during your visits to America Online. In the previous century, your resources for learning were confined to written material, such as books, newspapers, and magazines, or verbal descriptions. The twentieth century brought into play the audio and visual mediums as well. But interactive learning capabilities have come into their own with the advent of an online service such as America Online.

Because of the extent and scope of the educational resources available on America Online, a separate chapter would be needed for each of the Learning & Reference forums just to contain the full scope of their services. Consider this chapter a get-acquainted visit.

A visit to the Reference Desk

Keyword: **Reference**

The Reference Desk is your gateway to many resources on America Online. Many of the services listed in figure 11.1 are no doubt familiar to you. Some of the magazines, such as *Consumer Reports* and *Disney Adventures*, are discussed in more detail in other chapters. Other services offer huge databases of information that you'll want to explore. For now, stay with me if you want to begin a little sojourn for knowledge.

Fig. 11.1
The Reference Desk on America Online offers you a wide variety of information resources.

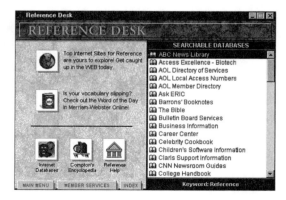

There are Internet sites for reference, too

There is a huge store of reference information available to you on the world wide Internet, with an emphasis on the World Wide Web. By clicking on the Top Internet Sites for Reference icon, you'll see a large list of specially selected World Wide Web and other Internet-based resources (see fig. 11.2).

Fig. 11.2
AOL's Reference Web opens the door to museums, reference works, and other fascinating information resources.

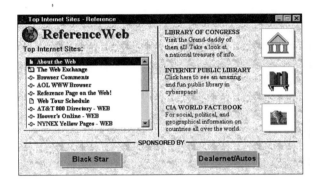

And the word you want is...

Keyword: **Thesaurus**

You can easily find the right word to make your written words more exciting by accessing Merriam-Webster's Thesaurus. Just enter the word for which you seek an alternative in the list field (see fig. 11.3), click on the Look Up button and you'll soon see a list of available alternatives.

Fig. 11.3
Merriam-Webster's online Thesaurus helps you find the right word.

One more thing: If you need to check the spelling of a word, the folks at Merriam-Webster can help you there too. The keyword: **Dictionary** will bring up *Merriam-Webster's Collegiate Dictionary*.

Ask ERIC

Keyword: **AskERIC**

ERIC is not a person. It's short for Educational Resources Information Center and it's an Internet-based information center, an electronic library containing thousands of information resources for educators. There's also a resource to have your education-oriented questions researched and answered by the ERIC staff.

Barron's Booknotes helps you with your studies

Keyword: **Barrons**

As you might already know, Barron's guides are useful abstracts about the great literary works. You can search the vast library of Barron's Booknotes on America Online.

A visit to Compton's NewMedia learning center

Keyword: **Comptons**

Not so long ago, looking up something in an encyclopedia meant a trip to the public library or purchasing a huge set of books for your home. Although you might not want to replace those voluminous, color-filled works on your bookshelves, consider America Online your second reference resource.

The folks at Compton's NewMedia have created a complete multimedia learning center on America Online (see fig. 11.4). All you have to do to tap that huge resource is click on one of the colorful icons.

If you've finished your studies for the day, or you just need a moment or two to recharge, click the Study Break icon for a fun-filled time. You'll find a Rap Room there, where you can have pleasant chats with other AOL members, or you can download a challenging puzzle or strategy game or two that you can play at your leisure.

Fig. 11.4
You can tap the resources of a huge encyclopedia, download multimedia learning materials, join chats, and more at the Compton's NewMedia forum.

The Career Center helps you reach a job decision

Keyword: **career**

One of the hardest tasks many young adults have to face is deciding what line of work to enter. Although some of you might have chosen your career during your early childhood, others work long and hard to find the line of work for which they are suited. And with cutbacks rampant in many industries, sometimes one has to make a mid-life career change.

America Online's Career Center is an electronic career and employment guidance forum (see fig. 11.5). The forum features an extensive lineup of services that can help you find the right career or even tap a huge database of available jobs.

Fig. 11.5
America Online offers a center for career counseling and employment opportunities. If you're looking for a job, you'll find a library of resume templates that you can alter to your personal needs.

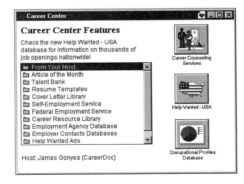

Court TV shows how courts really work

Keyword: **Court TV**

For most of us, knowledge about the workings of the court system is limited to such TV programs as *Matlock* or *Perry Mason*. In real life, trials are not resolved in 55 or so minutes plus commercials. The legal process is complex and convoluted and often difficult for the layman to understand.

The intense national attention over the O.J. Simpson murder case has placed such cable TV sources as Court TV (shown in fig. 11.6) into the spotlight. Court TV is a 24-hour network devoted solely to the legal process and how it works.

Fig. 11.6
Court TV is the popular cable TV network devoted to the legal system.

Access C-SPAN to see Congress in action

Keyword: **CSPAN**

Whenever an important hearing is being held in Congress, or a major address by the President or another important government figure is being given, C-SPAN (short for Cable-Satellite Public Affairs Network) is often there with gavel-to-gavel coverage.

Smithsonian Online is your interactive museum

Keyword: **Smithsonian**

Most of you probably never hear much about the Smithsonian Institution except when reading news about a particular exhibit that's on display. When visiting the Smithsonian Museums in person isn't possible, a visit to the

Smithsonian Online Forum on America Online provides a useful substitute (see fig. 11.7). You can even download GIF photos of some of these exhibits.

Fig. 11.7
You can visit the world's largest museum on America Online.

Let's explore the Education Center

Keyword: **Education**

America Online's Education department, shown in figure 11.8, complements the Reference Desk providing a wide range of information and tools to advance your education. Some of the resources are identified with colorful icons at the right of the Education department's main screen. The full roster of available facilities are listed in the directory at the right side of the department window.

Fig. 11.8
You can consider the Education department an online educational institution. Some of these facilities are also shared with the Reference Desk.

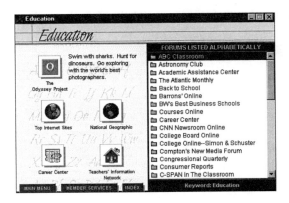

You can visit top education Web sites

You can explore museums and educational institutions, and view pictures of dinosaurs and planets using AOL's direct access to the World Wide Web. Just click on the Top Internet Sites icon in AOL's Education department to bring up a list of sites you'll want to explore further (see fig. 11.9).

Fig. 11.9
Explore museums and read the works of Shakespeare courtesy of the World Wide Web and AOL.

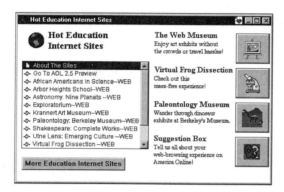

A visit to the Academic Assistance Center

Keyword: **homework, aac**

Whether you are pursuing higher education, preparing for the College Board exams, or just trying to figure out how to do a homework assignment, consider the Academic Assistance Center as one of your resources for help.

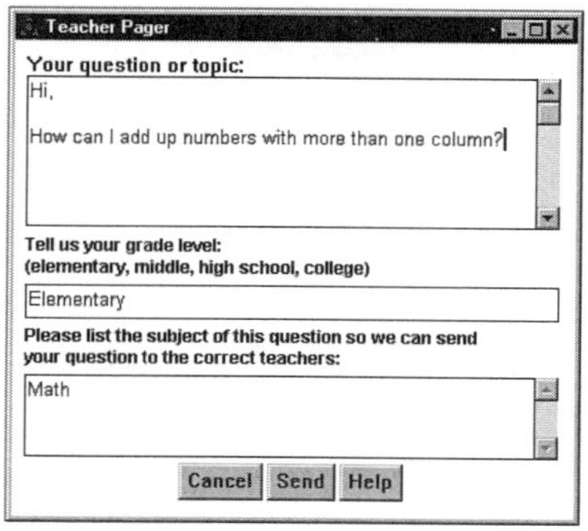

Fig. 11.10
AOL's Teacher Pager alerts an educator to help answer your questions or show you where you can find the answers.

A look at the CNN Newsroom

Keyword: **CNN**

CNN Newsroom is a daily 15-minute news program that is offered to schools by Ted Turner's Cable News Network. The online CNN Newsroom focuses on that program and related issues. The forum has message areas where you can communicate with other America Online members or with CNN staff.

Using College Board Online

Keyword: **College Board**

The College Board is a national organization devoted to the interests of secondary and higher education. You can use the online forum to order books and other materials to help prepare you or your child for college entrance exams and to deal better with some of the tougher academic subjects.

Paging a Teacher on AOL

Suppose that term paper or homework assignment is due tomorrow. You or a student in your family have worked for hours trying to put it into shape, and you still have questions you need solved. There's a real life teacher available on AOL to help you resolve the problem.

First use the keyword **Teacher Pager** to enter the this special area, then click on the Teacher Pager folder, then the Make a page listing, which brings up a message window where you or your child can make your request for help.

Here's how it works: Your child, a grade school student, asks the question posed in figure 11.10:

How do you add and subtract numbers with more than a single column? You ask your question, and then click on the button that reflects the grade level. Also indicate the time you want to meet with your online teacher. When you or your child asks the question, stay online for at least five minutes, because more often than not, your answer will be there in a jiffy in your mailbox. If not, you have the chance to meet with the instructor at the appointed time. In some cases, the student is invited into the Homework Help conference room for a one-on-one tutorial session.

Explore the Electronic University Network

Keyword: **eun**

Although attending college is often viewed as an exciting time for most students, sometimes traveling to classes just isn't possible. Work and family commitments might be preventing you from attending class for an advanced degree, new career studies, or a much-needed remedial course. If so, the Electronic University Network might be able to help you. It's a group of educational institutions that offer interactive learning programs on a variety of subjects (see fig. 11.11).

Fig. 11.11
AOL's Electronic University Network lets you attend college and stay home at the same time.

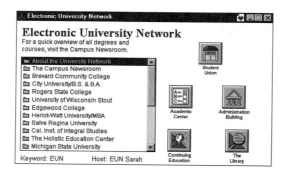

Attend the Komputer Klinic

Keyword: **Komando**

Kim Komando is a newspaper columnist and radio talk show host who has developed a line of tutorial videos designed to make the sometimes obscure world of personal computing understandable by using simple words instead of complex technospeak. You may have even seen the TV commercials about these tapes, entitled "Komputer Tutor." The Komando Forum is a resource of tips and secrets to help you use your computer more effectively (see fig. 11.12).

Chapter 11 Learning & Reference Sources Online **187**

Fig. 11.12
The Komputer Klinic is a place to get help with your computer-related troubles.

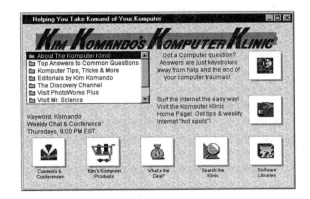

A trip to the Library of Congress Online

Keyword: **Library**

One of the largest information centers in the world is owned by the U.S. Government. It's the Library of Congress, and if you are ever in Washington, D.C., you can visit its teeming information archives in person. You can also explore this huge resource from right in front of your computer using America Online (see fig. 11.13).

Fig. 11.13
You can tap the huge information resources of the Library of Congress Online.

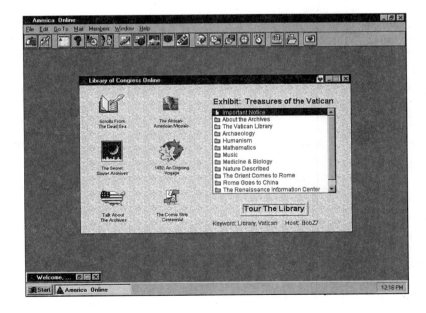

One popular Library of Congress area is devoted to the Dead Sea Scrolls. Since their discovery in the Judean Desert in 1947, scholars have spent countless hours researching their scope and meaning. You can access this area by clicking the Scrolls from the Dead Sea icon on the main forum window. This enables you to review the scholars' findings, plus learn the exciting background of this extraordinary archaeological find.

Join the National Geographic Society

Keywords: **geographic**, **ngs**

No doubt you've seen the elaborate, colorful *National Geographic* magazine. The magazine represents just a portion of the National Geographic Society's work, which is represented in its online forum, National Geographic Online.

Access National Public Radio Outreach

Keywords: **NPR**, **radio**

When you tire of silly disk jockey chatter, the same repetitive music over and over again, or endless confrontational and sometimes exploitive talk shows, and you want something a little more stimulating, National Public Radio is the way to go. It's not available in every town—but it should be.

The National Public Radio Outreach forum on America Online is your way to interact with this public broadcasting network.

A Visit to the Scholastic Forum

Keyword: **Scholastic**

The Scholastic Network Sampler is an online resource for teachers and students (see fig. 11.14). Professional educators can interact with their peers, and if you are a teacher, you can even join the network online.

Chapter 11 *Learning & Reference Sources Online* **189**

Fig. 11.14
From your child's classroom to America Online, the Scholastic Forum is the place for educators.

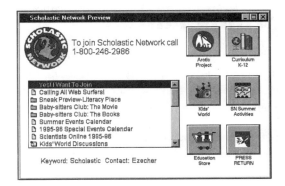

The Afterwards Cafe helps you relax

Keyword: **Afterwards**

Having spent these many hours deeply immersed in your studies on one subject or another, the time might come when you want to relax and perhaps meet with other students for a chat.

America Online's Afterwards Coffeehouse and Cafe is a pleasant, relaxing environment for serious discussions about all sorts of topics, from current events to literature and the arts (see fig. 11.15).

Fig. 11.15
When your studies are done, you can relax at the Afterwards Cafe. It's a place to get a virtual cup of coffee or a soft drink after completing a hard day's work.

AOL Makes Learning Fun

America Online's resources for education and reference aren't confined just to the forums mentioned so far in this chapter. The repositories are so huge that the surface has barely been scratched. You need to dig in and explore further on your own to find out what gems of knowledge you can find.

Both newspapers and magazines are valuable learning tools, too, and online resources for both are described in the next chapter.

12

Exploring Your Online Newsstand

● **Learn where to find:**

- **The latest news**

- **Late-breaking stories from Hollywood**

- **Current weather maps**

- **News and opinion journals**

- **Information resources**

- **Advice and information about business, stocks, and bonds**

A visit to America Online is like having many magazines and newspapers at your beck and call without having to travel to the corner newsstand. . . . . **>**

You can find a summary of the top news of the day, commentaries from your favorite columnists, or updates on how your stock portfolio is doing. And you don't have to travel to a newsstand or bookstore to locate any of this material. You can read it all in one place on America Online.

In this chapter, let's open up the pages of some of the magazines and newspapers AOL offers online. I have space to cover only a select portion of the publications that maintain online forums; many more are available for you to examine during your online visits.

A look at Today's News

Keyword: **News**

When you first sign on to America Online, you're greeted with the friendly, familiar In The Spotlight Welcome window and voice message (if you've got your computer's sound turned on, of course). The Top News Story of the day is always featured (and it may change from hour to hour, depending on new developments). You can see the major headlines by clicking the Top News icon (see fig. 12.1). What you have here is organized very much like the sections of your daily newspaper. We'll read through each section and give you an idea of what information you can find.

Fig. 12.1
America Online's Today's News department (referred to as Top News on the In The Spotlight screen) is organized in much the same way as a typical daily newspaper.

When you bring up the Today's News screen, you'll see the major stories of the day in a directory window, which you can scroll through for additional

Chapter 12 *Exploring Your Online Newsstand* **193**

information. By double-clicking a story listing, you'll be able to read the text of that news item. As with other America Online text windows, you can save the story or print it for later reference. Just like your daily newspaper, some of these stories include photos, too (see fig. 12.2).

Fig. 12.2
Some of the stories you'll read online include color pictures too, and they'll download to your computer in just seconds.

U.S. & World news

Keyword: **US News**

Now that you've read the front page, let's examine the table of contents of your daily newspaper and check out some of the other features (see fig. 12.3). During your online travels, you can set aside pages for reading later. You may also read the news of the world by category, simply by clicking the pop-up menu labeled Click Here for Categories. There are separate folders for National News, Washington News, Europe, and other categories. If you are seeking information about a particular topic, you'll want to click on the Search News icon.

Fig. 12.3
This is your online newspaper's table of contents, showing the stories you can read simply by double clicking the title.

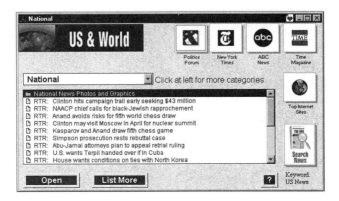

Business news

Keyword: **Business News**

Let's turn now to the business section (see fig. 12.4). All the information is divided into convenient categories, so you can easily locate material on a particular topic. The Search News icon at the right allows you to quickly access all the articles on a single topic. The Market News icon is useful for checking the goings-on in the world's various stock markets. Additional icons are used to access publications or forums with related interests, which you can access with a single click. These will change from time to time as AOL's forums are updated.

Fig. 12.4
Your online financial section covers the major business stories, plus related feature articles with a business orientation.

Reading news your way

Reading news on America Online can be done the way you want it. You can browse through the contents of each section simply by reviewing the directory of stories. Let's consider it the online equivalent of turning the pages in your daily paper. Or you can use the Search News feature to locate specific articles you want to read right away (and that listing will often show related articles containing material covering similar subjects).

As with other searchable databases on America Online, looking for a news item is a simple process. Just click the Search News icon to bring up the search window, enter the topic of your search, and you'll see a display of the available articles on that subject (as long as there are articles available, of course).

You'll also note that many of the news-related forums on America Online are interrelated. So if you open one screen, there will be icons that will allow you to switch to another area that has related information. An example is the Politics Forum icon at the right side of the U.S. & World news screen.

As an example of the sort of information one finds in the business news area, we selected the High Technology pages, where headlines separate current developments. You can access these articles from the pop-up menu labeled Click Here for Categories. You can select an article, double-click on the title, or click on the Open button. The entire article can be saved as a text file for printing later or for offline reading. Just choose either the File, Save or File, Print option.

Weather News

Keyword: **Weather**

Since we already read the sports and entertainment pages in chapter 6 (yes, I read them first, too!), let's skip the Entertainment and Sports icons in the Today's News screen and move on to the final category.

Although we can't do much to change the weather, we can at least be fully informed about it. By turning to the weather section in your virtual newspaper, you can review both articles and special forecasts countrywide (see fig. 12.5).

Fig. 12.5
When severe weather has a major impact, AOL has the latest information.

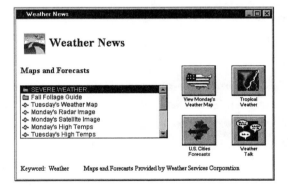

You can also see maps of weather trends right on your own computer, simply by selecting and downloading them. The forum updates the weather maps daily. You can see them in full color if you have a color screen. Choose from a satellite view or radar displays, and view charts of maximum and minimum temperatures not only for today, but for tomorrow and the next day as well (see fig. 12.6).

Fig. 12.6
See the latest weather maps displayed at this site.

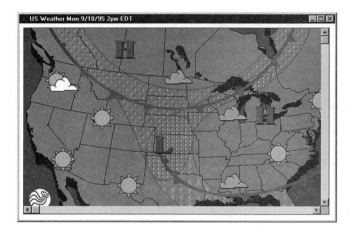

The forum offers these maps in the cross-platform GIF format (short for Graphic Interchange Format). Once you download the file to your computer, you can use the latest version of AOL's Windows software to open and view the file.

During the summer and fall seasons, there is a special area devoted to Tropical Storms and Hurricanes. You will want to check this section to see if any severe weather is expected in your area, and what the trends are for the very near future (within the limits of the science of weather forecasting, of course).

Q&A *Every time I want to view one of those fancy online maps, it takes so long for it to display on my computer. Why?*

Whenever you access new artwork from America Online, it has to be transferred to your computer. AOL uses a special artwork format for such features as weather maps to reduce file size, so you can retrieve them faster. But if you have an older modem that only works at 2400 bps, you may wait several minutes for the artwork to reach you.

The best solution is a fast modem. Since even 14,400 bps modems cost less than $100 these days, it's a great investment towards making your online visits more productive (and it also helps reduce your online bills too, which will cover the cost of a high speed modem in just a short time). And, for just a few bucks more, you can get a V.34 modem, providing up to 28,800 bps connections to America Online. Now that's really fast!

U.S. Cities Forecasts

Whether you are a regular traveler or a vicarious sojourner, you're no doubt curious as to the weather in other parts of the country. No problem—America Online's weather page has information about that, too, grouped by country or continent and updated regularly. If you're planning a trip abroad, consult this area before you pack your bags.

Top Internet sites

Not only can you explore AOL's own virtual newsstand, but you have quick access to the huge information resources available across the globe through AOL's World Wide Web feature. Just click on the Top Internet Sites icon (see fig. 12.7) to see a selection of current offerings.

Fig. 12.7
The major newspapers and information resources are quickly adding World Wide Web access.

The listing you see in figure 12.7 is subject to rapid changes, so you may expect to see a more diverse and larger offering when you begin to explore this area.

Browsing the online Newsstand

Keyword: **Newsstand**

Having read the latest news of the day, let's now pay a visit to America Online's huge newsstand. You can get there from anywhere on AOL with that single *keyword:* **Newsstand**. I described three of the major daily newspapers, the *Chicago Tribune,* the *San Jose Mercury,* and *The New York Times* in chapter 8. There, I focused on the features you find in daily newspapers. Double-clicking the appropriate directory listing under Publications, as shown in figure 12.8, will return you to those newspapers. Now I'll cover some other titles available from our virtual news dealer. Some of these publications, by the way, exist solely in cyberspace. You won't find them at your corner newsstand.

Fig. 12.8
The list of available magazines on AOL's newsstand is increasing rapidly.

The Atlantic Monthly

Keyword: **Atlantic**

Several important magazines regularly appear online at the same time they appear in your favorite bookstore. One of these is *The Atlantic Monthly* (see fig. 12.9). You'll find the entire content of the latest issue of this popular literary magazine on AOL, plus an active message board and live chats.

Fig. 12.9
Read *The Atlantic Monthly* on AOL.

Columnists & Features Online

Keyword: **Columnists**

You were exposed to the latest news and business reports in the Today's News department earlier in this chapter. Now let's pause for a few moments to review some commentary and opinion on the feature pages. Rather than poring through a pile of newspapers to find your favorite columnists, look in Columnists & Features Online. This forum is sponsored by the Newspaper Enterprise Association (NEA), featuring many popular columnists such as Hodding Carter, Nat Hentoff, William Rusher, and Bruce Williams.

Consumer Reports

Keywords: **Consumers, Consumer Reports**

Before you make a single purchasing decision, read *Consumer Reports*. This magazine offers comprehensive reviews on major new products of all types, from dishwasher detergents to new cars.

TIP **Many of the regular articles and columns of your favorite** magazines are available on AOL. You can save or print the text windows for reading at your leisure, as you can with other text files on America Online.

Cowles/SIMBA Media Information Network

Keyword: **CowlesSIMBA**

The word media connotes a variety of industries, from advertising agencies to broadcasting and publishing businesses. The Cowles/SIMBA Media Information Network is a major resource for information about this challenging and ever-changing business field.

The New Republic

Keyword: **New Republic**

The *New Republic* is a magazine of opinion that takes an unabashedly liberal viewpoint of the nation and the world. It covers politics, literature, and the arts with its own unique slant. The magazine is interesting, controversial, and always entertaining, whatever your political leanings.

OMNI Magazine Online

Keyword: OMNI

Whether you're interested in space exploration or in UFOs, you can explore scientific interests by visiting the *OMNI* Magazine forum on AOL (see fig. 12.10). In addition to reading many of the features from the latest issue of *OMNI*, you can attend a number of regular chats. One exciting and controversial section of *OMNI* is the Antimatter department, which explores the frontiers of science and features reports about psychic phenomena and strange things seen in the skies (generally referred to as UFOs).

Fig. 12.10
Science fact and science fiction are combined in *OMNI* magazine.

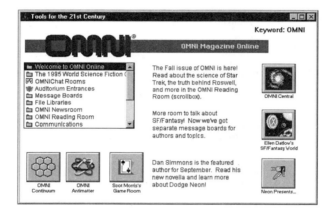

Saturday Review Online

Keyword: **Saturday Review**

Many of you probably remember *The Saturday Review* as a magazine of arts and culture that existed for many, many years, and folded in 1986. During over half a century of existence, this journal covered such subjects as politics, science, business, literature, and even the world of entertainment.

So what is a magazine that no longer exists doing on America Online? Well, unlike the other online magazines we've discussed so far in this chapter, *Saturday Review* Online doesn't exist as a printed publication—it's strictly an electronic magazine brought to you by the publishers of *OMNI* and *I-Wire* (which is also a magazine that only exists online).

Stereo Review Online

Keyword: **Stereo Review**

It started out years ago as *Hi-Fi Review,* and then it was *Hi-Fi/Stereo Review* when stereophonic audio became popular in the early 1960s. Now it's just *Stereo Review,* and it remains one of the most popular consumer audio magazines in the USA. If you are looking to buy a new stereo system, exploring the frontiers of home theater (surround sound), or you just want to read reviews about the latest recordings, you'll want to visit Stereo Review Online.

TIME Magazine Online

Keyword: **TIME**

When you want to find out how long you've spent on America Online, you might be inclined to type the keyword Time (rather than Clock, which is the correct choice). Instead of seeing time spent, you'll see the very latest issue of *TIME* magazine. The full content of the current issue is posted on America Online before the printed magazine hits the newsstands (see fig. 12.11).

Fig. 12.11
An issue of *TIME* on AOL.

WIRED

Keyword: **Wired**

The rise of the Information Superhighway means that we are all truly connected by telephone line, by satellite, or by our computers talking to one another. *WIRED* explores what it calls the "Digital Generation," which has grown up and experienced the joining of computers, telecommunications, and the media (see fig. 12.12).

Part IV *Information at Your Fingertips*

Fig. 12.12
The voice of the Digital Generation on AOL.

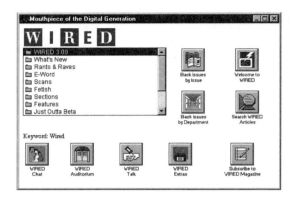

Woman's Day Online

Keyword: **Woman's Day**

From the recipe of the month to advice on health and special interests, *Woman's Day* has long provided an informative, optimistic outlook, and pages and pages of solid information (see fig. 12.13). The contents of each regularly scheduled issue are posted in the magazine's colorful online forum at the same time they appear at your local newsstand.

Fig. 12.13
Just a quick look at the contents of *Woman's Day* magazine on AOL will show recipes (one of the magazine's most popular features) and useful information about new developments in health care.

Worth Online

Keyword: **Worth**

Here's a different approach to presenting financial information. Instead of dealing with business news in a cold, dry, analytical fashion, *Worth* magazine attempts to take into account what it considers one's personal needs in providing financial information.

Say it with Flowers: Secrets of Online Shopping

● **In this chapter:**

- Search for products you want to buy
- Buy the items you want while online
- Join a service that will help you save money on your next car
- Have groceries and pharmaceutical items delivered right to your front door
- Place your own classified ad, free of charge

Shopping seems to become harder every day. You have to fight traffic, search for a parking space, wait on a checkout line. America Online offers an easier way. . . . . ▶

Do you want to save a few dollars on your next purchase? Perhaps you just want to get the most up-to-date information about a particular product or service before you decide whether to buy. America Online is the place to do both.

Until now, this book told you how to locate information resources on America Online. In this chapter, you'll go on an enjoyable shopping tour by way of the Information Highway. You'll make several brief stops at different shops in an online mall, and you'll even buy a few items along the way.

Your virtual marketplace

Keywords: **Marketplace, Shopping**

America Online's Marketplace department, shown in figure 13.1, is a gateway to AOL's huge shopping mall. Since my next chapter is devoted to using America Online for your travel plans, this little excursion is limited to the items that strictly concern shopping. Of course, the merchandise you buy during this trip may well be suited for that trip you're planning to take.

Fig. 13.1
When you first enter the Marketplace, you may also see a window labeled Spotlight, where you'll see a list of features you'll want to check further. Just click the Go to Marketplace button to return to the department itself.

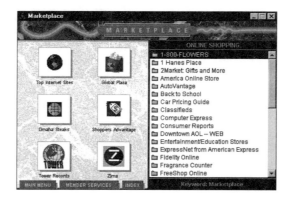

Before you go on, you should realize that the Marketplace, as with other online areas, is definitely a work in progress. Artwork is always being updated, and new shopping features are regularly being added to the mix. So the Marketplace you visit when you take your next online shopping tour might look a little different from the one described here. Some of the icons shown in figure 13.1, for example, represent nationally known chain stores who have established an online presence.

Top Internet Sites

Through AOL's convenient World Wide Web feature, you not only have access to shopping areas on AOL, but to other shopping areas across the globe. Just click on the Top Internet Sites icon in AOL's Marketplace (see fig. 13.2) to get a gander at some of the available shopping resources you can easily access with AOL's Web browser software (I'll explain what that's all about in chapter 19, "Getting Started on the Web").

Fig. 13.2
Double-click your way to World Wide Web shopping on AOL.

CAUTION In order to access sites on the World Wide Web (or WWW, for short), you need to have AOL's version 2.5 software, plus the WWW browser software. You can get both by accessing the Upgrade area (keyword: **Upgrade**) and downloading both software packages. If you already have AOL 2.5, you just need to download the browser software. To learn more about WWW access, read chapters 18, "Unmasking the World Wide Web" and 19, "Getting Started on the Web."

Placing an order with the AOL product center

Keyword: **AOL Store**

America Online has its own custom line of merchandise, which you can wear, send as a gift, or just keep as a souvenir. Since I collect fancy T-shirts myself, let's order one. The steps you're going to take here are similar to those you'll follow for most online ordering on America Online.

After you open the main screen for the AOL Store click the America Online Shop the Store icon in the main store directory (which comes up via the AOL

Store keyword), then click the A to Z Product Listing icon and you will see the screen shown in fig. 13.3.

Fig. 13.3
Choose the product that interests you from the directory listing; use the scroll bars or click the More button for additional offerings.

After I scrolled through the extensive list of products, I happened to come upon one labeled Logo T-shirt. To see a product description and a full color photo of the product, I double-clicked the product's name in the directory (see fig. 13.4).

Fig. 13.4
AOL's graphical interface lets you see the product before you buy.

The descriptive window gives you the very same sort of information you'd find in a mail-order catalog. I think I'm going to order one of these shirts, so let's select the Click Here To Order button (see fig. 13.5).

Choose the shirt size you want by double-clicking the entry in the directory window. After you've selected the merchandise you want to order, click the Continue button to continue the ordering process. You'll be asked to select how many shirts you wish to buy (see fig. 13.6).

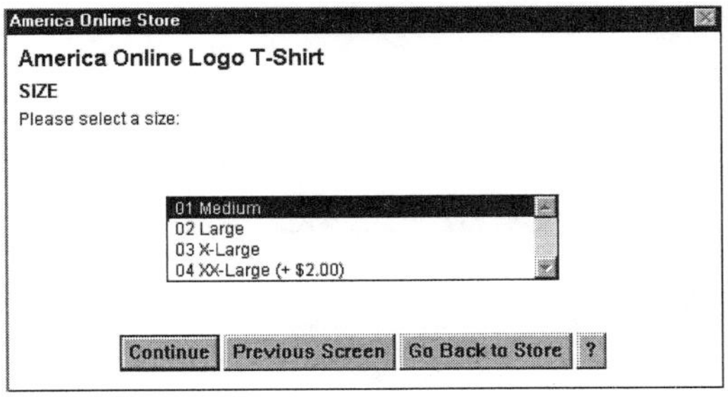

Chapter 13 *Say it with Flowers: Secrets of Online Shopping* **209**

Fig. 13.5
Before your order is completed, you need to select your shirt size first.

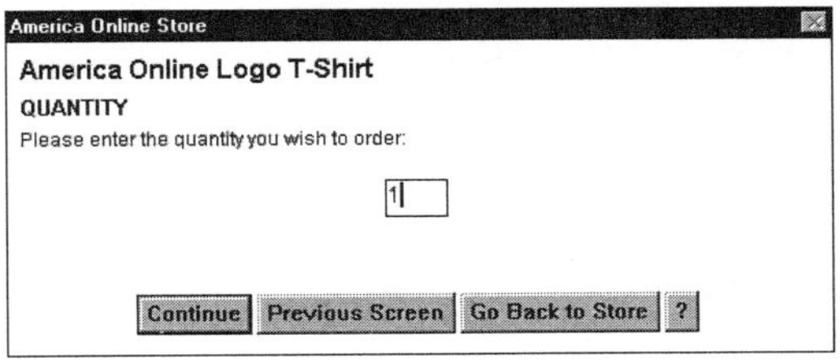

Fig. 13.6
Are you sure you just want one?

Before you tire of the information screens, you'll get one more, which confirms your order, and allows you to finish your stopping tour, if you're done. You can begin the final ordering steps simply by clicking the Checkout icon to bring up a window shown in figure 13.7.

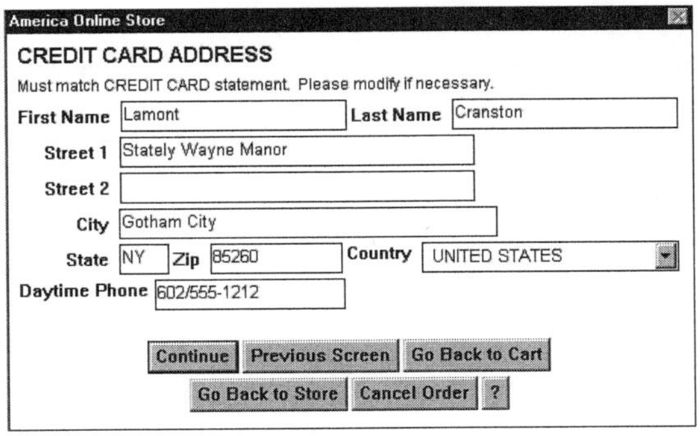

Fig. 13.7
Enter your billing and shipping information here.

 TIP **Before visiting your online shopping center, have your credit card** handy so that you can enter your billing information without delay.

After you've entered your billing information, enter your correct shipping address. By default, the address recorded for your online account is listed as the billing address (see fig. 13.8). Click the Continue button to add your shipping information. You can have the same address automatically entered for shipping or enter a different shipping location.

Fig. 13.8
Completing the order.

How to get an AOL software upgrade

From time to time, America Online upgrades its software to add new features and offer better performance. Whether you use a Mac or Windows, you can choose the software version you want and download either (or both, if you have computers from both platforms) from this download center.

Before you download the new version, you might want to refer to the file description for the new version to see what's being offered.

 TIP You can download the newest AOL software releases for free by using the keyword: **Upgrade**, selecting the upgrade you want, and choosing the Download Now option. If you choose Download Later, you will leave the free area and end up paying for the download time.

Buying a car

Keyword: **AutoVantage**

AutoVantage is an online database of new and used car information, and a center where you can arrange to service your car, buy accessories, and even order your new vehicle at a discount price (see fig. 13.9).

AutoVantage provides an interface that's very different from other areas on America Online, so this section discusses it in detail. If you have experience with a command-line (text) interface in DOS, you no doubt will find this setup familiar. This interface will seem a bit strange if you spend most of

Chapter 13 *Say it with Flowers: Secrets of Online Shopping* **211**

your computing time with Windows, but AutoVantage makes it really easy to navigate. You are prompted every step of the way, and your answers govern the information that's presented.

Fig. 13.9
AutoVantage is your online resource for automobile information.

To take advantage of AutoVantage's services, you have to join, but there's almost always a low-cost introductory membership available. To join, follow these steps:

1 Click the Access AutoVantage (Non-Members) icon (refer to fig. 13.9).

2 In the first window, specify how long your row of text should be. A good size is 60 or 80 characters, which will work effectively on the average 13 and 14-inch computer screen. The narrower the screen, the longer it takes to scroll through the section. If you don't make the correct selection, just close the window, open it again, and start over.

3 The Main Directory lists the services available to non-members (see fig. 13.10). Because this is a text-based interface, you cannot just double-click the item you want to select. You have to let the descriptions in the text window guide you on what to do next. In this case, you have 13 items from which to choose. Simply enter the number of the item you want to learn more about, and either click the Send button or press the Enter or Return key.

4 For each selection, you are asked to enter a number or further information. If you want to join, you'll be presented with a brief questionnaire that asks for your name, mailing address, and billing information. Pressing Enter or Return when you are finished entering the requested

Fig. 13.10
The AutoVantage main directory window is used to take you to different areas of the service.

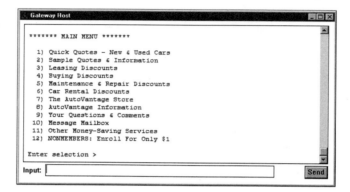

data sends it to AutoVantage's gateway, and you are then prompted for further information.

5 After you have completed your visit to AutoVantage, you can close the window to leave the text-based service behind and return to your familiar America Online icons and windows.

If you opt to join AutoVantage, you'll receive a letter and other material in a few weeks to confirm your membership and provide helpful hints on how to use the service.

Sending flowers

Keyword: **Flowers**

Your next stop along the Information Superhighway shopping mall is the flower shop shown in figure 13.11. Maybe a friend or relative is celebrating a special occasion, or you want to give a bouquet of roses to your significant other. You can place your order at 800-FLOWERS. That order is then transmitted to a local florist near the home of the person who will be receiving the flowers. That florist will deliver your order.

Fig. 13.11
Say it with flowers or other choice gifts.

 CAUTION **The quality of the image you see on your computer screen** depends on the size and quality of the monitor, and the capabilities of your computer to display an image at a specific resolution. The image is sent in full color, but whether it appears in black and white or clear, crisp, full color varies from installation to installation.

If you want to know more about the product being displayed, simply click the Featured Product Info button. You'll see a capsule description of the product, and have a chance to place your order through very much the same technique that was described earlier in "Placing an Order with the AOL Product Center." You'll have an opportunity to select your billing option and review your order before it's sent.

Buying books online

Keyword: **Bookstore**

America Online's Bookstore is stocked with shelves and shelves of the latest titles, both fiction and nonfiction, in all of the major categories (see fig. 13.12). There's a special database that allows you to search for a specific title; select the Search for Books icon in the upper-right corner of the Online Bookstore forum window. The Special Requests and Questions icon takes you to a message area where you can post your request for a book that might not be in stock, or simply ask for additional information about available volumes.

Fig. 13.12
Use the bookstore's database to look up that best-seller. Once you find it, you can place your order in just a minute or two.

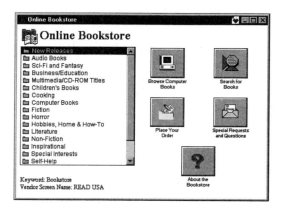

You can buy computer products online, too

You can get large discounts on many computer products on AOL. You can even order a brand new system and benefit from a big selection and good prices. Here is an example of an online resource for these products.

Computer Express

Keyword: **Computer Express**

Maybe you want to buy a neat new computer game, you need some hard drive utility software, or it's time to replace that old modem with one of those new high-speed models (and take advantage of America Online's 14,400 and 28,800 bps service). Computer Express (see fig. 13.13) is your resource for discount prices on all sorts of computer-related merchandise.

Fig. 13.13
Computer Express lets you search for a specific product or check out the newest software titles and special Hot Deals.

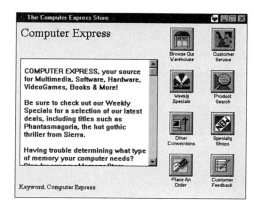

As with all stores in America Online's shopping mall, entering your order is simple. You list the items you want to buy (sometimes you have to also identify them by a part number), enter your billing information, recheck your order, and send it. The shopping service will usually have information text as to how long it takes to process orders.

The online gift shop

Keyword: **2Market**

America Online's 2Market department is quite literally an online gift shop. You can order special gifts for any occasion. (Figure 13.14 shows the promotions in effect just before New Year's Day, for example.) You can also take advantage of special deals on a variety of products.

Fig. 13.14
2Market is also available in CD-ROM form, so you can view colorful, interactive demonstrations on new products.

The most attractive way to order, though, is with the help of 2Market's CD. You can place your order for the CD during your online visit. It'll arrive in just a short time, and it provides entertaining, interactive demonstrations from many of the major manufacturers of the products offered through 2Market.

Even if you don't have the CD handy, you can still see a full-color picture of the product and a complete description showing the important features. Just click the Product Spotlight heading once, and then choose a product (see fig. 13.15).

Fig. 13.15
AOL's 2Market service offers a high quality photo and full product description.

 TIP **The popularity of CD-ROMs is not lost on the folks who run** America Online. Over time, you'll begin to see more CD-ROM-based offerings on America Online. Some of the art content for the service itself might also be offered on a CD. The advantage of this is that it allows the service to provide more detailed artwork and sound in a form that contains too much data to download to your computer efficiently.

Using Shoppers Advantage Online

Keyword: **Shoppers Advantage**

Shoppers Advantage is a discount buying service that lets you purchase up to 250,000 different items right from the comfort of your personal computer (see fig. 13.16). Like AutoVantage, the interface for Shoppers Advantage is text-based. That is, you navigate through the service by entering simple commands in the text field. By choosing numbers or typing simple words, you are able to view the vast catalog, read product descriptions, and place your order for prompt shipment to your home or office.

When you look over a product's description, you'll see two prices. One is for members; the other somewhat higher price is for non-members. When you find a product you want to order, you'll discover quickly enough whether the low membership fee covers the purchase of a single item (and quite often it does). Members also get a two-year warranty on the products they buy. A typical online shopping trip for a new computer can bring a huge list of choice products from Apple Computer, IBM, and other manufacturers.

Fig. 13.16
Shoppers Advantage Online is your interactive discount mail order catalog, offering over 250,000 items covering dozens of merchandise categories.

Using the Classifieds Online

Keyword: **Classifieds**

The Classifieds Online forum is the place to post your own ads or check out advertisements from fellow members and commercial outfits. You aren't limited to just the computer-related merchandise shown in figure 13.17; you also can place ads for home appliances, electronics, and other types of merchandise.

Fig. 13.17
America Online's buy/sell/trade center is a place where you can check out ads for all sorts of merchandise, not just computers.

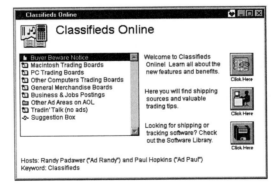

There are thousands of ads in the Classifieds message area. Most of them are placed by well-meaning firms and individuals; in most cases, you will receive the exact merchandise you order. But as with all mail order transactions, approach the deal with some healthy skepticism. It's a good idea, for example, to use a credit card when you make your purchase. That way, if you are not satisfied with the product or service, the credit card issuer will usually investigate the transaction on your behalf and even credit your account, if necessary.

Still more online shopping resources

Whenever you want to buy something new, you are faced with a bewildering array of choices. This section discusses one resource where you might find a little help in sorting through these choices to make the one that's right for you. You'll also find coverage about a nationwide buying service, a bill paying service, and an online resource for another kind of shopping—job hunting.

Home delivery from AOL

Keyword: **Shoppers Express**

Normally, when you have a prescription filled, you go to your local pharmacy and when you buy groceries, you go to a supermarket or convenience store. With Shoppers Express on America Online (see fig. 13.18), you can order the merchandise you want from the convenience of your personal computer and let the skilled buyers at Shoppers Express fill your order and bring it right to your home or office.

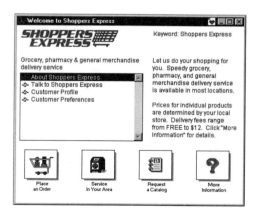

Fig. 13.18
Order food, pharmaceutical items, and general merchandise and have them delivered right to your home.

Shoppers Express works with merchants in your area to provide fast, home delivery of the products you want. Before deciding to try the service, click the Service In Your Area icon to see if Shoppers Express is represented by a store in your community.

Common sense tips for online shopping

Consider your online shopping tour a modern day equivalent of browsing through a mail order catalog. Although you can learn a lot about a product or service from the descriptions, there are occasions when the product you buy just won't meet your requirements or the merchandise you've received just doesn't work as it should.

Before you order...

- Read the product description thoroughly. If you have further questions, contact the staff of that particular shopping area.

- Read any posted Terms and Conditions carefully, in case you need to return the product for an exchange or refund for any reason.

- Merchandise sent via mail will usually include a shipping charge of some sort. If you're comparison shopping, be sure to include the shipping charge as part of the total price.

- Check the product description for estimated shipping times. Remember that shipments can be delayed as a result of conditions beyond the vendor's control, such as late delivery of merchandise from the manufacturer or delays on the part of the shipping agency.

- If you're ordering a product for a special occasion or as a gift, allow extra time for it to reach its destination.

- Make a copy of your order, so you can refer to it later in case you have a further question about the merchandise you've ordered.

- Bear in mind that you are ordering the merchandise directly from the vendor, not from America Online, who simply makes the vendor's service available. Complaints about products or services are best addressed directly to the vendor, and not to the online service.

- If you plan to buy merchandise from an AOL classified ad, don't be hesitant about asking the seller for some references. Remember, it's your money and you have a right to spend it carefully.

TIP **Some online order forms consist of multiple text fields, and** choosing File, Save might not save the complete text of your order. If this is the case, enter the full details of your order in a text document using AOL's memo feature, or use a screen image capture program to record the actual order screen itself.

After the package arrives

- When you receive your package, examine the box for signs of damage. If the box seems ruined beyond repair, contact the online vendor immediately about getting a replacement.

- If you have a problem with the merchandise you've received, follow the instructions that came with the package or are posted in the vendor area about whom to contact for customer service.

- If the product you ordered needs to be repaired, review the warranty information supplied with the package. Quite often, service must be done through a manufacturer's own authorized service center and not the vendor.

- If you use a credit card to make your purchase (and, in most cases, you will), you might also contact the card issuer to assist you if you run into problems dealing with a particular vendor. Remember that some credit cards provide extended warranties and other benefits when you use them to purchase large-ticket items.

Ready for that shopping tour?

Sometimes shopping is a headache, especially when you have to fight heavy traffic and search for parking spaces at a crowded suburban shopping mall. On America Online, however, there are no crowds and no lines. Simply browse through the virtual shopping aisles at your leisure, take the time you need to decide what you want to buy, and place your order. You can even get valuable information about selecting your next car.

14

Business or Pleasure: Travel with America Online

● **In this chapter:**

- **Check flight schedules and fares**

- **Make your airline, car, and hotel reservations**

- **Try a bed and breakfast establishment for a change**

- **Find out about attractions in your destination city**

- **Protect yourself by checking travel advisories**

Want to go to some exotic place for your honeymoon or a much deserved weekend getaway? From flight to hotel to rental car reservations—let AOL help you plan your trip. . . ●➤

Part IV *Information at Your Fingertips*

In this chapter, we'll explore AOL's Travel department. Instead of visiting the neighborhood travel agency when you're planning a trip, let's go to an agency located in cyberspace, available through the friendly interface of America Online. Following the simple steps I'm going to outline, you can pick a spot for a family vacation and gather information about the place you're going to visit without ever leaving your own home or office. You can select a hotel, make airline reservations, and even rent a car.

A visit to the Travel department

Keyword: **Travel**

Your first step in preparing for this vacation is to pay a visit to AOL's Travel department. To access this area, click the Travel icon in the Main Menu or use the keyword **Travel** (see fig. 14.1). Some of the online areas available in this department are described in the next few pages.

Fig. 14.1
The Travel department on AOL provides the resources you need before making a business or vacation trip.

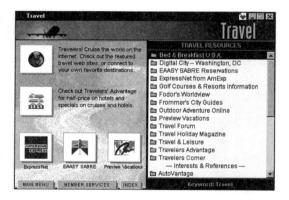

Cruise the world on the Internet

When you click on the little globe at the upper left of the Travel department window shown in figure 14.1, you see a directory of easily accessible travel resources on the World Wide Web (see fig. 14.2). You'll travel across the USA and around the world and locate fascinating, far-flung travel spots and valuable information that will serve you well on your next trip.

Fig. 14.2
WWW travel resources are easily accessed during your AOL visits.

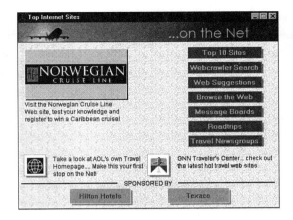

One resource you'll want to check out, shown at the upper-right side of the screen in fig. 14.2, is Webcrawler, an easy-to-use gateway that will help you locate WWW information of all sorts (not just related to travel, but to most any subject under the sun). Once you locate a specific place to visit, you can easily travel to that site by double-clicking on the entry. I'll tell you more about that in chapter 19, "Unmasking the World Wide Web."

Using the EAASY SABRE System

Keyword: **EAASY SABRE**

EAASY SABRE is an online travel agency, where you can make your airline, car rental and hotel reservations (see fig. 14.3). It's sponsored by American Airlines, but covers all the airlines in its lists.

Fig. 14.3
America Online's EAASY SABRE gateway is your entrance to full-featured travel reservation service.

If this is your first visit to this area, you'll want to briefly review the information texts in the forum directory window before you click that icon at the left of the screen that takes you to the EAASY SABRE main menu. This way, all of the new commands and procedures will be easy to get used to.

When you've located all the information you want, you can make your reservations, confirm those reservations, and bill the charges directly to your credit card. Your plane tickets and confirmation information will be mailed to your home or office.

TIP If you have a special preference, such as a nonsmoking window seat or a vegetarian meal, you need to list those preferences in your application. Getting correct reservations is much easier that way.

First you can view weather reports

If you're about to leave on that trip, you'll probably want to see a weather report for the city you're going to visit. Although the EAASY SABRE interface is text-based (like DOS), everything is clearly labeled in plain English. You just have to enter a number to correspond to a command you want (it's available under Other Information and Services). You can receive information not only about the current weather, but also about that day's forecast and the expected weather for the following day (see fig. 14.4).

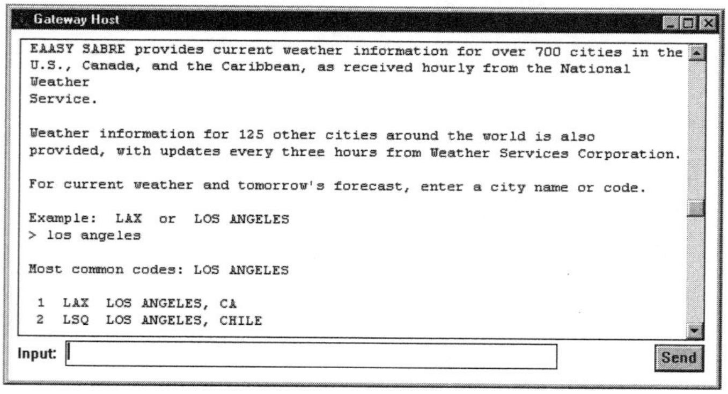

Fig. 14.4
EAASY SABRE provides the latest weather information on the places you want to visit.

Finding the best fares or flights

The ongoing airline price wars have made just about everyone (your cheerful author included) confused about airline fares. Each airline has its own schedule, with specific rules to obtain those highly touted discount fares. And the prices seem to change almost daily, in response to another airline's announcement about still lower and sometimes more confusing price schedules.

Before making your reservation, you'll want to find out just what the prices really are. First, click the Flights and Fares icon at the top left of the EAASY SABRE main menu. In response to the message prompts, you'll want to enter information about your planned flight. You are then asked the name of the city from which you're leaving, the final destination of your flight, the dates you plan to travel, along with the time you want to leave. Armed with that information, you'll be able to save money and get the flight that meets your needs. Using EAASY SABRE, you can also locate the latest discounts on car rentals and hotels.

TIP **If you want to bring your laptop computer with you, ask the hotel** if they provide a data port or other easy access to their phone lines, so you can easily get online to do your America Online sessions and other online transactions.

TIP **The national daily newspaper *USA Today* is a great source for** up-to-date news for travelers. Just select the USA Today Travel News folder from the main menu of the Travel window (you probably have to scroll down to see the folder). You then see a list of travel articles. And, don't forget, you can read, save, and print the latest news before planning your trip.

How to use ExpressNet from American Express

Keyword: **ExpressNet**

In setting up ExpressNet forum (see fig. 14.5), American Express has teamed up with the folks at America Online to provide a fully equipped interactive customer service center for you. If you're already an American Express card holder, you can use this forum to check your account status, and take advantage of some of the special shopping service offers. But even if you're not a card holder, you'll find valuable travel information that you'll want to know before you make your reservations. There's also a list of the company's own travel agencies throughout the world, where you can make your plans directly.

Fig. 14.5
Before you leave home, be sure you have your credit card ready.

A trip to Travelers Corner

Keyword: **Travelers Corner**

The next stopping point in this tour is the Travelers' Corner. This forum is hosted by the editors of Weissman Travel Reports. The Corner's main focus is comprehensive profiles of major U.S. and international destinations. You get a brief overview of the high points of a specific city and a list of its main attractions. The report not only describes these attractions, but also suggests the kinds of people who would most like to visit them. This information is especially important if you're taking your children with you.

To visit the Travelers' Corner, choose the Travelers' Corner icon from the Travel department window. The Travelers' Corner screen appears (see fig. 14.6).

If you want to read more travel-related material at your leisure, click the Travel Holiday icon to access the current issue of *Travel Holiday* magazine. The final icon in the Travelers' Corner, Order Travel Reports, gives you a special offer to purchase comprehensive professional profiles of the places you want to visit. These profiles are the same ones that are available through your local travel agency.

Fig. 14.6
The Travelers' Corner profiles some favorite travel spots and provides tips about local culture and etiquette.

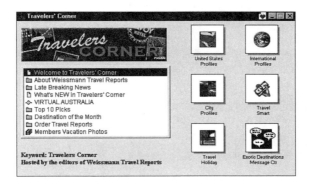

How to Preview Vacations Online

Keyword: **Vacations**

They say a picture is worth a thousand words, and while it's really nice to read text documents about travel locations online, wouldn't it be great to actually see what these far-off locales look like before you plan your trip?

That's what Preview Vacations Online is all about (see fig. 14.7). This forum lets you view full color photos of popular travel spots, and even participate in a real auction where you can bid on the vacation of your choice.

Fig. 14.7
Preview Vacations on AOL is a lot more than just a collection of travel photos.

A trip to the Travel Forum

Keyword: **Travel Forum**

The Travel Forum consists of a wealth of resources that contains much of the information you need to know before planning your trip (see fig. 14.8). The main window of this forum contains useful articles on many travel-related subjects. If you're going to travel by air, you receive up-to-date reports on the lowest fares. When you travel abroad, you need to know specific things about the country you are going to visit.

Fig. 14.8
America Online's Travel Forum is your first resource for information about the places you want to visit.

 TIP As with all America Online text windows, you can save the window by using the Save command, or you can print the text window by using the Print command.

Key resources of the Travel Forum, identified by colorful icons, include a What's New & Events department, where you can learn the latest tips and information. The Travel Cafe is a chat room where you can have online meetings with other members in a traveling frame of mind. You can exchange messages with other members in the Travel Boards area. The Travel Library includes downloadable text articles, and Travel Books provides news and views of books available at your neighborhood store.

Taking a Hike Online

Keyword: **Backpacker**

Not all travel plans involve cars, boats, or planes. Some involve traveling the old fashioned way, on foot. That takes us to *Backpacker* magazine on America Online (see fig. 14.9). This magazine caters to those who enjoy walking through the forests, trails, and deserts around the world in search of adventure.

Fig. 14.9
Backpacker magazine is a popular hiker's resource.

Experiencing Bed & Breakfast U.S.A.

Keyword: **Bed & Breakfast**

Bed and breakfast refers to a special kind of lodging that consists of private homes that rent out rooms to travelers, or inns that provide extra-special personal service. Sometimes they're referred to as guest houses or tourist homes. The Bed & Breakfast U.S.A. forum provides an up-to-date listing from across the country of this unique kind of accommodation (see fig. 14.10).

Fig. 14.10
Bed & Breakfast U.S.A. offers an alternative to conventional hotel/motel lodging.

Using DineBase Restaurant Listings

Keyword: **AOL Diner** (then double click DineBase in the directory at the left)

Whenever I travel to a new, unfamiliar part of the country, the first thing I seek out is a list of the best local restaurants. Goldwyn's DineBase makes this task easy (see fig. 14.11). This forum is a huge database that lists thousands of highly rated restaurants. You can search the listings by state, city, or even cuisine.

Fig. 14.11
DineBase is an easy way to find the best restaurants.

In search of an Outdoor Adventure Online

Keywords: **Adventure, OAO, Outdoor**

Some travelers are content to vacation in a hotel, or visit popular restaurants and shows. But if you want to take your travels to the great outdoors, you'll want to visit Outdoor Adventure Online (see fig. 14.12). It doesn't matter whether you're interested in hiking, skiing, scuba diving, or a host of other outdoor-related pursuits.

Fig. 14.12
Satisfy your quest for adventure with Outdoor Adventure Online. This is a forum that helps you tap a huge database of exciting outdoor excursions of all types.

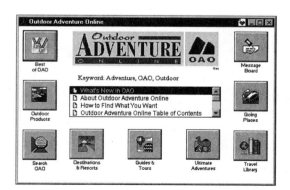

While planning your trip, you'll want to make sure you have just the right wardrobe and gear; for example, you might need a set of waterproof binoculars, or a set of skis. The Outdoor Products area offers hundreds of product reviews on field-tested equipment, and an active message board where you can read about the hands-on experience of other members who've tried these products.

Consulting the State Travel Advisories

Keyword: **Travel Advisories**

Because the world situation is apt to change at any moment, you'll want to view the official U.S. State Department travel advisories, shown in figure 14.13. You can tap into a huge database of information that covers the entire world, and learn if there are any special considerations for traveling to a specific country.

Fig. 14.13
The State Department's travel advisories can be searched on AOL.

The U.S. State Department Warnings folder contains the latest alerts about problems and limitations of traveling to specific parts of the world. It's a sad fact of life that some parts of the world may not always be safe places to visit. You'll want to review these text files before you plan your travel itinerary.

Ready to Leave?

Exploring America Online's resources for travelers is fun, not just for the vicarious voyagers among you, but also for those of you who are actually planning a vacation or business trip.

Part V: Getting on the Information Superhighway

Chapter 15: **The Internet Connection**

Chapter 16: **Internet E-Mail Made Easy**

Chapter 17: **The Lowdown on Internet Newsgroups**

Chapter 18: **Unmasking the World Wide Web**

Chapter 19: **Getting Started on the Web**

15

The Internet Connection

In this chapter:

- **What is the Internet?**

- **A fast Internet history lesson**

- **A look at AOL's Internet services**

- **How to learn more about the Internet**

The word Internet is plastered across our newspapers and TV screens. Here's what America Online is doing about this in-credible, global computer network . . . . >

Take a look at a typical business card, or an ad from any large company, or even from your local doctor, lawyer, or bagel baker. You'll see their phone number, their address, and something more, something about the Internet or World Wide Web. Now what's that all about?

Yes, what *is* this Internet stuff all about?

You read about it a while back. Congress was engaged in hot debate, not about the budget or about Social Security, but about whether to encourage censorship on the Internet. And all the online services are quickly jumping on the Internet bandwagon, led by America Online.

> *Plain English, please!*
>
> The word **Internet** means, basically, between networks. So the Internet isn't just a single amorphous entity, but a bunch of computer networks linked together, worldwide, consisting of millions and millions of computers, using not just the Windows or Mac operating systems, but Unix and other computer operating systems.

What you get from the Internet

The Internet allows you to use a whole range of features that extend beyond the ones you get on America Online, and it lets you get in touch with members of other networks and online services. Here's some of the Internet-based services offered through your AOL membership:

- You can send and receive e-mail across the world, even from users of other online services.

- You can search huge databases located at remote computer sites for files and information.

- You can join mailing lists and receive information on thousands of topics.

- You can engage in freewheeling, spirited discussions on newsgroup message boards.

- You can tap sources for hundreds of thousands of software files.

- You can access the colorful World Wide Web, the fastest-growing Internet service.

- You can easily build your own World Wide Web page, which can be accessed directly through AOL.

Just stay with me and I'll explain more about these features in this chapter and the ones that follow, chapters 16 through 19.

Let's pause for a quick history lesson

A lot of new developments came out of government projects, and the Internet is no exception. It started out in the 1960s as a government-sponsored experiment (directed by the U.S. Advanced Research Projects Agency) to discover the best methods to exchange data among remote computers. It was known then as ARPANET, not quite as exciting a name as Internet, and it consisted of computers installed at four educational institutions in California and Utah.

Unlike your normal, everyday computer network, the Internet had no hub or central control point. It was designed to operate under the assumption that the rest of the network was totally unreliable.

The fledgling Internet became a useful way for engineers and scientists to communicate with one another, by sending messages across the network. This process became known as electronic mail, or e-mail for short. In addition to sending messages, files were also placed on some of the computers, so that they could be shared among users of the network.

Over time, e-mail exchanges were shared among larger groups of users. In addition to simple messages, articles and reports were also included, and this became the beginning of the Internet mailing lists that are common today.

The Internet is still very much like the wild west of the 19th century. It's an open, largely unregulated frontier, and you may find files and discussions there that contain subject matter and language that goes against America Online's Terms of Service. So it's a good idea to carefully monitor your child's access to AOL's Internet areas (see chapter 7 for information on how to control your child's access to the Internet). And while it's true that most Internet veterans are only too happy to show new users (known as "newbies") the ropes, a few prefer to jealously guard their Net access and aren't so friendly to those unfamiliar with its procedures and traditions. Before you access America Online's Internet Connection, you'll want to read this chapter and perhaps the next four, and maybe explore some of the helpful information texts America Online has provided to introduce you to the Internet.

Let's explore AOL's Internet features

Keyword: **Internet**

America Online's Internet Connection is the focal point of its Net services (see fig. 15.1). All of AOL's Internet features are easily accessible simply by clicking on the labeled icon.

Accessing the Internet

Because of its wide reach, the Internet has become the place to be. Not too long ago, it wasn't so easy to get Internet access. You could only connect to the Internet from a scientific facility or educational institution, or pay a huge sum to set up your own computer to tap these resources.

But this isn't the case anymore. A number of Internet-based access services offer simple ways for users to get in the net. And America Online has been working feverishly to integrate the Internet with its own home-grown features, to provide the seamless access to all its users.

So now, get ready to travel across the Internet from the comfort of your own home or work area and your own personal computer.

Fig. 15.1
America Online has a special department that is designed to welcome you to the Internet and tap its resources.

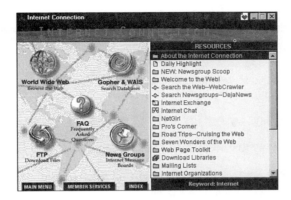

In addition, all of the major departments on America Online have their own direct Internet access. Throughout this book, I've described the little icons usually labeled Top Internet Sites that adorn many AOL areas. These icons put you a click away from some of the most popular sites on the Internet.

Throughout the rest of this chapter, I'll briefly cover AOL's Internet services. And the next four chapters will cover them in more detail. Over time, AOL will add still more Internet features, so stay tuned. The best is yet to come.

AOL's Mail Gateway is your Internet e-mail center

Keyword: **Mail Gateway**

America Online lets you send e-mail to your friends and business associates even if they aren't members of the service. AOL's Mail Gateway (see fig. 15.2) provides useful information on sending e-mail to members of other online services, businesses, universities, and more. Since the ground rules for setting up Internet e-mail are somewhat different than addressing mail to fellow AOL members, I've devoted chapter 16 to the subject.

Fig. 15.2
Learn more about sending your messages beyond AOL's borders from AOL's Internet e-mail center.

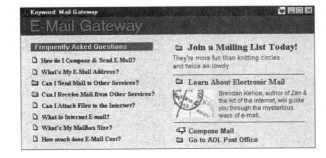

TIP You don't have to be in AOL's Mail Gateway or Internet Connection to compose Internet e-mail. All you have to do is open a blank mail form, address it, compose the message, and send it. You can even write your message while offline and send it via a FlashSession.

The wild world of UseNet Newsgroups

Keyword: **Newsgroups**

The closest thing to a message board on the Internet is UseNet, usually known as newsgroups. But the superficial resemblance to a message board doesn't extend to the content of the messages. Since it's largely uncontrolled, you'll find the discussions are often unfettered by any consideration of language or good taste, and America Online's Terms of Service are usually unknown in these discussion groups. You'll find thousands of newsgroups to choose from, and they cover most every topic under the sun, and a few (such as psychic phenomena and UFOs) that take you beyond the sun. Before getting involved, though, I suggest you read chapter 17, which covers the ground rules you'll want to check before you plunge in.

 Plain English, please!

UseNet is short for **User Network**, and it's one way of referring to the popular message boards that dot the Internet landscape. They're also known as newsgroups, which is the way I'll refer to them throughout this book.

The Internet provides huge resources of information

Keyword: **Gopher**

There's so much information to be found on the Internet, it's hard to know where to begin. Well, America Online makes it easy to find this information, by way of its Gopher and WAIS feature. Without leaving your home to consult a local library, you can easily access all this information. And you can use the same search capabilities I've described throughout this book. Just enter the topic you want to know about, and in seconds you see a directory of the information that matches your search string.

You can join an Internet Mailing list

Keyword: **Mailing Lists**

An Internet Mailing List is like a traveling discussion group. When you subscribe to such a list, you'll receive regular e-mail messages containing information on topics ranging from cars to restaurants (with lots of stuff in between). It's easy to locate a mailing list. Just access AOL's Mailing Lists area and use the search capability you'll find there. Once you locate a list that interests you and subscribe to it, your AOL e-mail box will be filled with lots of fascinating information. For the complete scoop on Mailing Lists, you'll want to check out chapter 16, "Internet E-Mail Made Easy."

When you first discover mailing lists that interest you, you might be tempted to go overboard and subscribe to lots of them. My advice is to be careful. Any single list can fill your mailbox with dozens of new messages each day. If you find your mailbox is becoming overwhelmed with new messages, you'll want to consider canceling your subscription to lists that produce messages you don't intend to read right away.

Transferring files on the Internet

Keyword: **FTP**

America Online's own software libraries have tens of thousands of software files. And there are hundreds of thousands more to choose from on the Internet. You'll be able to get files from commercial sources such as Apple, Microsoft, and Novell, and from private software libraries. Internet files are transferred using a technique called FTP, and AOL offers a gateway that lets you access these file sources (see fig. 15.3). Getting those files involves many of the same steps you use to download software direct from AOL's own libraries, which makes the entire process easy to learn.

> **Plain English, please!**
>
> **File Transfer Protocol**, usually known as **FTP**, describes the technique used to transfer files across the Internet. While the file transfer process on AOL doesn't seem much different, the underlying technology is much more complex, since allowances have to be made for different computing platforms and operating systems.

Fig. 15.3
Tap huge software repositories on the Internet via AOL's FTP gateway. Huge software libraries can be accessed through the Internet via FTP.

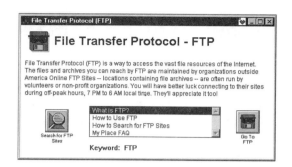

Experience graphics and sound on the World Wide Web

Keyword: **WWW**

The World Wide Web is the Internet's multimedia center. While other Internet services are text-based, the WWW (see fig. 15.4) combines text, graphics, and sometimes sound to provide a unique experience. The sample you see here is from my publisher's home page, and it's just an example of the sort of fancy stuff you'll find on the web. It's a place you'll want to visit often, as new sites are going up almost every day. There will be more about the subject in chapters 18 and 19.

 If you want to access the World Wide Web from America Online, you need version 2.5 of AOL's Windows software or a later version. You can download the latest AOL software free of online charges (if you use the Download Now feature). Just use the keyword Upgrade to get the software you need, if you don't already have it installed on your PC.

Fig. 15.4
The home page (starting point) of Macmillan Publishing's World Wide Web facility, as seen from AOL's web browser.

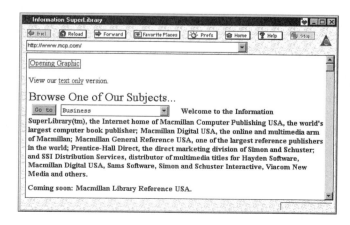

Chapter 15 *The Internet Connection* **243**

Q&A *Can I connect to AOL from the Internet?*

Yes you can, if you have direct Net access. Computers that hook up to the Internet speak a language called TCP/IP (Transmission Control Protocol/Internet Protocol).

If your computer network has such a connection (ask your network administrator about it), it's very easy to call up America Online through it. All you need is version 1.5 or later of AOL's Windows software. When you install AOL's software, the proper TCP/IP Winsock tools are also installed. If you're using other TCP/IP tools to browse the Internet, such as Netscape or Mosaic, your access to AOL through TCP/IP won't affect the use of these programs. Of course, with AOL's own Web capability, you may find yourself using those tools less and less.

To ring up AOL using TCP/IP, you just need to change your connection setup, using the instructions I provided in chapter 2. Just choose the Winsock version that matches the version of AOL software you're using (in your Location setup box), just as I've done in figure 15.5, below.

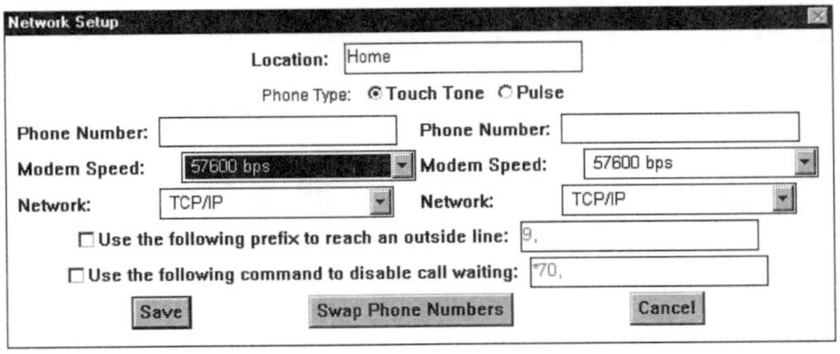

Fig. 15.5
It's easy to log onto AOL via a TCP/IP hookup.

When I visited AOL's headquarters recently, I logged onto the service via its direct TCP/IP connection. The speed was just incredible, much faster even than a regular 28,800 bps modem, so if you do have access to a high-speed TCP/IP line, you'll definitely want to use it to log onto AOL.

You can also sign up with a local Internet provider to get such a connection, but usually it's not worth the bother. First you have to remember that you are paying not just that provider's regular fee, but AOL's hourly charges too. Also, AOL offers direct 28,800 bps connections now, and you won't get any faster speed from an Internet service unless you invest in a high-speed network setup (which is much too costly to benefit a single user).

CAUTION **Direct Internet hookups to AOL may not be as secure as using your** regular modem and AOL's huge network of local access numbers. Information that passes back and forth between AOL and your computer via the Internet may be intercepted and read by computer hackers. This could include your account name and password, so if you connect to AOL via TCP/IP, it's a good idea to change your password on a regular basis. This will reduce the chances of anyone finding out what the password is.

If you want to know more

I've just scratched the surface of the Internet here, and the remaining chapters of this book will focus just on America Online's Internet features. If you want to know more, you'll want to stop over at your local bookstore and browse the bookshelves. There are lots of books to choose from.

When I wrote this section, I consulted *Special Edition Using the Internet*, published by Que, for background information about the Internet, and I recommend it to you highly. The second edition of this massive work (over 1,200 pages) includes a CD-ROM that provides over 100 Internet tools for Microsoft Windows.

Now that you've entered the on-ramp

America Online's Internet Connection takes all the fuss and bother out of Internet access. Without ever leaving the friendly confines of the service, you can go off and explore a worldwide collection of fascinating information. If your appetite has been whetted by my brief descriptions here, you'll want to read chapters 16 and 19 also. Those chapters provide much more information about AOL's exciting Internet features.

16

Internet E-Mail Made Easy

● **In this chapter:**

- **The easy way to send e-mail on the internet**

- **How to figure out an Internet e-mail address**

- **How to attach files to your Internet e-mail**

- **How to use Internet mailing lists**

- **How to keep your mailbox from being overwhelmed**

Sending e-mail and files to those who don't subscribe to AOL is as easy as sending it to those who do. . . . . ❯

When you use America Online's highly flexible and speedy electronic mail features, you are not restricted to sending your messages just to other AOL members. Through AOL's Internet Connection, you can send e-mail to members of other online services and, in fact, to anyone with Internet access. In addition, you can subscribe to any of thousands of mailing lists and place information on all sorts of topics in your AOL mailbox.

How to send and receive Internet e-mail

It's no surprise that e-mail is one of the most popular services offered not only by America Online, but through the Internet as well. Right now, you can send and receive electronic mail with anyone connected to the Internet. It makes no difference whether they use America Online. If you have friends who use one of the other online networks, such as Prodigy, eWorld, CompuServe, MCI Mail, AT&TMail, AppleLink, and others, you can send them e-mail by using America Online's regular e-mail feature through the Internet, simply by using their Internet e-mail address. America Online handles millions of Internet-based transactions each day.

America Online's Mail Gateway is a full service center that provides information and support on using Internet e-mail (see fig. 16.1). There you'll see updated listings that cover addressing and receiving e-mail, plus you'll have access to AOL's Internet search tools (such as Gopher and WAIS).

Fig. 16.1
AOL's Mail Gateway can be used to send e-mail throughout the world via the Internet.

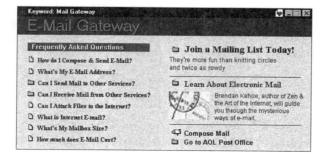

TIP You don't need to access the Mail Gateway to send Internet e-mail. Once you get the hang of the addressing techniques I'm describing in this chapter, you can just open your e-mail form directly and go to it.

Chapter 16 *Internet E-Mail Made Easy* **247**

You can begin the Internet e-mail process simply enough by opening a blank e-mail form (see fig. 16.2). Yes, it's the same e-mail form I described in chapter 5, "How to Stay in Touch with Other Members." The ground rules regarding content are the same; you enter an e-mail address, a subject line and the actual message. There's one difference, though: Don't bother using special typefaces, styles, or colors in your document. Everything will be converted to raw, unformatted (ASCII) text when your mail travels through the mail gateway. The use of ASCII text allows for total compatibility with millions of computers, using many operating systems and many kinds of telecommunications software.

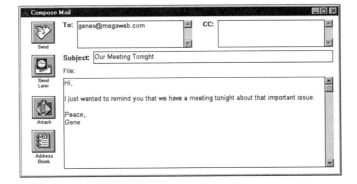

Fig. 16.2
Only the address differentiates Internet e-mail from regular AOL e-mail. You include a subject line and your message, and you can write these items in the same way you write any other e-mail.

> **TIP** The best way to learn the address of an Internet correspondent is to simply ask the person for it.

How to send Internet e-mail

Sending e-mail over the Internet works the same as sending normal America Online e-mail to other members. You just type the Internet address of your intended recipient rather than the America Online screen name you normally use to send mail to other AOL members.

Addressing Internet mail is that simple. However, there are a couple of rules, as follows:

- An Internet address never contains any spaces. If someone's mail system does allow spaces at the receiving end, the spaces are automatically replaced by underscores (_) in the Internet address. For example, you might see **john_smith@hugecorp.com**, in which the space between the user's first and last name is closed up with an underscore character.

248 **Part V** *Getting on the Information Superhighway*

- Also, every Internet address must have the user name and domain specified. For our purposes, the user name is everything before the **@** symbol, and the domain is everything after the **@** symbol. In the domain, a company name is followed by a suffix that describes what type of organization it is. A business, for instance, uses the suffix **.com**, educational institutions use **.edu**, military sites use **.mil**, and government offices use **.gov**.

> ❝ *Plain English, please!*
>
> **Domain** is a word that identifies the location or company running an Internet site. ❞

The following table shows how you can address Internet e-mail to your friends on other online services. Some additional information about each service has been added to help you address your e-mail for that service. If you follow the format provided here, you can easily address other services in much the same manner. But let me first explain the meanings behind some of those headlines:

- The Location is the name of the service.

- The Long Address is the full Internet e-mail address that you'd normally use.

- The Shortcut is an abbreviation you can use to save a few keystrokes when sending e-mail to some services.

The world of Internet-speak

Once you get the hang of all those Internet e-mail conventions, the places to put periods and all, there's one more thing to consider: just what do you say to your friends or business associates when they want you to tell them (not write) your Internet address?

Clearly all this dot and com stuff is meant to be written, right?

Well, you can say it, though it doesn't quite fall trippingly off the tongue. Just remember that the @ character is spoken as at. With that in mind, here's my Internet address:

It's written as aflgenes@aol.com, and you say: ay-ef-el-gene-es-at-ay-oh-el-dot-com.

Now try and say that three times, rapidly.

Chapter 16 *Internet E-Mail Made Easy* **249**

- The italicized entry labeled name indicates where you insert your own AOL screen name.

Location	Long Address	Shortcut	Example
AppleLink	applelink.apple.com	apple	**name@apple**
AT&TMail	attmail.com	att	**name@att**
America Online		aol.com	**name@aol.com**
BITNET	\<institution>.bitnet		**name@\<institution>.bitnet**
BIX	bix.com		BIXname@**bix.com**
CompuServe	compuserve.com	cis	**12345.678@cis**
Connect	connectinc.com		**name@connectinc.com**
Delphi	delphi.com		**name@delphi.com**
EasyLink	eln.attmail.com		**62\<name>@elattmail.com**
eWorld	eworld.com		**name@eworld**
Fidonet	p\<point>.f\<node>. n\<network>. z\<zone>.fidonet.org		**name@p\<point>.f\<node>. n\<network>.z\<zone>.fidonet.org**
GEnie	genie.geis.com	genie	**name@genie**
MCI Mail	mcimail.com	mci	**name@mci**
Prodigy	prodigy.com		**userid@Prodigy.com**
Well	well.com		**name@well.com**

Some organizations have a private area that uses CompuServe e-mail in their address. You can reach these locations using the format **name@organization.compuserve.com**.

 Plain English, please!
The **BITNET** network is a service involving various academic computers. The .bitnet designation provides an Internet address for these computers.

 **Each online service has its own requirements and limitations** as to how the offered Internet services work. AOL's Internet Connection contains help text that will help you address your e-mail to other services. As other services change their Internet offerings, these help texts will also be revised.

 Help! Why was my Internet e-mail returned by a MAILER-DAEMON? What's that, and what's it want with me?

If you do not address your Internet mail in the correct format, or it didn't reach its destination for some reason, the message will be returned by AOL's Internet mail computers.

First thing you want to do is look over the message, which spells out the reason why it was returned.

The most common cause is that the address is marked unknown. If this happens to you, verify the original recipient's correct e-mail address (even an error involving one letter or number is enough to bounce the letter). Internet e-mail can travel through a long, circuitous path on its way from AOL's mail server to its destination. Sometimes errors can occur during transmission (a blip on the information superhighway), and sometimes correctly addressed mail is returned for no apparent reason. The best solution (after verifying that the address is correct) is to send the letter again.

How to receive Internet e-mail

To receive mail from the Internet, you need to know your own Internet address. Your address is simply your America Online screen name, with any spaces removed, plus @aol.com. If your screen name is John User, for example, your Internet address is johnuser@aol.com.

 Internet addresses are almost always expressed in lowercase letters. Although this is not an absolute requirement, you should follow this convention for clarity and consistency with existing Internet practices.

A look at Internet file attachments

The really neat thing about AOL's Internet e-mail is that you can send and receive files in the very same way you send those files to other AOL members. But there are a few things to consider, especially when it involves someone on another service who may be getting the files you send from AOL:

- Files attached to your Internet e-mail are automatically converted to MIME format. In order to read those files, the recipient may need a separate program, but that's something that the recipient may have to check with the other service. One example of a good decoder utility is UUCODE by Sabasoft. A quick check of a shareware software library will yield lots of treasures of this sort.

> ❝ *Plain English, please!*
> **MIME** isn't something that refers to an actor performing without speaking. It stands for *Multipurpose Internet Mail Extensions*. It's a technique used to convert the file to text form, so it can be read on different kinds of computers. ❞

- If someone sends you a long text message (containing more than 27,000 characters), it will be converted to an attached file. You'll see the first 2,000 characters in the body of the e-mail message, and the full, original message will be attached as a file.

- Tell the person who is sending you files by the Internet not to attach more than one file to the message. Otherwise, you'll have to use another software program (a MIME converter) to change it back to its normal form. Instead, suggest to that person that they make the files into a single compressed archive, using one of the standard PC compression programs. You can find a MIME converter in AOL's software libraries using the File Search feature (click Search Software Libraries from the Go To menu).

CAUTION **Graphic files on the Internet do not have to follow America Online's Terms of Service regarding nude or sexually explicit content. Be sure to examine the article's header or look at the title and purpose of a newsgroup before transferring material from that area to your computer.**

A look at Internet mailing lists

Keyword: **Mailing Lists**

Internet mailing lists (see fig. 16.3) are e-mail discussions among groups of people on the Internet who share similar interests. Using regular Internet e-mail, information is exchanged in a continuing, interactive fashion with people all around the world. The entire text of these discussions will appear regularly in your AOL mailbox (don't overdo it, or your mailbox will fill up).

Fig. 16.3
Here's AOL's Internet Mailing Lists center.

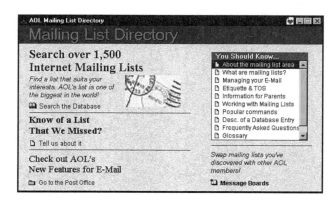

Thousands of Internet mailing lists exist today, encompassing almost every imaginable topic: computer technology, American literature, philosophy, cooking, chess, motorcycling, sports, the environment, rock music, UFOs, alternative lifestyles—take your pick.

TIP To learn someone's e-mail address without asking for it, I suggest you read the book, *A Directory of Electronic Mail !%@:: Addressing & Networks*, by Donnalyn Frey and Rick Adams, available in most bookstores. Business addresses can also be found in the book, *Internet Yellow Pages*, by Christine Maxwell and Czeslaw Jan Grycz, published by New Riders.

The Internet Mailing Lists area has various helpful text articles containing background and instructions on using the Mailing Lists features of the Internet Connection.

To locate specific mailing lists that might appeal to your interests, click the Search the Database button. You'll discover a database of mailing lists you can search by entering descriptive words (see fig. 16.4).

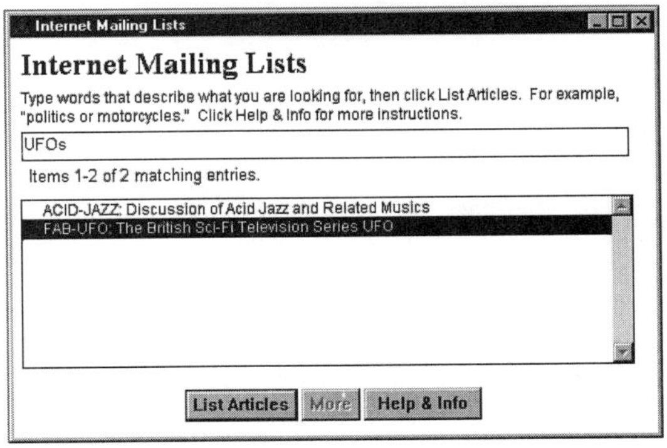

Fig. 16.4
Here's the Mailing List database search window with the results of your search for mailing lists on the topic of UFOs.

After a list of entries that match your search description appears, click the List Articles button (or press Enter). The items that appear after a successful search from this window contain the descriptions of Internet Mailing Lists available from the matches of your search words entered in the search window (see fig. 16.5).

Fig. 16.5
Here's a description of one of the Mailing Lists, containing information on the subject it deals with and how to subscribe.

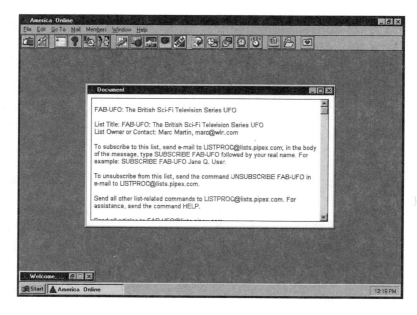

How to join an Internet mailing list

The descriptions of a mailing list contain instructions on how you can join the mailing lists that interest you by using your America Online Internet e-mail address. (Internet regulars call it "subscribe," but you don't pay anything to join these lists.) Follow the instructions carefully; they tend to differ slightly from list to list. Remember to also note how you can unsubscribe from any lists you join, in case you change your mind later. Most of these lists generate a large amount of mail and can quickly fill your online mailbox if you don't check it regularly.

Remember, also, that these mailing lists are sometimes run not by an individual reading your request, but by a software program that automates establishing and maintaining it, and sending the regular mailings to subscribers. Because you are communicating with another computer and not an individual, it's important that you make your requests follow the exact directions in the mailing list subscription.

Here are a few things to keep in mind when joining a mailing list:

- Use the exact commands specified in the instructions you read about joining a mailing list to subscribe and unsubscribe.

- Remember that Internet e-mail might take a couple of days to reach its destination, so be patient about getting a response. Also remember that mailings to subscribers might be sent at infrequent intervals.

- If a mailing list is also available as a UseNet newsgroup, you might prefer to use that option. With a UseNet newsgroup, you don't have to handle unsolicited e-mail, and you can easily limit reading messages to the ones that interest you within a given time frame and ignore messages dealing with topics you do not want to see. I'll cover UseNet in full detail in the next chapter.

How to respond to mailing list messages

The material you receive from a mailing list looks, for all intents and purposes, the same as any standard e-mail message (see fig. 16.6). And you respond to those messages in exactly the same way. Just choose the Reply option on your mailing list e-mail to incorporate your comments about a particular article in a subsequent group of messages. If you want to post an article to a mailing list, you'll want to consult the original instructions for that mailing list. Normally, this requires composing mail to the list address rather than responding to an individual message.

Fig. 16.6
Here's some typical e-mail from a mailing list.

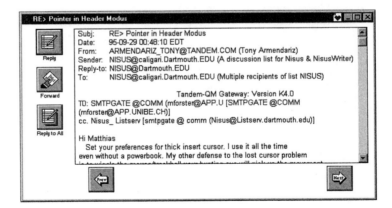

How to leave a mailing list

The instructions you receive when you first join a mailing list generally include online information on how to get off the mailing list, or unsubscribe. If the mailing list is run by an automated list server computer, you must make your request using the exact format contained in those instructions. Computers are very literal-minded. If the list is run by a person, you can just send a regular e-mail request.

CAUTION **When you want to leave a mailing list, consult the original** instructions on joining (in AOL's Mailing Lists area) to see how to unsubscribe. You don't just send a letter to the group with "unsubscribe" marked on it, as it won't accomplish anything but raise the wrath of some of the mailing list regulars.

CAUTION **If you change your screen name or cancel your AOL account, be** sure to unsubscribe all of your mailing lists (the mail won't be forwarded). If the list is maintained by a person, you can send whatever mail-forwarding information is appropriate. You'll have to resubscribe to the mailing lists from which you want to continue getting e-mail.

What to do if your mailbox is filled

There are so many fascinating mailing lists that you will no doubt be tempted to join a number of them. It's not uncommon to overdo it a bit, and you might find your mailbox clogged with messages still unread. FlashSessions can produce huge incoming mailboxes. The best advice is to be judicious about managing your mail so that you aren't overwhelmed.

Presently, your AOL mailbox is limited to 550 items. This number includes not only the mail you have read, but also the mail you have not yet seen. The list of mail you've sent remains in your mailbox for 28 days; mail you've read is deleted after 4 days (at least as of the time this book was written).

CAUTION **If the number of read and unread mail exceeds 550, the oldest** mail is deleted automatically by AOL's host computer system. By managing your mailbox carefully, you'll avoid losing mail you might want to keep. And bear in mind that the amount of time your AOL mail is kept may change from time to time to make the mail server computers run better.

Here are some common-sense tips to help you keep your mailbox down to usable proportions:

- Be sure you subscribe only to mailing lists you really want to read.

Chapter 16 *Internet E-Mail Made Easy* **257**

- Take note of directions on how to unsubscribe to a mailing list when you join, in case the mailing list doesn't meet your expectations or you find your mailbox getting a little too crowded.

- Check your e-mail regularly to keep your mailbox as small as possible.

TIP **If you've lost directions on how to subscribe or unsubscribe to a** mailing list, simply search for that mailing list—again using the search feature in the Internet Mailing Lists area. The results of your search can be saved and printed for later review.

Bigger than the Post Office

As you can see, sending and receiving e-mail on the Internet is hardly more complicated than sending e-mail to another America Online member. Subscribing to a mailing list follows basically the same steps. And, from the comfort of America Online's graphical interface, participating in all the Internet's exciting features is just as easy.

17

The Lowdown on Internet Newsgroups

● **In this chapter:**

- ● **What Internet newsgroups are**

- ● **What Netiquette *really* means**

- ● **How to find the newsgroups in which you're interested**

- ● **How to participate in newsgroups**

For hot-and-heavy discussions about most any subject under the sun (and then some), there's nothing like a UseNet newsgroup. . . . . ⊘

America Online's own message boards are one source of information exchange. But for really intense debate you'll want to head for the global Internet network. The discussion boards on the Internet, unlike those on AOL, are not restricted by the boundaries and requirements of a single online service (or even their rules and regulations).

Some of the most interesting parts of the wide world of the Internet are newsgroups, also known as UseNet newsgroups (see fig. 17.1). **Newsgroups** are popular and active exchanges. Just as with mailing lists, there are newsgroups covering almost any topic you can think of, and then some.

Fig. 17.1
One of the most exciting Internet features is newsgroups, where the discussions often get heated.

> **Plain English, please!**
> **UseNet** is short for user network, which summarizes the essence of these discussion boards, in which Internet users speak their minds about the subject at hand.

How to set up AOL's newsgroup reader

Now let's dive in and get ready to explore the wacky world of newsgroups.

If you've used a newsgroups reader on another online service, you're apt to find some differences, because America Online is a graphical service, and many dedicated Internet providers still use text-based software.

Chapter 17 The Lowdown on Internet Newsgroups

> **Plain English, please!**
> A **news reader** is, simply speaking, software used to read, organize, and post messages in a newsgroup. AOL's news reader is integrated into its client software, so you can seemlessly switch from a regular message board to a newsgroup without having to access another program.

Over the next few pages, I'll show you how to set up AOL's newsreader for best performance. Then, I'll cover some of the rules of online etiquette, and then you'll want to seek out and participate in some popular newsgroup discussions.

First, let's set your newsgroup preferences

The opening Newsgroups window (see fig. 17.1) has two sets of preferences. There is yet a third set of preferences, but you can't access that until you open a list of messages. This third set is described later in this chapter. For now, look at the two rectangular buttons at the bottom of the Newsgroups window.

First, there's Parental Controls, which can be used to limit access to certain Internet features. If you want to explore that further, you'll want to read chapter 7.

The Set Preferences button produces a collection of preferences you can set (see fig. 17.2). Using these preferences, you can create a signature that automatically appears at the bottom of your newsgroup messages and you can dictate how you want those messages to appear.

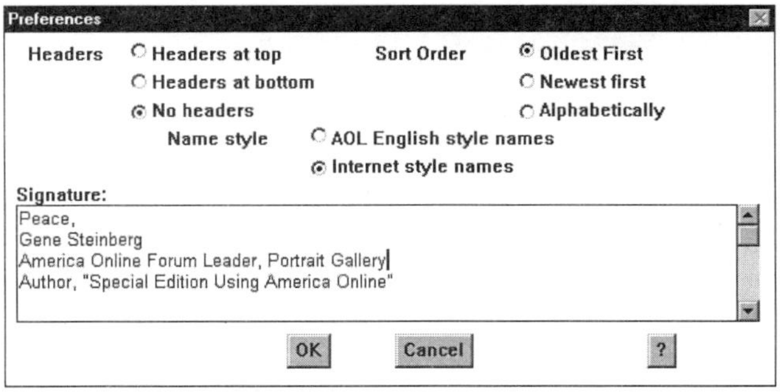

Fig. 17.2
Set your global newsgroup preferences in this dialog box.

The three types of preferences are covered in order.

How the messages are displayed

Internet transactions go through a circuitous route, from computer to computer, on their way to America Online. You can choose whether you want to see any of this header information, which displays the long, roundabout path your message takes (you might want to leave it off, to keep message windows free of clutter). Here are the header options to choose from:

- *Headers at top.* The path your message travels is included at the top of your message window.

- *Headers at bottom.* The path your message travels is included at the bottom of your message window.

- *No headers.* Ah, that's more like it. The headers are stripped from the messages you see. The header is limited to the date and time the message was sent, the message ID information, and the Internet address of the message's author.

Then, the order of display

In what order would you like your messages to appear? By default, you see the oldest first, and then you move through them, in chronological order, with messages grouped by thread (topic). Here are your choices:

- *Oldest first.* The default setting enables you to read the messages in their normal sequence.

- *Newest first.* This choice might seem like reading the end of a book before the beginning, but if you have a huge number of messages to read through you may find it convenient to look at the latest messages first. This option makes following a message thread difficult, however, because you will see the response before you see the question (sounds similar to what Johnny Carson used to do when he hosted the *Tonight* show).

- *Alphabetically.* This option groups messages by topic, in alphabetical order.

What's in a name

The names of a newsgroup follow a specific naming convention, which might seem confusing if you are visiting the Internet for the first time. You have two options as to how the names in your Newsgroups list are shown. Here's what they do:

- *AOL English style names.* For this setting, a newsgroup might be identified as Help with Newsgroups.

- *Internet style names.* When you select this option, Help with Newsgroups is shown as **aol.newsgroups.help**.

As you see, the Internet name, despite its odd syntax, is really not difficult to comprehend, but whether to choose this option is up to you. Why not try both methods? You can change your preferences at any time by opening the Set Preferences window, making your alterations, and then opening your list of newsgroups again. The changes take effect immediately.

TIP **If you are viewing your newsgroups with English-style names, you** can see the actual Internet name by clicking the Internet Names icon at the top of the newsgroup message window. This action brings up a window showing the Internet name versions.

Internet Newsgroups—the Ground Rules

No doubt when you first visit AOL's Newsgroups area, you'll want to jump right in and get involved in a discussion board yourself. Before you do so, though, you should learn something about newsgroups in general and how to introduce yourself to a discussion group. Over the years, the Internet, although largely unregulated and unsupervised, has developed some forms and conventions you'll want to learn more about.

So here are a few tips based on hard-won experience on the Net:

- You'll be tempted to plunge in to a discussion that interests you. Don't. Spend a little time reading messages or following the discussions (which experienced Net visitors sometimes call lurking). Often you'll find a set of FAQs, a set of text files that provide a list of ground rules for a specific discussion group, and responses to typical user questions. After you've developed a feel for the flavor of a particular group, it's time to consider posting a message of your own.

Plain English, please!
FAQ is short for **Frequently Asked Questions**, which is usually a list of commonly asked questions and answers about a specific subject or range of subjects.

- There are literally thousands of newsgroups. The number of messages you are likely to encounter will be in the hundreds of thousands. You can quickly become overwhelmed by the sheer volume of information if you don't pick and choose carefully. To begin with, you should restrict yourself to only a small number of discussion groups, take time to digest the messages, and add more only when you think you can devote the time necessary to follow up on all the information you'll receive.

- When you respond to a message, consider that you are posting a response to not just a single person, but an audience that could number in the millions. If you decide you want to restrict your audience to a single person, send that person e-mail instead. The option to reply to just the author rather than the group is available in America Online's newsgroup reader.

- Before writing your message, carefully choose the appropriate forum. It wouldn't necessarily be a good idea to promote the use of a Macintosh in a discussion group oriented toward users of Microsoft Windows, for example, unless you want to risk generating a lot of ill will.

- Show respect and be polite when you post a message. If you disagree with someone's statement, try to stick to the issues and refrain from personal attack. Such attacks are regarded as flaming, and although they might be entertaining on some television talk shows, they are not considered good taste on the Internet.

 Plain English, please!
Flaming is a term that is the online equivalent of a shouting match, which involves making personal attacks and using abusive language. It's not considered good online etiquette under any circumstance.

- When responding to someone else's message, quote the relevant portions of that message at the beginning of your response, or before each part of your message that refers to that message (don't just quote the entire message). The text you select first is automatically quoted in your message form.

- It is customary to use your Internet address (described in chapter 16, "Internet E-Mail Made Easy") as your personal signature, but your name and affiliations can be placed there, too (see figure 17.3). Some folks also include their address and phone number, but before you do this, consider whether you feel that you'd want to really give this information out to millions of strangers. Others add a statement or motto that reflects some aspect of their personality. Before preparing your own signature, you might want to see how others do it first.

Fig. 17.3
This is a typical UseNet newsgroup signature. The information below the signature shows the long and twisted path that was taken by that message before it reached its destination.

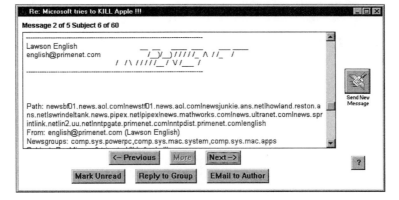

- Keep your messages short and to the point. You are reaching an audience of millions, and you don't want to waste anyone's time, because many users pay high charges for Internet access. Also, try not to cross-post, or send your message to more than one newsgroup at a time (unless you think it's really necessary).

TIP When you create an online signature for yourself, try to keep it brief (such as your name and, if needed, company affiliation or a short motto). Long signatures, with elaborate artwork, simply waste bandwidth and may upset users who pay large amounts for Internet access.

- Choose a subject title that specifically describes the topic of your message. It is better to use General Protection Fault in Word 6.0c than System Crash if you are seeking advice on solving a problem in a Windows-based applications newsgroup.

- Express emotions and humor with care. When you speak with someone in person, very often body language and the inflection of your voice would reveal whether you are serious, angry, or happy about something. But in your messages, your words alone must be the mirror of your feelings. Experienced online users express emotions with smileys :). See chapter 5, "How to Stay in Touch with Other Members," for a list of common online shorthand characters (known as smileys and emoticons).

- Before you respond to a message, take the time to see whether someone else has already answered it. Time on the busy Internet is at a premium, and reading the same sort of message over and over wastes everyone's time, including your own.

How to participate in Internet newsgroups

To repeat what I said earlier, there are thousands upon thousands of newsgroups that cater to interests of all sorts. Many newsgroups overlap in terms of content, too, so you probably will want to select more than a single newsgroup that caters to topics that interest you.

America Online maintains a list of the most popular newsgroups in its own database. Just click the Add Newsgroups icon in the main Newsgroups window. You'll see a directory listing, shown in figure 17.4, that displays many subjects of interest.

Fig. 17.4
The first step in locating a newsgroup is to get a list of groups that cater to your favorite subjects.

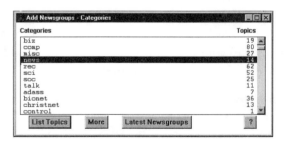

After you've picked a subject, click the List Topics button to bring up a list of newsgroups that fit the description. To find the newsgroup itself, click the listing once more, and then you'll see the display shown in figure 17.5. Now you've gotten to the heart of the matter.

Fig. 17.5
Here's a list of newsgroups catering to a particular interest.

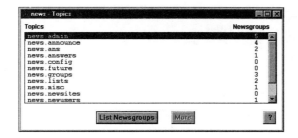

You don't have to join any newsgroup yet, but if you want to dive in you can automatically subscribe to the selected newsgroup by clicking the Add button (shown in the list of newsgroup titles). If you'd rather sample the flavor of a particular discussion group, just click its name and you'll see a list of the available messages, as shown in figure 17.6. You can read those messages, but because you are just sampling the newsgroup for now, you cannot actually post a response to a message or create a topic of your own. To do either of these things, you must actually add the newsgroup to your list.

Fig. 17.6
Before you actually join a newsgroup, you might want to look over some of the messages.

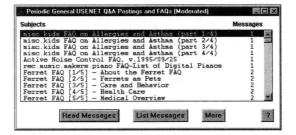

When you've actually added a newsgroup, it appears under the Read My Newsgroups listing, which is discussed later in this chapter.

How to find a newsgroup

If you don't find a newsgroup that interests you, you'll want to perform a more thorough search of the available newsgroups. Click the Search All Newsgroups icon in the Newsgroups area to bring up a search window, as shown in figure 17.7. Enter the subject for which you want to locate a newsgroup in the list field.

Fig. 17.7
Search from among thousands of newsgroups for one that piques your curiosity.

If there is a newsgroup that meets your search criteria (and sometimes you have to refine the phrases a bit or even try related ones), that newsgroup title appears in a window. From there, you can read a capsule description by double-clicking the newsgroup's title. You'll find, however, that many newsgroups do not actually have any description other than the titles themselves, which those newsgroups usually consider sufficient to describe their mission.

Unlike the Add Newsgroups feature, the searching mechanism doesn't give you the ability to sample a newsgroup before adding it to your list. Because you can remove a newsgroup later if you choose, by the simple click of a button, this is not a major shortcoming.

TIP If you want to search for more than a single item, you should insert **and** between words and phrases to separate subjects. You also may expand your search with the word **or** when you wish to look for one option or another, but not both; and you can exclude an item with the word **not** to designate a subject or word you don't want to use in the search result listing.

Use Expert Add if you know the name

As with e-mail addresses, the titles of newsgroups are identified by a special syntax, with words generally separated by a period. An example is **comp.sys.mac.advocacy**, which, as the title suggests, is a discussion group with active debates on the subject of using the Apple Macintosh versus other computing platforms. If you know the exact title of a newsgroup, you can bypass the search mechanism or America Online's own listing and join by using the Expert Add feature, shown in figure 17.8.

Fig. 17.8
If you know the name of the newsgroup you want to join, enter it here.

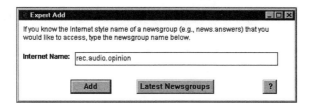

CAUTION America Online's Expert Add feature is quite literal-minded. For it to work, you need to enter a newsgroup's name using the exact spelling and punctuation. Otherwise, the newsgroup won't be located, or worse, you'll add the wrong newsgroup.

After you've subscribed to the newsgroups that interests you, it's time to read the messages.

How to read your newsgroup messages

Click the Read My Newsgroups icon at the main screen of the Newsgroups area, and you'll see a list of all the newsgroups to which you've subscribed, as shown in figure 17.9. When you enter this area for the first time, you'll see a list of popular newsgroups that America Online has automatically included, but you can remove them at any time by highlighting the name of the newsgroup and clicking the Remove button. The Mark Read button enables you to flag the messages in a selected group as read without actually opening the messages themselves (use this feature with caution if you want to read those messages later).

Fig. 17.9
Here are the newsgroups you've joined. Looks to me like you've got lots of reading to do.

Before you begin to read the messages in your selected newsgroups, you'll want to review the section on Netiquette earlier in this chapter. Then take some time to read the messages themselves. The first time you read the messages, you might find there are literally thousands in a single newsgroup alone. But because the messages are grouped by topic (also known as message threading), as shown in figure 17.10, you'll easily be able to pick the messages you want to read.

Fig. 17.10
Newsgroup messages are threaded, or grouped according to topic.

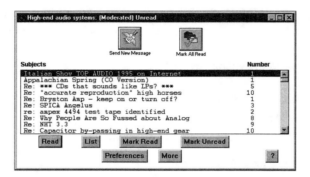

How to follow a message thread

All newsgroup messages are normally sorted by date and then by topic. You can choose to display messages in a different order, using the Set Preferences feature described previously. But in this description, the messages will be referred to in their regular order.

 Plain English, please!
> The process of organizing the messages into topics is known as threading. It enables you to read messages and responses about a single topic without having to read through messages on other subjects.

After you've read all the messages in a single thread, the next message you bring up (by clicking the Next button) takes you to a new thread. If you want to bypass that subject, just close the message window. You can then look over the directory of unread messages for another topic you want to follow.

TIP Because messages in a single thread are often posted at widely varying times, you might actually find two or more separate listings for messages concerning a single topic.

Setting message preferences

Another set of newsgroup preferences covers the time frame of messages shown when you open a message window. It's very similar to the Find Since feature that you use on a regular AOL message board (see chapter 5, "How to Stay in Touch with Other Members"). By clicking the Preferences option in a newsgroup message window (see fig. 17.11), you'll have options that will serve you now and in the future.

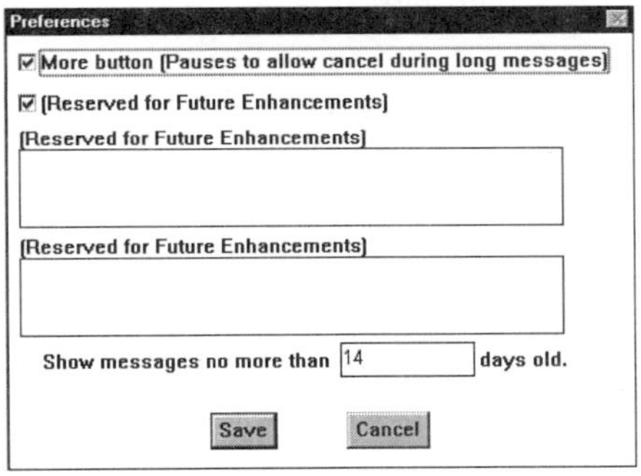

Fig. 17.11
Choose the time frame under which messages will be displayed, as well as other options.

At the time this book was written, some of the message preferences hadn't been activated. The sole option that was available was the one at the bottom, in which you can select the time frame in which messages are displayed. This option can save you the drudgery of having to pore over thousands of accumulated messages during your first visit to a newsgroup or when visiting a newsgroup after a few days' absence from AOL.

 **CAUTION** The message-board options you choose apply only to the individual newsgroup in which you select them. Preferences must be selected separately for every newsgroup to which you subscribe.

Q&A *Help! I selected the option to show messages for no more than a day or so, yet I'm still seeing thousands of messages displayed after I click the Save button and close the preference window. Why?*

You need to reload the message list on your computer. Here's how:

1 Close the window containing the message list that appears when you select Read messages.

2 Open the Read My Newsgroups window (if it's not already open), and then double-click the newsgroup window you just closed.

You'll then see only the unread messages posted within the time frame you set on your message preferences.

See it all with the List All feature

When you first open your personal newsgroup list and select a topic, double-clicking the topic name or pressing the Enter key brings up a list of unread messages. To review messages you've read previously, click the List All button instead, which brings up a display of all recent messages available in that newsgroup, whether or not you've read them.

How to reply to a newsgroup message

After you've read the messages in your favorite newsgroup, no doubt, you'll be tempted to respond to a particular message. Use the Reply to Group button to add your message to the existing thread so that others will see your response, also. There are two ways to respond to a message. First is simply to click the Reply button, which brings up the screen shown in figure 17.12. If you want the author of the original message to receive a reply by e-mail, check the box at the lower left corner of the message window.

The second option is Reply to Author, which enables you to send your response as e-mail instead. You still have the choice of having the same message posted in the newsgroup, by clicking the check box in the Reply to Author window.

The Use signature (set in global preferences) check box automatically adds the signature you set in the newsgroup preferences box to your message. If you prefer not to use this signature, or to use a different signature, click the check box to disable this option.

Fig. 17.12
The Reply to Group window is where you respond to someone who has written a newsgroup message.

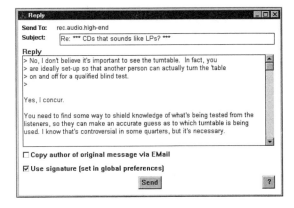

About cross-posting

Although cross-posting the same message to different newsgroups isn't always a good idea, some of the messages to which you respond are already posted in more than once place. If you respond to any of these messages, you also see a message that your reply will also be posted in another newsgroup. There is nothing you can do to change the route of the response, so just click the OK button.

How to post a newsgroup message

If you are not responding to a message in a particular thread and you want to create a new topic, click the Send New Message icon at the top of a message window. This action brings up a blank message window, into which you can insert the topic and then the body of your message.

After you've finished reading the messages in your selected newsgroup and responding to the ones that interest you, click the Mark All Read icon at the top of the directory of available messages. That way you won't be presented with the same list of messages the next time you visit your newsgroup.

Q&A *Help! The message I posted still hasn't shown up in the newsgroup I sent it to. What's wrong? Where did it go?*

The Internet e-mail and messages you send must pass through a number of computer networks before they make their way to your newsgroup, or to the recipient of your message. Your message can sometimes get to the other side of the world in a matter of minutes, yet other times it may take a day or two to arrive. This is to be expected, and you should be patient and give the message some time. In very few cases, a message does get lost in cyberspace, but because the systems are quite reliable that doesn't happen very often.

 **When you are in the Read My Newsgroups window, before you** actually select an individual newsgroup to browse through, using the Update All As Read icon marks all messages in all the discussion groups on your list as having been read. Be careful when you choose this option; otherwise, none of the messages in those newsgroups will be available for reading unless you select the List All option. The latter option forces you to plow through literally thousands of messages (even ones you've read before).

 Help! I'm getting offensive messages from the Internet. What do I do?

America Online's Terms of Service, of course, do not apply to members of other services (although, they do govern your conduct on the Internet, so be careful). But if you get objectionable or threatening material, you often do have a way to protect yourself. The easiest way to deal with this situation is to check the sender's return address, especially at the domain or location of the service that person is using (such as @<service>.com).

If you received the material as e-mail, you can use AOL's forward feature to send the offensive message in e-mail form directly to the folks who administer that service—in this case, it would be postmaster@<service>.com. If the material was contained in a message posted in an Internet newsgroup, select the entire message, choose Edit, Copy, and insert the message into the body of an e-mail form using the Edit, Paste command, along with your own request that the problem be dealt with.

Many Internet-based services have rules and regulations for their users, and they do not consider such conduct any more acceptable than you do. They will act against that member in accordance with the rules covering their service.

Some services, I hasten to add, may not object to a message unless its content indicates a possible illegal act. Over the years, I've encountered a very few Internet-only services who care only if the messages aren't being received, not what's contained in the messages.

If the newsgroup has no unread messages

If you've read all the messages in a newsgroup and closed the message window, and then you decide you want to add a message of your own, here's what to do:

1 Double-click the directory listing for that newsgroup, which brings up a sequence of two messages, shown in figure 17.13 and figure 17.14. You must click the OK button of the first message to see the second.

Fig. 17.13
You're notified that no unread messages are available.

Fig. 17.14
Decide whether you want to post a new message.

2 If you want to add a new message of your own, click the OK button, which brings up a standard blank newsgroup message window.

3 If you decide not to prepare that message, click the Cancel button.

Let AOL record your keystrokes

You don't have to manually log on to read and send newsgroup messages. There's another way, and it involves using AOL's FlashSession feature. When you've added newsgroups to the material that you want to send and receive during your automatic log-ons, there's one more thing you want to do. And that is to choose the newsgroups you want to include during these sessions (see fig. 17.15).

Fig. 17.15
Choose the newsgroups you want to read during your AOL FlashSessions and then add them to the list on the right of this screen.

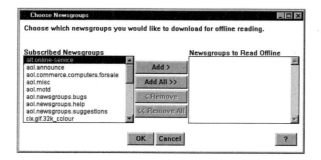

Click the Add button to add a single newsgroup to the list. If you want to include them all (and I'd think carefully about that if you want to avoid being overwhelmed with hundreds of messages in your mailbox), click on the Add All button instead.

Secrets of AOL's File Grabber

Some newsgroup messages are too large to display in a message window. Others consist of a file rather than a message. In either case, AOL's File Grabber feature will sort this all out for you. When you open such a message window, you'll get the message shown in figure 17.16.

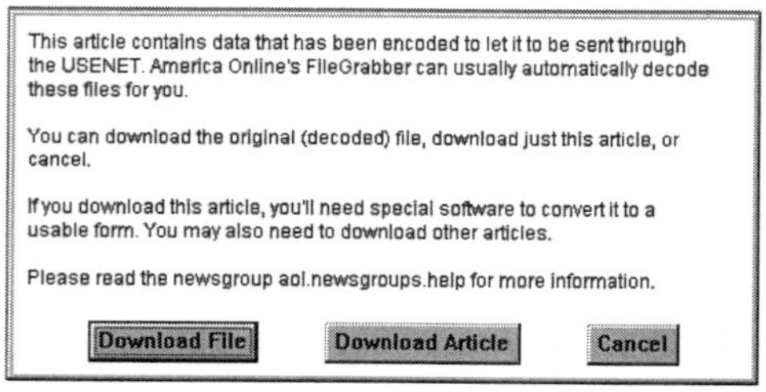

Fig. 17.16
The message is too long, or it consists of a file rather a message. What action should you take? Click Download Now.

When you click the Download Now button, AOL's File Grabber will work behind the scenes to translate the file to its original form. Then you'll get a dialog box asking to where you'd like the file to be downloaded. The rest of the process is more or less the same as downloading a file from AOL's regular software libraries.

TIP **You can rate your favorite newsgroups, using AOL's Newsgroup** Scoop area (*Keyword:* **Scoop**). Just provide a review of the ones you like in the Scoop message window and send it on its way. Each week, the Scoop staff will go over the member reviews they get, and give three of them a complete write-up. Ratings are done by Content, Traffic, Heat Index (from Tea to Lava) and Camp Value.

A favorite newsgroup list

Literally thousands of Internet newsgroups are active at any one time. New ones are always being introduced, and others are being discontinued. When you first visit AOL's Newsgroups area, you'll find a list of several newsgroups automatically included in your list (some of them are oriented toward educating you further about Internet practices). Over time, you can change or add to this list.

18

Unmasking the World Wide Web

In this chapter:

- What a Web page is made of

- How to use AOL's Web browser

- How to surf the Web

- Common sense solutions to common problems

The World Wide Web is hot news now. Let's see what it's all about and how it relates to America Online. . . . . >

If you've read about the Internet in previous chapters, you've no doubt discovered it's an exciting and sometimes intimidating place to visit. Except for AOL's fancy graphic windows, everything on the global information superhighway is text-based. Even graphic files consist simply of text, unless you download them or run them through one of those handy decoder programs.

The World Wide Web (often simply referred to as the Web, or WWW) is something different. It adds full-color pictures, and sometimes sound, to the otherwise drab Internet interface, which explains why Web access is becoming one of the fastest growing Internet services. The Web is not only a constant source of information about a huge range of subjects, but also an area where you can observe the creative efforts of a growing number of computer artists.

To understand how the Web works, I want to describe something that's near and dear to most of you. It's your Windows 95 Help menu (see fig. 18.1). And it's made up of pages of information that you are able to access just by clicking an underlined title, which allows you to zoom right to the article linked to that title.

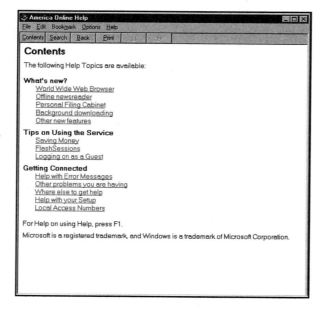

Fig. 18.1
Your own Windows 95 help screens give you a taste of navigating through the World Wide Web. Just click on a few titles on the Contents screen and see what I'm getting at.

Chapter 18 Unmasking the World Wide Web — **281**

Although the technique isn't terribly different, when you access a page on the World Wide Web (the equivalent of moving from one information screen to another in your Help menu), you are not necessarily moving to another part of a single file, but often to another item, located on another computer, in another part of the world. Furthermore, the entire process is transparent; you never see the complex, sometimes convoluted path the data must travel before it reaches your PC.

Hello, Web site!

Before we take apart a Web page, let's visit one. And that requires opening America Online's browser, which, unlike other online services, is a part of your AOL software. To get to the World Wide Web, all you need is a keyword—WWW.

> **66** *Plain English, please!*
>
> A **browser** is an application that can locate documents on the World Wide Web. These documents, known as pages, are retrieved by the browser program, which then translates them into a form that's readable by your computer. **99**

Hold on a second—something's missing!

You're right (caught me in the act!). There's one more thing you may need the first time you use your Windows AOL software to surf the World Wide Web, and that's a little addition that provides WWW features (see fig. 18.2).

CAUTION In order to access AOL's **WWW** features, you need version 2.5 or later of AOL's software. If you have an older version, you can download the latest one from AOL's free Upgrade area (*keyword:* **Upgrade**). Remember that selecting the Download Now option to retrieve software in a free area keeps you in that area, so your download is free.

Fig. 18.2
Yes, you have to download an update to your AOL software the first time you try to access the World Wide Web.

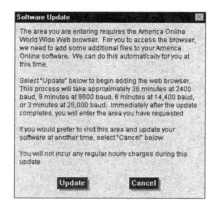

Just click the Update button to start the process of transferring the WWW software to your computer.

Once you've downloaded the software update (and how long it takes depends on the speed of your connection to AOL), you'll be ready to surf the Web in earnest. Your first stop on the Information Superhighway will be AOL's own home or introductory page (see fig. 18.3).

Fig. 18.3
AOL's home page on the World Wide Web has a huge number of resources that are just a mouse click away.

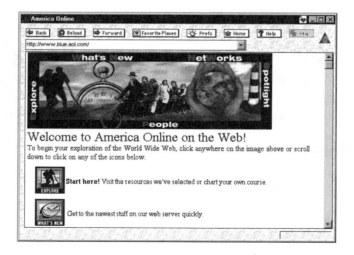

How to get from here to there

Traveling around AOL's home page is just a matter of clicking once on the labeled icon or on an underlined title. Either step will magically transport you to another WWW page that's linked to that site.

Chapter 18 *Unmasking the World Wide Web* **283**

This process of moving from one page to another is done behind the scenes. AOL's WWW browser will look up another page or site address, known as its URL.

 Plain English, please!

> **URL** is short for **Uniform Resource Locator**. The URL information you enter is a shortcut for the location of the site. Here's the format of a typical URL (which happens to be the AOL home page we've just connected to):
> **http://www.blue.aol.com**

Before going any further, let's dissect that URL to see what it's made of:

- The letters http are short for Hypertext Transfer Protocol, which is the technique developed by the architects of the World Wide Web to locate and access Web sites.

- The colon (:) and the two slashes (//) inform the software that the information that follows is the actual Internet address of the site being accessed (www stands for World Wide Web).

- The last extension added to this particular Web site, .com, identifies it as a commercial enterprise. If the extension is .edu, it's an educational institution. You'll find more information about Internet site naming conventions in chapter 15, "The Internet Connection."

 **Be sure to enter the exact URL information shown to visit one of these sites.** Even a single incorrect character will result in failure. The author and publisher are not responsible for errors, however, so if you cannot find a particular site using the information provided in this and the next chapter, you can contact that source directly for additional assistance or use one of the search tools described in this chapter for up-to-date information.

If you want to visit another Web site, simply enter the URL or site address in the Current URL list field, or use AOL's keyword feature (Ctrl+K) and enter a site address as the place to which you want to go.

Then press Enter and AOL's Web browser will attempt to access the site. If the browser is successful at finding the site (and usually it is), the image of the new site will begin to appear on your PC's screen in just a moment or two. It will always take a little while for the entire page to be displayed, depending on the speed of your AOL connection.

Q&A Why can't I connect to a site?

To connect to a Web site on your PC, it isn't enough to be running your AOL software. You must also be logged on to AOL. If you log off, get disconnected, or if AOL's Internet access is interrupted, you won't be able to access the site you've selected.

If you are logged on when you cannot access a site, try logging off and on again. If the problem continues, you might want to try using the World Wide Web at a later time. It's always possible that the site's server isn't running or has crashed (just like your PC may do sometimes).

Q&A Why does it take so long for Web images to appear on my computer's screen, especially compared to the images I see on AOL?

There are a couple of reasons. First of all, the images retrieved by AOL's Web browser are sent from a remote computer, and the transmission process is not as efficient as it would be on AOL's host computers.

Also, the speed at which you connect to AOL is a major factor in the time it takes for a Web page's images to appear. At the very least, you need a 14,400 bps modem and 14,400 bps AOL connection to get adequate speed on the World Wide Web. The new generation of V.34 (28,800 bps) modems are worth considering if there's an AOLNet access number in your city. If you are limited to a 9600 bps modem or access number or something slower, my suggestion is that you use the World Wide Web feature judiciously because you will be disappointed with its performance.

Let's get past that Home Page

Once you've hooked up to a Web site's home page, you can easily navigate to other pages by clicking an icon or underlined text. You need not know the URL to locate the additional pages—that's the beauty of those behind-the-scenes links used by the browser to move from one page to another.

TIP You can navigate directly to a specific Web page other than a home page if you know its full URL (including the name of the actual page). For example, **http://www.blue.aol.com/preview/welcome.html** accesses AOL's own Web site, and the part of the address following the com/ takes you to a specific page at that site.

A fast way to get there again

If you want to return to a WWW site again and again, you'll want to use AOL's Favorite Places feature to store the information on how to get to the site. That keeps it just a click away.

Click the Favorite Places icon at the right side of the WWW site's window (that little heart-shaped icon). You'll get a message on your PC's screen that the site has been added to your Favorite Places listing (see fig. 18.4).

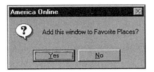

Fig. 18.4
AOL will let you know when you've added a site to your Favorite Places listings.

From here on, just click the Favorite Places button at the top of your WWW document window. Your personal listing will appear in just a moment (see fig. 18.5). Then double click on the site's name and you're in.

Fig. 18.5
Here's my list of Favorite Places. You'll build up one of your own as you become used to navigating AOL's highways and biways.

What do all those fancy buttons mean?

The rectangular buttons at the top of the Web document window let you control which pages are displayed, and a few other features. Here's what they do (from left to right):

- **Back.** Click to return to the previous page.
- **Reload.** Click to reload the current Web page onto the program's document window. You may have to use this option if a transmission problem prevents the page from displaying properly.

• **Forward.** Click to go to the next page.

 • **Favorite Places.** Click to bring up the listing of your Favorite Places, for quick access to the WWW sites and other areas you want to return to.

 • **Preferences.** Click to bring up a window showing your settings for AOL's Web browser. You can pretty much leave the settings as they are for normal use (and play with them at your leisure).

 • **Home.** Click to return to AOL's home page.

 • **Help.** Click to bring up AOL's online assistance.

 • **Stop.** Click if you want to halt the process of retrieving a Web page (in case you change your mind and don't want to wait till the page finishes displaying).

TIP **AOL's Windows Web browser will transparently go to FTP or Gopher sites that are directly accessed through a WWW site.** You won't have to enter a separate site address to access them. All that's necessary is to click a picture or underlined text—the same technique you use to go to another WWW page. When you choose a file to download via FTP from a Web site, you'll see a progress display window showing the status of your file download, similar to the one you see when you download software via AOL's regular software.

Secrets of speeding up Web access

Under any circumstances, the World Wide Web can tax the fastest computer's CPU with its roster of photos, sounds, and animation. As convenient and useful as WWW access is, don't expect speedy performance. Sometimes, heavy network traffic will slow image displays to a crawl, and there's nothing you can do about it—other than trying to log on to AOL at a different time or using a different access number. But there are ways to make AOL's Web software perform better. Here are a few considerations:

- Get a faster modem.

- Find a faster access number. Use keyword Access to get a list of connection numbers. Because AOL's new AOLNet network, with 28,800 bps access, is expanding, you'll want to check occasionally for newer phone connection choices.

- Get a faster computer. It goes without saying that PCs are getting faster and cheaper. If you have an older model, it might be time to look at a new computer equipped with a Pentium microprocessor. These new models can outperform older models by a huge factor.

- Get more RAM. Windows 95 will run with 8MB of RAM, but it won't give your programs much elbow room before information has to be swapped to your hard drive (which can bring things down to a crawl). If you want to use multimedia features such as the World Wide Web, upgrading to 16MB RAM, minimum, is a good idea.

- Turn off the option to show graphics. This choice is available as part of your Graphics preferences, which is represented by an icon that you can select from the Personal Choices window (*Keyword*: **Personal Choices**). It's a last resort, and is recommended only if you have serious performance problems viewing graphics, but it's worth a try.

TIP **Some AOL departments offer access to a Web site by double** clicking a directory listing or clicking once on an icon. The areas that offer this capability usually have an icon labeled Top Internet Sites or something similar. You can also access a WWW site during your online session by using Ctrl+K to bring up the keyword window, and entering the URL as the keyword. Once you click Go, the WWW browser will be opened (if necessary), and you'll be magically transported directly to that site.

And that's not all

The World Wide Web provides a ripe area for you to explore a huge range of subjects. Now that you've seen just how easy it is to use AOL's WWW browser features, you can go off on your own and travel across the world without ever leaving the comfort of your personal computer's screen. In the next chapter, I'll introduce you to a few of my favorite Web sites, which you can add to your list of Favorite Places, or use as a jumping off point to find more cool places to explore.

19

Getting Started on the Web

● **In this chapter:**

- **About popular computer-related Web sites**

- **About some of the coolest Web pages around**

- **A quick way to search for additional Web sites**

- **And some more troubleshooting tips**

Now that you know how to get on the World Wide Web, you'll want to find some fun places to visit while you're there . . . ❯

In the last chapter, I unmasked some of the elements of the World Wide Web. I explained how you can install and use AOL's WWW browser to access all those color sites. A few popular World Wide Web sites were described to illustrate how particular features of the software are used.

There are literally thousands of sites from which to choose on the World Wide Web, covering every conceivable category—from your favorite forms of entertainment to areas where you can learn about the latest products from your favorite computer manufacturer. This chapter is devoted to listing just a few of the popular Web sites along with their URLs (locations). You can easily visit these sites by entering the URL information (precisely as shown) in AOL's Web browser (or just by a keyword). You navigate through these sites by clicking the underlined titles or descriptions, which provide quick access to the named areas.

TIP **Some Web sites offer the ability to display material in text or** graphic form. If you don't have a 14,400 bps or faster modem (and an AOL connection to match that speed), choose the text option where possible to improve performance and reduce the time it takes for material to appear on your computer.

CAUTION **To visit one of the WWW sites described in this chapter, be sure to** enter the exact URL (Web site address) information shown. Even a single incorrect character will result in failure to access these locations. The author and publisher are not responsible for errors, however, so if you cannot find a particular site using the information provided, you can contact that source directly for additional assistance or use the Yahoo search site, described at the end of this chapter, for up-to-date information.

Just a few favorite computing sites (and some other good stuff)

Since I started surfing the Web, I've built up a list of sites I like to revisit often. I'm going to share a few of those locations with you (plus a few others some friends have suggested). The selections that follow were chosen arbitrarily and are only meant as a guide to get you started. No doubt, you'll find others equally compelling during your online travels.

IBM

URL address: **http://www.ibm.com/**

IBM's Web site (see fig. 19.1), or at least the version that was used when this book was written, is designed to look like the front page of a company magazine. The icons show a list of features, followed by headlines of the top company news.

Fig. 19.1
IBM's Web site offers stories about the company's activities, as well as product and technical information.

Remember that visiting a Web site doesn't just involve reading text and looking at pretty pictures. It represents a valuable resource for software, and you might actually find that downloading from a Web site seems easier than rummaging through various folders or directories to locate the files you want.

Help! How can I get to the World Wide Web sites you describe in this book?

The Web is a fluid place, and sites are always being added, removed, and changed. If a site address shown in this book is no longer correct, use the Yahoo search site (URL: **http://www.yahoo.com/**), described at the end of this chapter, to locate a site's correct URL.

Microsoft

URL address: **http://www.microsoft.com**

Microsoft's Web site is valuable to both Mac and PC users because Microsoft's software is so popular on both computing platforms. You'll find this site (see fig. 19.2) a helpful resource for further information about both Windows-related issues and matters concerning the publisher's popular productivity software, such as Excel and Word.

Fig. 19.2
Microsoft's Web site offers support and information on their products.

Novell, Inc.

URL address: **http://www.novell.com**

Novell (see fig. 19.3) is the well-known publisher of networking software for both the PCs and Macs. Novell is also the publisher of WordPerfect, which is available in versions for DOS, Mac, and Windows. The company's Web site takes full advantage of the terrific graphics you can create on the World Wide Web.

Fig. 19.3
Pay a visit to Novell's Internet-based support facility.

Software Ventures Corporation

URL address: **http://www.svcdudes.com/**

Software Ventures (see fig. 19.4) is a publisher of telecommunications software for both the Windows and Macintosh environments. The publisher's Web site is designed to offer helpful technical information, updates for modem drivers and other utilities needed by the program, and ways to interact with the publisher to help you solve your own telecommunications problems.

Fig. 19.4
Get support for telecommunications software from Software Ventures.

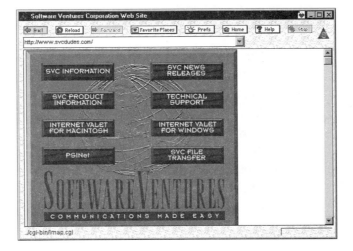

Ziff-Davis

URL address: **http://www.ziff.com**

Many of you are probably regular readers of some of the various Ziff-Davis computer magazines, such as PC User, MacUser, PC Week and MacWeek (see fig. 19.5). The publisher's Web site offers a colorful repository of the latest material from all of these publications. If you want to read more about the newest software from Microsoft or a hot announcement about a new computer from Compaq, navigate through the Ziff-Davis site.

Fig. 19.5
The popular Web site run by Ziff-Davis offers text from many of their computer magazines and software for you to download.

The Howard Stern Show

URL address: **http://krishna.cs.umd.edu/stern/**

What can you say about one of the most controversial figures in broadcasting? Howard Stern (see fig. 19.6), the self-proclaimed King of All Media, has been praised and vilified (sometimes by the same people at roughly the same times) for a radio show that can be irritating, controversial, exciting, funny, or none of the above. This site is run by Howard's fans to report on his activities and those of his sidekicks.

Fig. 19.6
Where radio has never gone before: *The Howard Stern Show.*

Star Trek: Voyager

URL address: **http://voyager.paramount.com/**

Star Trek: Voyager's Web site offers information about past episodes, the cast and crew, and the strange and wonderful beings who appeared on the show. It also enables you to experience some of the finest moments of the program, and it offers insights into new developments (such as possible movie projects). The site shown here, by the way, is one of several devoted to various *Star Trek* programs.

Fig. 19.7
Star Trek: Voyager's holographic doctor takes you on a tour of this Web site. You access this page by clicking the Voyager picture on the home page.

The Young and the Restless

URL address: **http://www.digimark.net/wow/yr/**

The plot of the typical television soap opera is often difficult to describe in a pithy paragraph or two, so I won't even try. *The Young and the Restless* (see fig. 19.8) has been on the air for more than 20 years. It involves the lives of dozens of characters whose activities intermingle in many related (and sometimes unrelated) story lines. At this site, you'll find a complete description of some of the most popular story lines, learn about the doings of your favorite characters, and locate descriptions about what you might expect in future shows.

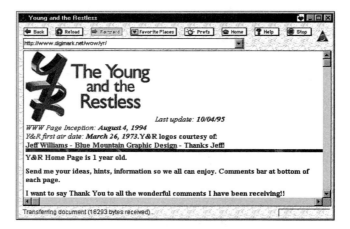

Fig. 19.8
Fans of *The Young and the Restless* will find a lot to read about here.

The X-Files

URL address: **http://www.rutgers.edu/x-files.html**

The Fox television program, *The X-Files* (see fig. 19.9), has garnered a level of interest that is reminiscent of *Star Trek* fandom. The show details the exploits of two FBI agents who choose to investigate weird or unusual cases that might involve UFO visitation or psychic phenomena (ghosts and things that go bump in the night). This Web page describes everything from show plots to background information on the stars of the program.

Fig. 19.9
Learn about the most popular episodes of The *X-Files* and even download a sound file that contains the show's theme.

The Central Intelligence Agency

URL address: **http://www.ODCI.gov**

What's this? A Web site devoted to the CIA? You won't find any top-secret information here, but you will find online publications about the agency's mission and place in the world (see fig. 19.10). One useful resource is the Factbook on Intelligence, which you can read while visiting this Web site. It tells of the CIA's early history, provides a basic overview of its purpose in the world, and informs you about the setup of its headquarters—or at least as much as can be described without compromising national security. The Factbook is indexed by topic, and just clicking the appropriate item brings up additional information. One topic worth reading about is entitled "Key Events in CIA's History."

Fig. 19.10
Learn about the CIA by visiting its Web site.

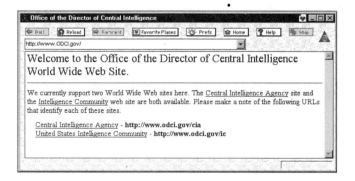

Finding Web sites on your own

The above selections are but a few of thousands of Web sites that can be found across the world. The question is, How do you find a particular site or find out if a particular business or educational concern has a Web site?

Fortunately, this is becoming easier to do because more and more representatives of such firms include their URL on their business cards and stationery. You also find WWW listings in popular magazines and newspapers. Press releases announcing new products or services will also mention the Web site address somewhere in the text.

If you cannot easily find the name of a site, you'll want to have a look at the search tools I'm about to describe.

Q&A *Why do I get a Fatal Error message when I try to access a WWW page?*

Take heart: The message doesn't mean your PC has crashed, or that you have encountered a really serious problem.

Most of the time, you get that error when the page you are trying to reach isn't available, or you've entered the URL site address information incorrectly. When you get this message, recheck the URL and make sure that every character is accurately entered. Remember, there are no word spaces, for example, in an URL. If you've confirmed that the URL is correct, you might want to recheck the source from which you got that site location to make sure the address hasn't changed. Or maybe you should just try again. Sometimes network glitches (or simply a system problem on the site's own server) along the Internet will make a site easily available one day, and unavailable the next.

Paying a visit to Yahoo

URL address: **http://www.yahoo.com**

If you want a convenient way to look up additional sites that you might want to visit, pay a visit to the Yahoo Web site (see fig. 19.11).

Fig. 19.11
You can use Yahoo to search through a directory of thousands of Web sites.

You'll find using Yahoo's Web facility similar to searching for data on America Online. If you want to find sites dealing with a specific topic, simply click the underlined item representing the category, or click the Search tool (see fig. 19.12). After you find the area that you want to visit, click the underlined reference to go directly to that site.

Not just a casual pursuit

The Yahoo search site is a classic case of a hobby blooming into a real business. It was started by two undergraduate students, David Filo and Jerry Yang. They created the search database for their own personal use so they could keep tabs on their favorite Internet sites.

The site has mushroomed into a huge Internet searching facility that tracks literally thousands of Internet sites worldwide. Also, it has corporate sponsors, which is why you'll see ads displayed on various Yahoo pages. Although the name, Yahoo, is reported to stand for Yet Another Hierarchical Officious Oracle, Filo and Yang maintain that they chose the name because they regard themselves as yahoos.

The tale of the creation of Yahoo has drawn the attention of the national news media. Stories about it have appeared in *USA Today* and other newspapers.

Fig. 19.12
This is an efficient way to search for other Web sites that might warrant further exploration.

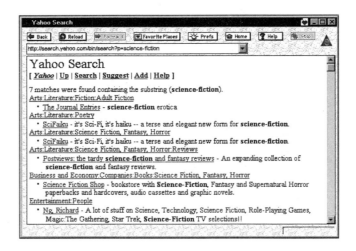

More search tools

America Online provides links to other popular WWW search tools at its own site, which you can reach via the URL address: **http://www.blue.aol.com/preview/search.html**. When you enter that site address (or just choose the Search icon from AOL's regular Preview page), you'll see the selections shown in figure 19.13.

Fig. 19.13
AOL offers a selection of Web sites that provides an extensive range of search tools.

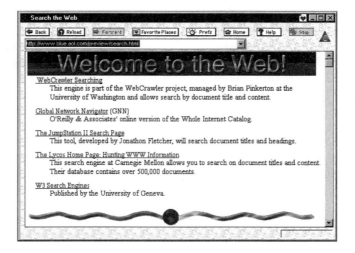

Chapter 19 *Getting Started on the Web* **301**

Clicking each of the items shown on this page will provide a different tool for seeking information on the Internet.

Here's a quick summary of what's offered at these sites:

- WebCrawler Searching. This site allows you to locate a specific site by its name and topic. It also provides a Top 25 Sites listing and helpful advice on how to locate sites that may interest you. (AOL was so impressed with this search tool, by the way, that they bought the product.)

- Global Network Navigator. This is the online version of The Whole Internet Catalog, and it lists a large number of sites by subject. By clicking on a subject, you get a list of sites meeting that criteria. The next step, clicking on the site's name, gets you a one-paragraph description and the option to go right to that site to see it for yourself.

- JumpStation II Front Page. Here's another valuable search tool that helps you quickly locate sites that may interest you. Before you give it a try, you'll want to review some of its text documents to learn all about the search procedures.

- The Lycos Home Page. Clicking on this entry takes you to Carnegie-Mellon University's Web site, which lets you search a database of over 500,000 documents.

- W3 Search Engines. This may be the best search tool in AOL's list. It gathers a number of search engines into one handy interface, listing the most popular sites, a text entry field, and a Submit (request) button that lets you access that particular search function to locate the site or information you seek. The illustration shown here (see fig. 19.14) depicts but a few of the search functions you can access from this site.

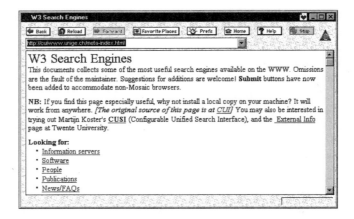

Fig. 19.14
W3 Search Engines provide a big selection of search tools to help you locate the information you want.

Do it your way

The World Wide Web can be a useful resource where you'll spend many, many enjoyable hours learning more about your favorite subjects, locating software updates, or discovering ways to use your computer more effectively. Its bright, colorful interface represents the latest, best, and perhaps easiest-to-use Internet resource. As you continue to use AOL's Web browser, you'll locate many additional sites you'll want to add to your list of favorites.

How to make your own WWW page the easy way

Keyword: **My Home Page** or **Personal Publisher**

If you want to get really involved in making your own Web pages, AOL has a quick solution for you. It's called My Home Page. It's a place where you can easily assemble the text and pictures to make your own WWW page, and then have it made available to other AOL members (or to the entire Internet if you prefer). It will give color and depth to your online profile, so it's definitely worth checking out.

Let's build a page from scratch (mine) and see how easy it is. In order to start the process, let's bring up AOL's My Home Page construction area (which is also called Personal Publisher, as shown in fig. 19.15).

Fig. 19.15
AOL's Personal Publisher area easily guides you through the process of making your own WWW page.

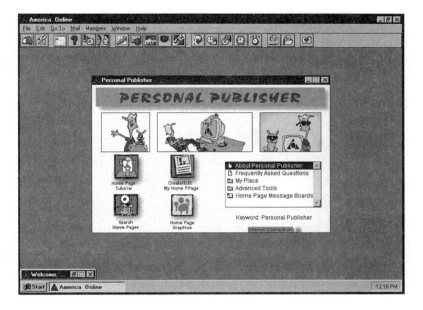

First, the ingredients for our stew

Your AOL web page begins with your online profile. If you haven't created one yet, you'll want to check out chapter 4, "The Easy Way to Meet People Online," where I take you through the process. Once your profile is created, you can use that as the foundation of your personal web page.

With your profile finished, you click the Create/Edit My Home Page icon in the Personal Publisher area (see fig. 19.16), and begin to assemble the building blocks.

 TIP **If you reach a sticking point in your WWW page creation process,** just click the Tutorial or Help icons that are sprinkled about various places of the page creation area, and you'll get additional assistance.

Fig. 19.16
Your personal WWW page uses your online profile as the first ingredient.

The creation page is long, so you'll have to scroll through it to see all of its elements (I've only shown the top portion in fig. 19.16). At this point, you can modify your online profile if you find it doesn't suit you by entering new text in the boxes that apply to each category of the profile. You'll also be presented with the choice of whether to make it available just to other AOL members, or as a WWW page that's accessible throughout the Internet.

Of course, text is only the starting point with a WWW page. In order to make it sparkle, you need to add pictures, too. If you want to provide a more colorful Web page, scroll to the bottom of the window, and click the Add button.

Fig. 19.17
To include additional elements in your Web page, click the Add icon at the bottom of the Create/Edit window.

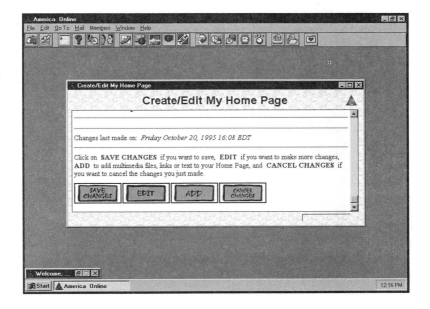

Here's some items you may want to include:

- Web links. You enter the URL of your favorite Web sites and they'll be added to your home page.

- Graphics. You can transfer photos and drawings (in GIF and JPEG formats). In addition to graphics you may have on hand, you can find some useful clipart by clicking the Home Page Graphics icon in AOL's Personal Publisher area.

- Text. You can add text captions to the photos, and provide information about you, your family, your philosophy of life, your business. You can write about anything you think would interest AOL's members or the Internet at large, so long as you keep it in good taste (within the bounds of AOL's Terms of Service).

Getting to the finish line

Once you've put all of the pieces of your WWW page together, you can save your changes (see fig 19.18).

Fig. 19.18
Success at last! Here's the URL of your own Web page, ready to be viewed by your friends on AOL.

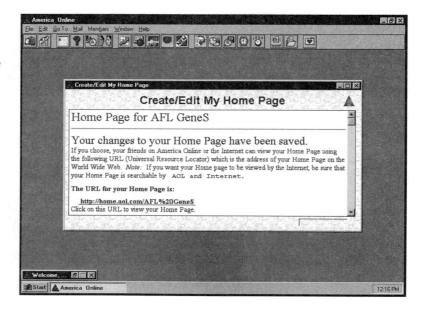

You can update your Web page whenever you like, of course. As you continue to look over your page (or receive comments from your friends on AOL), you may find ways to make it better.

The WWW page you make on AOL is simple and highly structured. If you are truly interested in exploring the possibilities of making Web pages, you may want to check out software that can make an HTML document. Some programs are add-ons to existing desktop publishing or word processing software. Other programs take those documents and add the appropriate information so they can be used for a Web page. From time to time, AOL offers for download the WWW publishing tools from its NaviSoft division. You can use the keyword *NaviSoft* to find the latest version of their NaviPress program.

 Plain English, please!

> **HTML** stands for hypertext markup language, and it's the WWW technique of tagging or identifying the elements of a document containing graphics and text so that it can be translated to a Web page.

How to find AOL member home pages

To view the page you've created for yourself, or access one belonging to another member, use this **URL: http://home.aol.com/<screen name>**.

If you're not sure whether a member has such a page, use this URL: **http:// home. aol.com/**. You'll bring up a document window in which you can enter the screen name of the person whose page you're trying to find.

The steps I've outlined above will help you become your own publisher on the World Wide Web. It's an exciting new prospect that you'll want to check out further. I know I'll be working over my WWW page from time to time. If you have the chance, check it out and tell me what you think about it.

Index

A

abbreviations, 69
Academic Assistance
Center, 184
access numbers
changing, 28
troubleshooting, 56-57
accessing
artwork maps, 196
files, downloading,
172-173
Hollywood forum, 100
Internet (children), 111
newsgroups (UseNet
newsgroups), 266-267
World Wide Web
(WWW), speeding up,
286-287
accounts
billing, 17-18
deleting, 19
ordering, 16-18
passwords, 16, 19
registration number, 16
troubleshooting, 116
adding newsgroup
messages, 275
addresses, 18-20
Address Book,
75, 80-81
entering, 80-81
e-mail, 74
Internet, 247-249
Afterwards Cafe forum,
189
airlines
Aviation forum,
134-135
prices, 224-225

America Online
Highlights icon, 23-24
ancestry (Genealogy
Club forum), 131
animals (Pet Care
forum), 134
AOL (America Online)
accounts
billing, 17-18
deleting, 19
ordering, 16-18
passwords, 16, 19
registration
numbers, 16
addresses, 18-20
connecting to, 15-16
history of, 10
Internet, connecting to,
243
modem profiles, 14
starting, 21-23
store, 207-210
TOS (Terms of
Service), 20, 61
Welcome screen, 42
AOL software
installing, 11-15
ordering, 12
requirements, 11
applications, launching,
27
areas (free), 21
Astronomy Club forum,
129
Atlantic Monthly, 198
attachments (defined),
76

Audio/Video forum,
137-138
auditoriums (Center
Stage Auditoriums),
63-65
automobiles
(*Car & Driver*), 137
AutoVantage forum,
210-212
joining, 211-212
Aviation forum, 134-135

B

Baby Boomers forum,
127
BackPacker, 228-229
Barrons Booknotes
forum, 180
Bed & Breakfast USA
forum, 229
Better Health &
Medical forum, 133
billing, 17-18
binary downloads,
blocking, 115
BITNET network
(defined), 250
blocking
binary downloads, 115
expert add
newsgroups, 115
instant messages, 112
newsgroups, 115
rooms, 112
conference, 112
members, 112
Book Bestsellers forum,
107

310   *books*

books
Address Book,
75, 80-81
Book Bestsellers, 107
Bookstore forum,
213-214
**Bookstore forum,
213-214**
**brochures (child safety
brochure), 122-124**
browsers (defined), 281
**Business news forum,
194-195**

C

C-SPAN, 182
**call waiting, turning
on/off, 15, 29**
**Capital Connection
forum, 130**
Car & Driver, **137**
Career Center, 181
**Cartoon Network
forum, 119**
**Center Stage
Auditorium, 63-65**
chats
abbreviations, 69
Kids Connection,
120-121
rules, 121-122
starting, 122
logs, 65
closing, 66
recording, 65-66
session logs, 65
system logs, 91
protocol, 91
rooms, 61-62
children, 111-113
logs, 65
Travel Cafe, 228
shorthand, 69-71
windows, 90-91
**Check Mail I've Read
command (Mail
menu), 79**
Chicago forum, 139
Chicago Tribune,
139-140

children
Kids Only department,
50, 117
Cartoon Network
forum, 119
Disney Adventures,
118
Games &
Computers, 120
Kids Connection,
120-122
*Tomorrow's
Morning* forum,
119-120
note to parents, 116
Parental Controls
(setting preferences),
114-116
safety online
child safety
brochure, 122-124
face-to-face
meetings, 110
harassment, 111
inappropriate
material, 110
internet access, 111,
113-114, 238
National Parenting
Center, 123-124
Parents'
Information
Network, 122-123
TOS (Terms of
Service), 113
**CIA (Central
Intelligence Agency)
web site, 297**
**cities (Chicago forum),
139**
**Classifieds forum,
217-218**
closing logs, 66
**Clubs & Interests
department, 126**
Astronomy Club, 129
Audio/Video forum,
137-138
Aviation forum,
134-135

Baby Boomers forum,
127
Better Health &
Medical forum, 133
Capital Connection,
130
Car & Driver, 137
Chicago, 139
Chicago Tribune,
139-140
Consumer Electronics,
138
Cooking Club, 129
Environmental forum,
133
Exchange forum, 130
Genealogy Club, 131
Issues in Mental
Health, 133
Mercury Center,
140-141
Military & Vets Club,
135
National Multiple
Sclerosis Society
forum, 128
National Space Society,
135-136
Network Earth, 133
New York Times,
141-142
Pet Care forum, 134
Photography forum,
131
Religion & Ethics
forum, 128
*San Jose Mercury
News*, 141
Science Fiction &
Fantasy, 131-132
SeniorNet forum, 128
Star Trek Club, 132
TicketMaster, 139
**CNN Newsroom forum,
185**
**College Board forum,
185**
**colleges (Electronic
University Network
forum), 186**

Columnists & Features forum, 199
commands
  Edit menu
    Copy, 274
    Paste, 274
    Show Tools, 33
  File menu
    Logging, 65
    Logs, 91
    Open, 67
    Print, 80
    Save, 65
    Save As, 80
  Mail menu
    Check Mail I've Read, 79
    Edit Address Book, 81
    FlashSessions, 82
    Read Incoming Mail, 80
  Members menu
    Edit Your Online Profile, 55
    Send Instant Message, 84
    Set Preferences, 31
  Start menu (Programs), 27
commercial software, 173-174
companies, finding, 158
compressing
  defined, 78
  files, undoing, 172-173
Compton's NewMedia learning center, 180-181
Computer Express forum, 214-215
computers
  Applications forum, 146
  Communications forum, 147
  Computer Express forum, 214-215
  Computing department, 45

  Developers forum, 147
  DOS forum, 148
  Games forum, 149
  Graphics forum, 149
  Home Office Computing, 155
  HomePC, 155
  Mobile Office Online, 156
  Music & Sound forum, 151
  OS/2 forum, 152
  PC Hardware forum, 150
  PC Multimedia forum, 150
  PC World, 156
  Personal Digital Assistants forum, 152
  User Groups forum, 153
  Windows 95 forum, 154
  WordPerfect, 157
  Games & Computers, 120
  Help Desk, 146
  IBM web site, 291
  Industrial Connection (technical support), 158, 160-161
  Industry Connection, 158
  Komputer Komando forum, 186-187
  Microsoft web site, 292
  Novell web site, 292
  Software Ventures Corporation web site, 293
  Virus Information Center, 167
  Wired, 201-202
  Ziff-Davis web site, 294
Computing department, 45
concerts (TicketMaster online), 139
Conference Center, entering, 105

conferences
  chat windows, 90-91
  rooms, blocking, 112
connecting
  AOL (America Online), 15-16
  settings, changing, 27-29
  World Wide Web (WWW), troubleshooting, 284
construction area (My Home Page), 302
Consumer Electronics forum, 138
***Consumer Reports*, 199**
controls (Parental Controls), 111-113
Cooking Club forum, 129
Copy command (Edit menu), 274
Court TV, 182
Cowles/SIMBA Media Information Network, 199
Create Topic icon, 88
credit cards (ExpressNet forum), 225-226
Critics forum, 103
cross-posting messages, 273

D

decompressing files, 172-173
deleting
  accounts, 19
  e-mail, 78
demoware, 174
departments
  Clubs & Interests, 126
    Astronomy Club, 129
    Audio/Video forum, 137-138
    Aviation forum, 134-135

Baby Boomers forum, 127
Better Health & Medical forum, 133
Capital Connection, 130
Car & Driver, 137
Chicago, 139
Chicago Tribune, 139-140
Consumer Electronics, 138
Cooking Club, 129
Environmental forum, 133
Exchange, 130
Genealogy Club, 131
Issues in Mental Health, 133
Mercury Center, 140-141
Military & Vets Club, 135
National Multiple Sclerosis Society forum, 128
National Space Society, 135-136
Network Earth, 133
New York Times, 141-142
Pet Care forum, 134
Photography forum, 131
Religion & Ethics forum, 128
San Jose Mercury News, 141
Science Fiction & Fantasy, 131-132
SeniorNet forum, 128
Star Trek Club, 132
TicketMaster, 139
Computing, 45
Education, 49, 183
Academic Assistance Center, 184

Afterwards Cafe forum, 189
Electronic University Network forum, 186
Komputer Komando forum, 186-187
Library of Congress forum, 187-188
National Geographic Society forum, 188
National Public Radio Outreach forum, 188
Scholastic forum, 188-189
Entertainment, 48, 96-97
Book Bestsellers forum, 107
CNN Newsroom forum, 185
College Board forum, 185
Conference Center, 105
Critics forum, 103
Federation, 105
Grateful Dead forum, 102
Hollywood forum, 100
music forums, 101
MusicSpace forum, 98
PC Games forum, 104
radio forums, 99
RockNet forum, 101-102
Sports forum, 106
Sports Grandstand forum, 107
television forums, 99
What's Hot icon, 97
Kids Only, 50, 117
Cartoon Network forum, 119

Disney Adventures, 118
Games & Computers, 120
Kids Connection, 120-122
Tomorrow's Morning forum, 119-120
MarketPlace
2Market forum, 215-216
Bookstore forum, 213-214
Classifieds forum, 217-218
Computer Express forum, 214-215
flowers, 212-213
Shoppers Advantage forum, 216-217
Shoppers Express forum, 218-219
Marketplace, 47, 206
AutoVantage forum, 210-212
shopping, 219-220
Newsstand, 47-48
Personal Finance, 44
Sports, 50
Today's News, 44
Travel, 46-47, 222
airlines, 224-225
BackPacker, 228-229
Bed & Breakfast USA forum, 229
DineBase Restaurant listings forum, 229-230
EAASY SABRE, 223-224
ExpressNet forum, 225-226
Outdoor Adventures forum, 230-231
State Travel Advisories forum, 231
Travel Cafe, 228

Travel forum,
227-228
Travelers' Corner
forum, 226-227
Vacations forum,
227
dialog boxes
General Preferences,
31
Logging, 65
Network Setup, 29
Open, 66
**DineBase Restaurant
listings forum,
229-230**
Disney Adventures, **118**
**displaying messages,
262-263**
**Dolby Audio/Video
forum, 137-138**
domains (defined), 248
DOS forum, 148
**Download Manager,
170-172**
downloading
artwork,
troubleshooting,
97-98
blocking, 115
Download Manager,
170-172
files, 79, 169-170
accessing, 172-173
defined, 166
queue, 169
saving, 169-170
finish later button, 170
interrupted, 173
photographs, 67-68
software, 169-170
saving, 169-170
upgrades, 210
troubleshooting, 173

E

e-mail
addresses, 74
Address Book, 75,
80-81

attachments, 76
deleting, 78
files, downloading, 79
FlashSessions
(preferences), 82-83
forwarding, 77
ignoring, 78
Internet, 237
addresses, 247-249
file attachments,
251-252
graphic files, 252
Mail Gateway,
239-240, 246
mailboxes, 256-257
mailing lists, 252-254
receiving,
246-247, 251
returned, 250
sending, 246-250
messages
boards, 86-90
instant, 84-85
posting, 88-89
saving, 78
threading, 89-90
you have a mail
message, 77
printing, 80
reading, 77
receiving, 76-78
saving, 79-80
flashbox, 80
sending, 75-76
files, 78-79
later, 76
troubleshooting, 83
writing, 74-75
**EAASY SABRE forum,
223-224**
airlines, 224-225
weather, 224
**Edit Address Book
command
(Main menu), 81**
Edit menu commands
Copy, 274
Paste, 274
Show Tools, 33

**Edit Your Online
Profile command
(Members menu), 55**
editing
graphics tools, 33-34
photographs, 33-34
**Education department,
49, 183**
Academic Assistance
Center, 184
Afterwards Cafe forum,
189
Barrons Booknotes,
180
Career Center, 181
CNN Newsroom forum,
185
College Board forum,
185
Compton's NewMedia
learning center,
180-181
Education department,
49
Electronic University
Network forum, 186
ERIC (Educational
Resources
Information Center),
180
Komputer Komando
forum, 186-187
Library of Congress
forum, 187-188
National Geographic
Society forum, 188
National Public Radio
Outreach forum, 188
Reference Desk, 178
Scholastic forum,
188-189
Smithsonian, 182-183
thesaurus, 179-180
**Electronic University
Network forum, 186**
**electronics (Consumer
Electronics forum),
138**
engines (search), 301

314 *entering*

entering
Address Book, 80-81
Conference Center, 105
Lobby, 61
**Entertainment
department, 48, 96-97**
Book Bestsellers, 107
Federation forum, 105
games forums, 104-105
Conference Center,
105
PC games forum,
104
movie forums, 99
MusicSpace, 98
music forums, 101
Grateful Dead
forum, 102
RockNet forum,
101-102
radio forums, 99
Saturday Review, 200
Sports forum, 106
Sports Grandstand
forum, 107
television (Critics
forum), 99, 103
What's Hot icon, 97
**Environmental forum,
133**
Network Earth forum,
133
**ERIC (Educational
Resources
Information Center),
180**
ethics (Religion &
Ethics forum), 128
Exchange forum, 130
**exiting Mailing Lists,
255-256**
**Expert Add (UseNet
newsgroups),
searching, 115,
268-269**
**ExpressNet forum,
225-226**

F

**face-to-face meetings,
110**
**FAQ (Frequently Asked
Questions), 264**
**fatal error message,
298**
Favorite Places, 45, 285
Federation forum, 105
**fiction (Science Fiction
& Fantasy forum),
131-132**
File Grabber, 276-277
File menu commands
Logging, 65
Logs, 91
Open, 67
Print, 80
Save, 65
Save As, 80
files
attachments
defined, 76
Internet e-mail,
251-252
sending, 78
compressing, 78
decompressing,
172-173
downloading,
79, 169-170
accessing, 172-173
defined, 166
Download Manager,
170-172
saving, 169-170
troubleshooting, 173
e-mail, sending, 78-79
editing photographs,
33-34
File Grabber, 276-277
file search window,
167-168
ftp (file transfer
protocol), 241-242
graphics (Internet), 252
missing, 171
modem profiles, 14
queue, 169

saving text, 80
uploading, 175-176
defined, 166
process, 175-176
where to, 175
Virus Information
Center, 167
financial
Business news forum,
194-195
Personal Finance
department, 44
Worth, 203
Find New icon, 88
Find Since icon, 88
finding
companies, 158
forums (messages),
87-88
members, 60-61
newsgroups (UseNet
newsgroups), 267-268
profile members, 57-59
flaming, 264
**FlashBars (icon
listings), 34-37**
flashbox
defined, 80
e-mail, saving, 80
FlashSessions
messages, 275-276
preferences, setting,
82-83
**FlashSessions command
(Mail menu), 82**
**flowers, sending online,
212-213**
**flying (Aviation forum),
134-135**
**folders (message
boards), 88**
**food (Cooking Club
forum), 129**
forecasts
US Cities Forecasts
forum, 197
Weather news forum,
195-196

forums **315**

forums
  ancestry (Genealogy Club forum), 131
  animals (Pet Care forum), 134
  automobiles (*Car & Driver*), 137
  books
    Book Bestsellers forum, 107
    Bookstore forum, 213-214
  children
    Cartoon Network forum, 119
    Games & Computers, 120
    Tomorrow's Morning forum, 119-120
  cities (Chicago forum), 139
  clubs
    Astronomy Club forum, 129
    Baby Boomers forum, 127
    Capital Connection forum, 130
    Cooking Club forum, 129
    Exchange forum, 130
    Genealogy Club forum, 131
    Military & Vets Club forum, 135
    National Space Society forum, 135-136
    Photography forum, 131
    Science Fiction & Fantasy forum, 131-132
    Star Trek Club forum, 132
  computers, 144-145
    Computer Express forum, 214-215

    Komputer Komando forum, 186-187
    Wired, 201-202
  cooking (Cooking Club forum), 129
  education
    Academic Assistance Center, 184
    Afterwards Cafe forum, 189
    CNN Newsroom forum, 185
    College Board forum, 185
    Electronic University Network forum, 186
    Komputer Komando forum, 186-187
    Library of Congress forum, 187-188
    National Geographic Society forum, 188
    National Public Radio Outreach forum, 188
    Scholastic forum, 188-189
  electronics (Consumer Electronics forum), 138
  elements, 84-86
  entertainment, 96-97
    Car & Driver, 137
    Critics forum, 103
    Saturday Review, 200
    Sports forum, 106
  environments
    Environmental forum, 133
    Network Earth forum, 133
  ethics (Religion & Ethics forum), 128
  fiction (Science Fiction & Fantasy forum), 131-132

  financial (*Worth*), 203
  food (Cooking Club forum), 129
  games forums, 104-105
    Conference Center, 105
    Federation, 105
  PC Games forum, 104
  geography (National Geographic Society forum), 188
  governments
    Library of Congress forum, 187-188
  health
    Better Health & Medical forum, 133
    Issues in Mental Health forum, 133
    National Multiple Sclerosis Society forum, 128
  hobbies
    Astronomy Club forum, 129
    Cooking Club forum, 129
    Exchange forum, 130
    Photography forum, 131
  icons
    Create Topic, 88
    Find New, 88
    Find Since, 88
    List Messages, 88
    Read 1st Message, 88
  interests (*Woman's Day*), 202
  leisure
    Car & Driver, 137
    Saturday Review, 200
  medical (Better Health & Medical forum), 133

316 *forums*

message boards, 86-90
  finding, 87-88
  posting, 88-89
movies, 99
  Hollywood forum, 100-101
music, 101
  Dolby Audio/Video forum, 137-138
  Grateful Dead forum, 102
  MusicSpace, 98
  RockNet forum, 101-102
news
  Business news forum, 194
  CNN Newsroom forum, 185
  Columnists & Features forum, 199
  New Republic, 199
  Newsstand forum, 197-198
  OMNI, 200
  Time, 201
  US & World news forum, 193
  US Cities Forecasts forum, 197
  Weather news forum, 195-196
  Worth, 203
newspapers
  Chicago Tribune, 139-140
  Mercury Center forum, 140-141
  New York Times, 141-142
  San Jose Mercury News, 141
photographs (Photography forum), 131
politics
  Capital Connection forum, 130

Library of Congress forum, 187-188
professions (Aviation forum), 134-135
radio
  National Public Radio Outreach forum, 188
  Stereo Review, 201
religions (Religion & Ethics forum), 128
science (Astronomy Club forum), 129
shopping
  2Market forum, 215-216
  AutoVantage forum, 210-212
  Bookstore forum, 213-214
  Classifieds forum, 217-218
  Computer Express forum, 214-215
  Shoppers Advantage forum, 216-217
  Shoppers Express forum, 218-219
space
  National Space Society forum, 135-136
  OMNI, 200
sports (Sports Grandstand forum), 107
television, (Star Trek Club forum), 132
travel (EAAsy Sabre forum), 223-224
travelling
  Bed & Breakfast USA forum, 229
  DineBase Restaurant listings forum, 229-230
  ExpressNet forum, 225-226
  Outdoor Adventures forum, 230-231

State Travel Advisories forum, 231
Travel forum, 227-228
Travelers' Corner forum, 226-227
Vacations forum, 227
videos (Dolby Audio/Video forum), 137-138
weather
  EAAsy Sabre, 224
  US Cities Forecasts forum, 197
forwarding e-mail, 77
free areas, 21
freeware, 174-175
Frequently Asked Questions, *see* **FAQ**
ftp (file transfer protocol), 241-242

G

Gallery, 66
  downloading, 67-68
games, 104-105
  Conference Center, 105
  Federation forum, 105
  Games & Computers, 120
  PC Games forum, 104
Genealogy Club forum, 131
General Preferences dialog box, 31
geography (National Geographic Society forum), 188
GIF (Graphic Interchange Format), 67, 196
Global Network Navigator, 301
Gopher, 240
governments (Library of Congress forum), 187-188
Graphic Interchange Format (GIF), *see* **GIF**

Internet **317**

graphics (tools,
editing), 33-34
Graphics forum, 149
Grateful Dead forum,
102

H

harassment (safety
online), 111
health
Better Health &
Medical forum, 133
Issues in Mental Health
forum, 133
National Multiple
Sclerosis Society
forum, 128
Help Desk, 146
hobbies
Astronomy Club forum,
129
Cooking Club forum,
129
Exchange forum, 130
Photography forum,
131
Hollywood forum,
100-101
*Home Office
Computing*, 155
home pages
creating, 303-305
defined, 145
finding, 307
My Home Page
(construction area),
302
saving, 305-306
updating, 305-306
World Wide Web
(WWW), creating,
302-303
HomePC, 155
Howard Stern Show
web site, 294-295
HTML (Hypertext
Markup Language),
306
http (Hypertext
Transfer Protocol),
283

I

IBM web site, 291
icons
America Online
Highlights icon, 23-24
Create Topic, 88
Find New, 88
Find Since, 88
FlashBars
listings, 34-37
List Messages, 88
What's Hot, 97
ignoring e-mail, 78
Industry Connection
(technical support),
158, 160-161
installing
AOL software, 11-12
modems, 14-15, 26-29
software (AOL), 12-15
instant messages, 84-85
blocking, 112
replying to, 84
interests
Clubs & Interests
department, 126
Baby Boomers
forum, 127
Internet
abilities, 236-237
AOL (America Online),
connecting to, 243
children, 113-114
access , 111
safety online, 238
defined, 236
e-mail, 237
addresses, 247-249
file attachments,
251-252
graphic files, 252
mailboxes, 256-257
mailing lists,
252-254
receiving, 246-247,
251
returned, 250
sending, 246-250
history, 237

Internet Connection,
238-239
ftp (file transfer
protocol), 241-242
Gopher, 240
Mail Gateway,
239-240, 246
Mailing Lists, 241
newsgroups
(UseNet
newsgroups), 240
languages, 248
newsgroups (UseNet
newsgroups)
accessing, 266-267
finding, 267-268
offensive messages,
274-275
rules, 263-266
Parental Controls
(setting preferences),
114-116
shopping sites, 207
TCP/IP (Transmission
Control Protocol/
Internet Protocol),
243-244
travelling, 222-223
World Wide Web
(WWW), 242-244,
280-281
browsers, 281
buttons, 285-286
CIA (Central
Intelligence
Agency), 297
Favorite Places, 285
Howard Stern
Show, 294-295
HTML (Hypertext
Markup Lan-
guage), 306
IBM, 291
images, 284
Microsoft web site,
292
navigating, 284
Novell, 292-293
Software Ventures
Corporation, 293

318 *Internet*

Star Trek: Voyager
web site, 295
system
requirements, 281
URL (Uniform
Resource
Locator), 283
X-Files web site,
296-297
*Young and the
Restless*, 296
Ziff-Davis, 294
**Issues in Mental Health
forum, 133**

J-K

**joining mailing Lists,
254-256**
**JPEG (Joint
Photographic Experts
Group), 67**
**JumpStation II Front
Page, 301**

keywords, 20-21, 45
**Kids Connection,
120-121**
chats
rules, 121-122
starting, 122
**Kids Only department,
50, 117**
Cartoon Network
forum, 119
Disney Adventures,
118
Games & Computers,
120
Kids Connection,
120-122
starting, 122
Tomorrow's Morning
forum, 119-120
kids, *see* **children**
**Komputer Komando
forum, 186-187**

L

launching
applications, 27
programs, 27
leisure
Car & Driver, 137
Dolby Audio/Video
forum, 137-138
Entertainment
department, 48
Saturday Review, 200
TicketMaster online,
139
libraries
software
commercial, 173-174
demoware, 174
freeware, 174-175
public domain, 175
searching, 167-169
shareware, 174
uploading, 175-176
**Library of Congress
forum, 187-188**
List Messages icon, 88
Lobby, 58-59
chat rooms, 61-62
entering, 61
**Logging command
(File menu), 65**
Logging dialog box, 65
logs
chat logs, 65
closing, 66
session logs, 65
system logs, 91
tape recorders, 65-66
**Logs command
(File menu), 91**
lurking, 58
Lycos, 301

M

magazines
Atlantic Monthly, 198
BackPacker, 228-229
Consumer Reports, 199
Disney Adventures,
118

*Home Office
Computing*, 155
HomePC, 155
Mobile Office Online,
156
New Republic, 199
OMNI, 200
PC World, 156
Saturday Review, 200
Stereo Review, 201
Time, 201
Wired, 201-202
Woman's Day, 202
WordPerfect, 157
Worth, 203
**Mail Gateway,
239-240, 246**
Mail menu commands
Check Mail I've Read,
79
Edit Address Book, 81
FlashSessions, 82
Read Incoming Mail, 80
mailboxes
flashbox, 80
full, 256-257
MAILER-DAEMON, 250
**mailing addresses,
18-20**
mailing Lists, 241
Internet e-mail, 252-254
exiting, 255-256
joining, 254-256
messages, 255
unsubscribing, 256
maps, accessing, 196
**MarketPlace
department, 47, 206**
2Market forum, 215-216
AutoVantage forum,
210-212
Bookstore forum,
213-214
Classifieds forum,
217-218
Computer Express
forum, 214-215
flowers, 212-213
Shoppers Advantage
forum, 216-217

news **319**

Shoppers Express
forum, 218-219
**medical (Better Health
& Medical forum), 133**
members
finding, 60-61
profiles
finding, 58-59
locating, 57
viewing, 59-60
rooms, blocking, 112
signatures, 265
**Members menu
commands**
Edit Your Online
Profile, 55
Send Instant Message,
84
Set Preferences, 31
**Mental Health forum
(Issues in), 133**
**Mercury Center forum,
140-141**
messages
boards, 86-90
Create Topic, 88
defined, 86
Find New icon, 88
Find Since icon, 88
folders, 88
List Messages, 88
posting, 88-89
Read 1st Message,
88
threading, 89-90
e-mail, saving, 78
forums, finding, 87-88
instant, 84-85
blocking, 112
replying to, 84
mailing lists,
responding to, 255
newsgroups (UseNet
newsgroups)
adding, 275
cross-posting, 273
displaying, 262-263
File Grabber,
276-277
FlashSessions,
275-276

offensive, 274-275
posting, 273-275
preferences, 271-272
reading, 269-270
replying, 272-273
threading, 270-271
troubleshooting,
272-274
threading, 89-90
defined, 270
World Wide Web
(WWW) fatal error
messages, 298
You Have a Mail
message, 77
Microsoft web site, 292
**Military & Vets Club
forum, 135**
**MIME (Multipurpose
Internet Mail
Extensions), 251**
missing files, 171
Mobile Office Online,
156
modems
AOL (America Online),
connecting to, 16
call waiting, turning
on/off, 15, 29
connection settings,
changing, 27-29
defined, 11
installing, 14-15, 26-29
modem profiles, 14
system requirements,
11
troubleshooting, 29-30
movies, 99
Hollywood forum,
100-101
**multimedia (defined),
11**
**Multipurpose Internet
Mail Extensions,** *see*
**MIME (Multipurpose
Internet Mail
Extensions)**
**museums
(Smithsonian), 182**

music, 101
Dolby Audio/Video
forum, 137-138
Grateful Dead forum,
102
Music & Sound forum,
151
MusicSpace, 98
RockNet forum,
101-102
TicketMaster online,
139
**Music & Sound forum,
151**

N

**names (UseNet
newsgroups), 263**
**National Geographic
Society forum, 188**
**National Multiple
Sclerosis Society
forum, 128**
**National Parenting
Center, 123-124**
**National Public Radio
Outreach forum, 188**
**National Space Society
forum, 135-136**
**navigating (World Wide
Web), 284**
**netiquette (UseNet
newsgroups), 263-266**
**network, connecting to,
27-29**
**Network Earth forum,
133**
**Network Setup dialog
box, 29**
New Republic, **199**
New York Times,
141-142
news
Atlantic Monthly, 198
Business news forum,
194-195
CNN Newsroom forum,
185
Columnists & Features
forum, 199

Consumer Reports, 199
New Republic, 199
Newsstand
  department, 47-48,
  197-198
OMNI, 200
readers (defined), 261
Time, 201
Today's News, 44
Today's News forum,
  192-193
US & World news
  forum, 193
US Cities Forecasts
  forum, 197
Weather news forum,
  195-196
newsgroups, 115
blocking, 115
**newsgroups (UseNet
  newsgroups), 240**
accessing, 266-267
defined, 260
File Grabber, 276-277
finding, 267-268
FlashSessions, 275-276
messages
  adding, 275
  cross-posting, 273
  displaying, 262-263
  offensive, 274-275
  posting, 273-275
  preferences, 271-272
  reading, 269-270
  replying, 272-273
  threading, 270-271
  troubleshooting,
    273-274
names, 263
news readers, 261
preferences, 261-262
rules, 263-266
searching
  Expert Add, 268-269
  multiple, 268
troubleshooting, 272

newspapers
Chicago Tribune,
  139-140
Mercury Center Forum,
  140-141
New York Times,
  141-142
*San Jose Mercury
  News*, 141
Tomorrow's Morning,
  119
**Newsstand department,
  47-48, 197-198**
Atlantic Monthly, 198
Columnists & Features,
  199
Consumer Reports, 199
Cowles/SIMBA Media
  Information Network,
  199
New Republic, 199
OMNI, 200
Saturday Review, 200
Stereo Review, 201
Time, 201
Wired, 201-202
Woman's Day, 202
note to parents, 116
**Novell web site,
  292-293**
**numbers (access,
  changing), 28**

O-P

OMNI, **200**
**online profiles,
  creating, 54-57**
**Open command
  (File menu), 67**
Open dialog box, 66
ordering
AOL store, 207-210
software (AOL), 12
**organizing (UseNet
  newsgroups), 270-271**
OS/2 forum, 152
**Outdoor Adventures
  forum, 230-231**

**Parental Controls,
  111-113**
blocking
  binary downloads,
    115
  expert add
    newsgroups, 115
  instant messages,
    112
  member rooms, 112
  newsgroups, 115
  rooms, 112
Internet (setting
  preferences), 114-116
newsgroups, 115
note to parents, 116
parents
child safety brochure,
  122-124
National Parenting
  Center, 123-124
note to parents, 116
Parental Controls,
  111-113
**Parents' Information
  Network, 122-123**
passwords, 16, 19
defined, 19
preferences, 32
**Paste command
  (Edit menu), 274**
**PC Applications forum,
  146**
**PC Communications
  forum, 147**
**PC Developers forum,
  147**
PC Games forum, 104
**PC Hardware forum,
  150**
**PC Multimedia forum,
  150**
PC World, **156**
**PDA (Personal Digital
  Assistants) forum,
  152**
People Connection
auditoriums, 63-65
chat rooms, 61-62

rooms (chat) **321**

Gallery, 66
Lobby, 58
    entering, 61
    lurking, 58
people, _see_ **members**
**Personal Finance
department, 44**
Pet Care forum, 134
photographs
    downloading, 67-68
    editing, 33-34
    Gallery, 66
    Photography forum,
        131
    thumbnails, 67, 68
Photography forum, 131
pictures, _see_
    photographs
politics
    Capital Connection
        forum, 130
    Library of Congress
        forum, 187-188
posting
    messages, 88-89
    newsgroups
        (UseNet
        newsgroups),
        273-275
preferences
    messages (UseNet
        newsgroups), 271-272
    newsgroups (UseNet
        newsgroups), 261-262
    Parental Controls,
        114-116
    passwords, 32
    software (AOL), 31-32
    World Wide Web
        (WWW), 33
**Print command
    (File menu), 80**
printing
    e-mail, 80
    information windows,
        110
**private chat rooms,
    61-62**
**product center,
    ordering, 207-210**

**professions (Aviation
    forum), 134-135**
profiles
    members
        finding, 57-59
        viewing, 59-60
    online, creating, 54-57
    People Connection,
        58-59
    troubleshooting, 56-57
**Program command
    (Start menu), 27**
programs, launching, 27
protocol (chats), 91
**public domain software,
    175**

Q-R

queues, 169

radio, 99
    National Public Radio
        Outreach forum, 188
    Stereo Review, 201
**Read 1st Message icon,
    88**
**Read Incoming Mail
    command (Mail
    menu), 80**
reading
    e-mail, 77
    .newsgroups (UseNet
        newsgroups), 269-270
receiving
    e-mail, 76-78
    Internet, 246-247,
        251
recorders (logs), 65-66
Reference Desk, 178
references, _see_
    resources
**registration numbers,
    16**
**Religion & Ethics
    forum, 128**
**religions (Religion &
    Ethics forum), 128**
replying
    instant messages, 84
    Mailing Lists, 255

messages newsgroups,
    272-273
**requirements
    (AOL software), 11**
resources
    Academic Assistance
        Center, 184
    Barrons Booknotes,
        180
    Career Center, 181
    CNN Newsroom forum,
        185
    College Board forum,
        185
    Compton's NewMedia
        learning center,
        180-181
    Court TV, 182
    Electronic University
        Network forum, 186
    ERIC (Educational
        Resources
        Information Center),
        180
    Komputer Komando
        forum, 186-187
    National Geographic
        Society forum, 188
    National Public Radio
        Outreach forum, 188
    Scholastic forum,
        188-189
    Smithsonian, 182-183
**restaurants (DineBase
    Restaurant listings
    forum), 229-230**
**RockNet forum,
    101-102**
rooms (chat), 61-62
    blocking, 112
        members, 112
    chat logs, 65
    children (safety),
        111-113
    conferences, blocking,
        112
    logs, closing, 66
    Travel Cafe, 228

rules (UseNet newsgroups)

rules (UseNet newsgroups), 263-266

S

safety online
children
child safety
brochure, 122-124
face-to-face
meetings, 110
harassment, 111
inappropriate
material, 110
Internet, 113-114,
238
National Parenting
Center, 123-124
Parental Controls,
111-113
Parents'
Information
Network, 122-123
San Jose Mercury
News **forum, 141**
Saturday Review, **200**
Save As command
(File menu), 80
Save command
(File menu), 65
saving
downloading
files, 169-170
software, 169-170
e-mail, 79-80
flashbox, 80
messages, 78
home pages, 305-306
text files, 80
Scholastic forum,
188-189
science (Astronomy
Club forum), 129
Science Fiction &
Fantasy forum,
131-132
screens
(Welcome screen), 42

searching
file search window,
167-168
multiple items, 268
newsgroups (UseNet
newsgroups), 267-268
Expert Add, 268-269
software libraries,
167-169
troubleshooting, 171
World Wide Web
(WWW), 298, 300-302
Global Network
Navigator, 301
JumpStation II
Front Page, 301
Lycos, 301
search engines, 301
WebCrawler, 301
Yahoo, 298-300
Send Instant Message
command
(Members menu), 84
sending
e-mail, 75-76
files, 78-79
Internet, 246-250
later, 76
SeniorNet forum, 128
session logs, 65
Set Preferences
command
(Members menu), 31
shareware, 174
Shoppers Advantage
forum, 216-217
Shoppers Express
forum, 218-219
shopping
2Market forum, 215-216
advice, 219-220
AutoVantage forum,
210-212
Bookstore forum,
213-214
Classifieds forum,
217-218
Computer Express
forum, 214-215

flowers, 212-213
Marketplace
department, 47
Shoppers Advantage
forum, 216-217
store, 207-210
shortcuts
defined, 28
keywords, 20-21, 45
shorthand, 69-71
Show Tools command
(Edit menu), 33
signatures, 265
signing on (accounts,
troubleshooting), 116
Smithsonian museums,
182-183
software (AOL)
commercial, 173-174
demoware, 174
downloading, 169-170
saving, 169-170
upgrades, 210
freeware, 174-175
installing, 11-15
libraries, searching,
167-169
ordering, 12
preferences, 31-32
public domain, 175
requirements, 11
shareware, 174
uploading
process, 175-176
where to, 175
Virus Information
Center, 167
World Wide Web
(system
requirements),
281-282
Software Ventures
Corporation web site,
293
sorting (UseNet
newsgroups), 270-271
space
National Space Society
forum, 135-136
OMNI (Italic), 200

UseNet newsgroups   **323**

Sports department, 50
Sports forum, 106
Sports Grandstand
   forum, 107
Star Trek Club forum,
   132
Star Trek: Voyager
   web site, 295
Start menu commands
   (Programs), 27
starting (America
   Online), 21-23
State Travel Advisories
   forum, 231
Stereo Review, 201
system logs, 91
system requirements
   modems, 11
   software (AOL), 11
   World Wide Web
      (WWW), 281-282

T

tape recorders (logs),
   65-66
TCP/IP (Transmission
   Control Protocol/
   Internet Protocol),
   243-244
Teacher Pager, 184, 185
technical support
   (Industry
   Connection),
   158, 160-161
television, 99
   C-SPAN, 182
   Court TV, 182
   Star Trek Club forum,
      132
   Star Trek: Voyager
      web site, 295
   X-Files web site,
      296-297
   Young and the Restless
      web site, 296
Terms of Service, *see*
   TOS (Terms of
   Service), 20
text, saving files, 80

thesaurus, 179-180
threading
   messages, 89-90
   defined, 270
   newsgroups
      (UseNet
      newsgroups),
      270-271
thumbnails, 67-68
TicketMaster online,
   139
Time, 201
Today's News, 44
Today's News forum,
   192-193
Tomorrow's Morning
   forum, 119-120
tools (graphics,
   editing), 33-34
TOS (Terms of
   Service), 20, 61
   children, 113
Transmission Control
   Protocol/Internet
   Protocol, *see* TCPIP
Travel department,
   46-47, 222
   airlines, 224-225
   BackPacker, 228-229
   Bed & Breakfast USA
      forum, 229
   DineBase Restaurant
      listings forum,
      229-230
   EAAsy Sabre, 223-224
      weather, 224
   ExpressNet forum,
      225-226
   Outdoor Adventures
      forum, 230-231
   State Travel Advisories
      forum, 231
   Travel Cafe, 228
   Travel forum, 227-228
   Travelers' Corner
      forum, 226-227
   Vacations forum, 227
Travel forum, 227-228
Travelers' Corner
   forum, 226-227

travelling (Internet
   sites), 222-223
troubleshooting
   access numbers, 56-57
   accounts, 116
   downloading, 173
      artwork, 97-98
   e-mail, 83
   messages (UseNet
      newsgroups), 273-274
   modems, 29-30
   newsgroups (UseNet
      newsgroups)
      messages, 272
   profiles, 56-57
   software libraries, 171
   World Wide Web
      (WWW), 291
      connecting, 284
turning on/off
   (call waiting), 15, 29

U-V

universities
   College Board forum,
      185
   Electronic University
      Network forum, 186
updating home pages,
   305-306
uploading
   files, 175-176
   defined, 166
   process, 175-176
   where to, 175
URL (Uniform Resource
   Locator), 290
   defined, 283
   http (Hypertext
      Transfer Protocol),
      283
   parts of, 283
US & World news
   forum, 193
US Cities Forecasts
   forum, 197
UseNet newsgroups,
   240
   accessing, 266-267
   defined, 240, 260

File Grabber, 276-277
finding, 267-268
FlashSessions, 275-276
messages
  adding, 275
  cross-posting, 273
  displaying, 262-263
  offensive, 274-275
  posting, 273-275
  preferences, 271-272
  reading, 269-270
  replying, 272-273
  threading, 270-271
  troubleshooting, 273-274
names, 263
preferences, 261-262
rules, 263-266
searching
  Expert Add, 268-269
  multiple, 268
troubleshooting, 272
User Groups forum, 153
User Network, 240

Vacations forum, 227
videos (Dolby Audio/ Video forum), 137-138
viewing member profiles, 59-60
viruses
  files, 166
  Virus Information Center, 167

W

weather
  EAAsy Sabre, 224
  US Cities Forecasts forum, 197
Weather news forum, 195-196
  maps, accessing, 196
web, *see* World Wide Web (WWW)
WebCrawler, 301
Welcome screen, 42

windows
  file search window, 167-168
  information, printing, 110
Windows '95 forum, 154
***Wired*, 201-202**
***Woman's Day*, 202**
Word Wide Web (WWW), 242-244
***WordPerfect*, 157**
World Wide Web (WWW), 280-281
  browsers, 281
  buttons, 285-286
  CIA (Central Intelligence Agency), 297
  connecting (troubleshooting), 284
  Favorite Places, 285
  home pages
    creating, 302-305
    defined, 145
    finding, 307
    saving, 305-306
    updating, 305-306
  Howard Stern Show, 294-295
  HTML (Hypertext Markup Language), 306
  IBM, 291
  images, 284
  messages (fatal error), 298
  Microsoft, 292
  navigating, 284
  Novell, 292-293
  preferences, 33
  searching, 298, 300-302
    Global Network Navigator, 301
    JumpStation II Front Page, 301
    Lycos, 301
    search engines, 301
    WebCrawler, 301
    Yahoo, 298-300

shopping sites, 207
software (AOL)
  requirements, 281-282
Software Ventures Corporation, 293
Star Trek Voyager web site, 295
travelling, 222-223
troubleshooting, 291
URL (Uniform Resource Locator), 290
  defined, 283
  http (Hypertext Transfer Protocol), 283
  parts of, 283
X-Files web site, 296-297
Young and the Restless, 296
Ziff-Davis, 294
***Worth*, 203**
writing e-mail, 74-75
WWW (World Wide Web), *see* World Wide Web (WWW)

X-Y-Z

***X-Files* web site, 296-297**

Yahoo, 298-300
***Young and the Restless* web site, 296**

Ziff-Davis web site, 294

GET CONNECTED
to the ultimate source of computer information!

The MCP Forum on CompuServe

Go online with the world's leading computer book publisher! Macmillan Computer Publishing offers everything you need for computer success!

Find the books that are right for you!
A complete online catalog, plus sample chapters and tables of contents give you an in-depth look at all our books. The best way to shop or browse!

➤ Get fast answers and technical support for MCP books and software

➤ Join discussion groups on major computer subjects

➤ Interact with our expert authors via e-mail and conferences

➤ Download software from our immense library:
  ▷ Source code from books
  ▷ Demos of hot software
  ▷ The best shareware and freeware
  ▷ Graphics files

Join now and get a free CompuServe Starter Kit!

To receive your free CompuServe Introductory Membership, call **1-800-848-8199** and ask for representative #597.

The Starter Kit includes:
➤ Personal ID number and password
➤ $15 credit on the system
➤ Subscription to *CompuServe Magazine*

Once on the CompuServe System, type:

GO MACMILLAN

for the most computer information anywhere!

PLUG YOURSELF INTO...

THE MACMILLAN INFORMATION SUPERLIBRARY™

Free information and vast computer resources from the world's leading computer book publisher—online!

FIND THE BOOKS THAT ARE RIGHT FOR YOU!
A complete online catalog, plus sample chapters and tables of contents!

- **STAY INFORMED** with the latest computer industry news through our online newsletter, press releases, and customized Information SuperLibrary Reports.
- **GET FAST ANSWERS** to your questions about QUE books.
- **VISIT** our online bookstore for the latest information and editions!
- **COMMUNICATE** with our expert authors through e-mail and conferences.
- **DOWNLOAD SOFTWARE** from the immense Macmillan Computer Publishing library:
    - Source code, shareware, freeware, and demos
- **DISCOVER HOT SPOTS** on other parts of the Internet.
- **WIN BOOKS** in ongoing contests and giveaways!

TO PLUG INTO QUE:

WORLD WIDE WEB: **http://www.mcp.com/que**

FTP: ftp.mcp.com

Complete and Return this Card for a *FREE* Computer Book Catalog

Thank you for purchasing this book! You have purchased a superior computer book written expressly for your needs. To continue to provide the kind of up-to-date, pertinent coverage you've come to expect from us, we need to hear from you. Please take a minute to complete and return this self-addressed, postage-paid form. In return, we'll send you a free catalog of all our computer books on topics ranging from word processing to programming and the internet.

Mr. ☐   Mrs. ☐   Ms. ☐   Dr. ☐

Name (first) ☐☐☐☐☐☐☐☐☐☐☐☐ (M.I.) ☐ (last) ☐☐☐☐☐☐☐☐☐☐☐☐☐

Address ☐☐☐☐☐☐☐☐☐☐☐☐☐☐☐☐☐☐☐☐☐☐☐☐☐☐☐☐
        ☐☐☐☐☐☐☐☐☐☐☐☐☐☐☐☐☐☐☐☐☐☐☐☐☐☐☐☐

City ☐☐☐☐☐☐☐☐☐☐☐☐☐☐ State ☐☐ Zip ☐☐☐☐☐☐☐☐☐☐

Phone ☐☐☐ ☐☐☐ ☐☐☐☐ Fax ☐☐☐ ☐☐☐ ☐☐☐☐

Company Name ☐☐☐☐☐☐☐☐☐☐☐☐☐☐☐☐☐☐☐☐☐☐☐☐☐

E-mail address ☐☐☐☐☐☐☐☐☐☐☐☐☐☐☐☐☐☐☐☐☐☐☐☐☐

1. Please check at least (3) influencing factors for purchasing this book.

Front or back cover information on book .... ☐
Special approach to the content .... ☐
Completeness of content .... ☐
Author's reputation .... ☐
Publisher's reputation .... ☐
Book cover design or layout .... ☐
Index or table of contents of book .... ☐
Price of book .... ☐
Special effects, graphics, illustrations .... ☐
Other (Please specify): _____ ☐

2. How did you first learn about this book?

Saw in Macmillan Computer Publishing catalog .... ☐
Recommended by store personnel .... ☐
Saw the book on bookshelf at store .... ☐
Recommended by a friend .... ☐
Received advertisement in the mail .... ☐
Saw an advertisement in: _____ ☐
Read book review in: _____ ☐
Other (Please specify): _____ ☐

3. How many computer books have you purchased in the last six months?

This book only .... ☐   3 to 5 books .... ☐
2 books .... ☐   More than 5 .... ☐

4. Where did you purchase this book?

Bookstore .... ☐
Computer Store .... ☐
Consumer Electronics Store .... ☐
Department Store .... ☐
Office Club .... ☐
Warehouse Club .... ☐
Mail Order .... ☐
Direct from Publisher .... ☐
Internet site .... ☐
Other (Please specify): _____ ☐

5. How long have you been using a computer?

☐ Less than 6 months   ☐ 6 months to a year
☐ 1 to 3 years   ☐ More than 3 years

6. What is your level of experience with personal computers and with the subject of this book?

	With PCs	With subject of book
New	☐	☐
Casual	☐	☐
Accomplished	☐	☐
Expert	☐	☐

Source Code ISBN: 0-7897-0594-x

7. Which of the following best describes your job title?

Administrative Assistant .... ☐
Coordinator .... ☐
Manager/Supervisor .... ☐
Director .... ☐
Vice President .... ☐
President/CEO/COO .... ☐
Lawyer/Doctor/Medical Professional .... ☐
Teacher/Educator/Trainer .... ☐
Engineer/Technician .... ☐
Consultant .... ☐
Not employed/Student/Retired .... ☐
Other (Please specify): _____ ☐

8. Which of the following best describes the area of the company your job title falls under?

Accounting .... ☐
Engineering .... ☐
Manufacturing .... ☐
Operations .... ☐
Marketing .... ☐
Sales .... ☐
Other (Please specify): _____ ☐

9. What is your age?

Under 20 .... ☐
21-29 .... ☐
30-39 .... ☐
40-49 .... ☐
50-59 .... ☐
60-over .... ☐

10. Are you:

Male .... ☐
Female .... ☐

11. Which computer publications do you read regularly? (Please list)

_____
_____
_____
_____
_____
_____
_____
_____
_____
_____

Comments: _____
_____
_____

Fold here and scotch-tape to mail.

BUSINESS REPLY MAIL

FIRST-CLASS MAIL PERMIT NO. 9918 INDIANAPOLIS IN

POSTAGE WILL BE PAID BY THE ADDRESSEE

ATTN MARKETING
MACMILLAN COMPUTER PUBLISHING
MACMILLAN PUBLISHING USA
201 W 103RD ST
INDIANAPOLIS IN 46209-9042

NO POSTAGE
NECESSARY
IF MAILED
IN THE
UNITED STATES